FACE AND SHADOW

APPROACHES TO
THE MODERN
REVOLUTIONARY IMPULSE

by JUDAH STAMPFER

SIMON AND SCHUSTER / NEW YORK

FOR MY BROTHER JOSHUA, GOLDIE,
AND THEIR CHILDREN

CONTENTS

PREFACE

LET ME here acknowledge a debt never to be paid in its entirety. This book was touched off, at a distant remove, by Paul Tillich, whose friendship I enjoyed in Cambridge some twelve or thirteen years ago. The man communicated a rapport with the ways of the human spirit in ways deeper than words. In a profound man, the courage to be requires an elegance of spirit. Paul Tillich's courage to be was exceedingly elegant.

Once, shortly before a lengthy visit of his to Europe, I made a request of him to which no immediate answer was possible. More than half a year later, walking along the Harvard stacks, I was startled to see him coming down the long ramp in my direction, blushing slightly, hanging his head like a truant boy. When we met, he simply granted my request, spontaneously, without a word from me, as though I had asked him that morning. His friendship had no seam.

From Tillich, I learned, as by a contagion, to read silences, to trust the instincts of my ear about social energies and what makes them go demonic, to demand the meaning of their wayward shifts.

The immediate occasion of this book is a deep sense of sadness at the loss of nerve that pervades our country, at the silences that gather and spread in a sullen opacity, at fumbling corrections that die in well-meaning irrelevance. I should like to clarify some aspects of the modern temper, the way it tends to shift as groups approach the establishment and slip away. Writing, I struggled to keep my tongue as free as possible from clichés, metaphysical structures and political commitments, to skip and move about, flushing my quarry, to sense how things taste as much as what they mean.

I recall, in a conversation of some years back, a New York psychoanalyst telling me that he and his colleagues spent their lives treating the neuroses prevalent when they were in high school; he only trusted they approximated whatever was bothering his patients. So, I keep having a sense we have blinded and petrified our thinking with outdated definitions of the proletariat, of the myth of progress, the mystique of labor, of the style, controls and solidity of the establishment, and of what makes revolutionary material. There words have shifted their meaning too little in the last hundred years, while everywhere the reality to which they refer has undergone a sea change. We do not pursue the implications of the consumer mentality and the incredible expansion of electric force in our country. We pietistically avoid a dialogue with our own black citizens. Against our full knowledge, we allow an entrenched establishment like Soviet Russia to stand as a revolutionary center, and read its slow, conservative, expansionist power in terms of the proletarian urgency it had at the time of Lenin. Everywhere, ossified insights hamstring our minds and fault our every attempt at a fresh start, until revolutionary impulses turn as stale as they are well-meaning.

This book is not a detailed map; nor is it just a loose collection of material. It is rather an attempt to examine the present temper with an instinct for social habits large and loose enough to catch a variety of material. If its net has collected some oddly relevant material in fresh associations, or made available some useful terms, it will have fulfilled its function.

Let me here acknowledge an immediate debt to Dr. Ruth-Jean Eisenbud, who was open-handed and insightful in discussing some of my psychological material, and to David Hoddeson, who read the last chapters with uncommon editorial skill.

JUDAH STAMPFER
State University
Stony Brook, New York
November 6, 1970

PART I

THE TERMS
WE WORK WITH

1

FACE AND SHADOW

I WORRY about history. I live by a fairly routine schedule, but dead events snag my mind and won't let go. Sometimes I wish I hadn't learned to read. I'd simply flow through love, work, rejection, achievement. I'd eat, sleep, move about, stay put awhile, and then die. That would be a pretty life, to stir through the years like an elm tree; but no elm tree knows its history—it just lives it. Me, I know the history I live; or do I? Every road has threads, tangles, that can catch my feet and tumble me on my face; but even with a clean, straight road, I know where events are buried, suddenly to swarm from the soil like seven-year locusts. And yet the land seems open, the past dead.

Our country nourishes us as an alfalfa field grows alfalfa; but its spirit is odd, kinky and changing, shifting in unpredictable ways. Its impulses work stubbornly, surprisingly, with a bent, a will, a stupidity of their own. Yet its impulses are what we are after—history, some ghostly, essential social process we can establish and wrestle with. We want to grasp the impulses that tell us where we are, what we have become, and how to look at our neighbors. We want history, and not simply a quaint tombstone from before the Civil War, a rhyming script that graces a museum. We'll visit an antiquarian shop when we have time.

Countries come through to us with an uncanny variety and feel. England unfolds like an elm tree, its common-law roots gripping rock and soil, its institutions rising in a tough trunk to support a

15

careful foliage of crafts and industries, arts, sports and husbandry. A small island, England casts a seed to sail with the wind, to float on the waves, to blow around the world. The seed lodges on a distant shore—Canada, Australia, New Zealand—it sinks roots, and a fresh elm tree begins to grow.

Russia comes through more as a bush than a tree, but a huge winter bush, spreading over the land. Sliced at by the Mongols, the Teutonic Knights, the Poles, the Turks, the Swedes, the Nazis— torn out altogether—it shoots back up as the pressure eases. Russia grows by throwing out runners that sink fresh root, as it pushes its massive presence in a continuous sprawl across Siberia, around China, overgrowing the Iron Curtain, reaching down into Egypt, spreading outward from the Russian heartland.

Rooted people grow with their land, each in its way. Beyond the Arctic Circle, the land grows its trees like Eskimo empires, in miniature.

America is more an open area than a vegetable growth. The first Puritans had no mystique about virgin land. They started a colony by chopping a clearing in the primeval forest; then building homes around a central square that left an open area for town meetings, markets and fairs; and finally, throwing up a last-ditch defense against the surrounding wilderness. Just so, crossing the great plains of the American heartland, the wagon caravans camped each night around an empty circle, where children played, buffalo meat was roasted over an open fire, and plans were laid for the next day's journey. Outside the clearing were tribes of Indians, buffalo and coyote runs, and the endless stir of the plains.

The frontier and the oceans around it gave America a sense of living apart. The Canadian border was quiet, Mexico of another civilization; we grew up an only son in North America, to work out our own destiny, without a close constant fight over every item in the larder. Did Shakespeare see England as a "precious stone set in the silver sea?" America was mountain range and virgin farmland "from sea to shining sea," a clearing in the wilderness, to be organized as the land was settled. We started from scratch.

Today, all America is wide-open; but the American clearing is filling with clutter, and the sea with indestructible garbage. Inside our heartland swing cars, trucks, planes, telephone wires and TV antennae; around our borders, acres of atomic rockets bristle against the wilderness of the starved, resentful foreign world. The sense of a clearing remains; but now it stands embattled. Americans like to move, to follow the stir of new places; but suburbs swallow up and choke out our cities. In one generation, California has become our most populated state, as, all over, sections of farmland go back to the bush. But for all our stirring, our jet planes and rockets to the moon, we're headed no place now. Our open area is filling up into a crowded parking lot.

Human nature moves differently from nation to nation; what is more important, it moves differently depending on its social location. Thus, society registers in our experience as consisting of a Face and its various Shadows. By a Face, we mean the elite of a society, its established, legitimate power, that has grown in an organic way out of its historic past, the clan or economic style celebrated when patriotic songs are sung in school. The Face of a country is the group that never thinks to define itself or justify its existence—it just is. By a Shadow, we mean any group which is legally tolerated, however generously, but remains self-consciously marginal and irregular, with no authority growing organically out of its past. The Shadow may be economic, for example, private enterprise in Soviet Russia; or it may be social and biological, like the blacks or women in this country. To make my meaning more clear, in America a homosexual might say, "I am as good as any heterosexual"; but no heterosexual will say, "I am as good as any homosexual." In this country, then, heterosexual is Face; homosexual is Shadow.

Local accident can be a factor. An Italian is Shadow at a Jewish wedding, a Jew Shadow at an Italian wedding. The pecking order among human beings is not as tight as in a flock of chickens, but the distinction holds tolerably well. On a Sunday morning, I once visited a black church in New Orleans, a singing church, with drums, castanets, and cymbals scattered through the pews, and an organ and a piano behind the pulpit. I was welcomed with deep, subdued dignity and warmth, an intangible élan that spread as I sat down, a joyous snap to the hymn. It was part of the deep faith of the worshipers to make a stranger welcome; yet an intangible sense came through that in that church, I was not a Shadow, but Face.

It must be emphasized that Face and Shadow need not conform with real power, though they generally do. Our concern here is with a bent in human nature, and not with its institutions. The British House of Lords has Face by its history and public esteem, though its power has steadily dwindled through the centuries. Indeed, a powerless Face can be very useful, since it does not mobilize the hostility and mistrust citizens generally feel for institutions. Thus, a government vulnerable to election can use a powerless Face like the House of Lords to initiate unpopular reforms, like easing the laws dealing with homosexuality or abolishing capital punishment. So Bertrand Russell, a man raised as Face but politically powerless, could a generation ago, undertake a broad defense of sexual freedom as social policy. So Albert Einstein, who became Face by his discoveries in physics, could tell a UN committee that its hearings were trivial since neither the United States nor Russia had revealed its plans. Once Face is established, its utterance carries authority.

Indeed, a powerless Face can be exceedingly attractive. Not having to justify his existence, a Face has a great deal of rope available, to shift and adjust his position; yet having no real power, he need account for no decisions and can therefore speak freely. All he has to do is give advice. This is the stance of the senior professor who refuses departmental office so he can speak his mind on all occasions. He may have great moral force, but that force has not been institutionalized. His strength lies in trenchant originality, the power to organize fresh approaches to problems. Thus, the pronouncements of a paid consultant, an established engineer or a doctor, have a stamp of finality, not only objectively, because of his training, but subjectively, because the acknowledged expert speaks with disinterested authority and then turns away with clean hands. Thus, the Rand Corporation can afford incisive originality; it gives only advice, it makes no decisions.

The authority of Face, once it has learned its style, cannot be overestimated—its mysterious savoir faire, its instinct for timing and for managing the undercurrents of tension. The "Face" of modern English poetry during the first half of our century was T.S. Eliot, by his essays, his sensibility, his public posture. He was followed in that role by Robert Lowell, who was nominated for the poetry chair at Oxford University formerly held by Robert Graves. That the great New England names of Eliot and Lowell should preside over the English as well as the American muse testifies to the potency of unattached Face, its authenticity, its sense of pace and style. The maneuvering of the French government not to arrest Sartre rested on his moral Face, not on his political power. So in Soviet Russia, the scientist, being Face, is the best hope for some degree of freedom of thought. The more talented writers can be kept Shadow until they are safely dead.

But just as a Face can continue without institutional power, so a Shadow can seize institutional power and yet remain in shadow. The Face of the country is then masked or hidden. This occurs when two elements coincide: first, a group or sect that has seized power by a cabal or accident rules by institutional secrecy; second, the traditional temper of the society regards that group or sect as inferior or alien. The psychology of Shadow in power then sets in, insular, careful, unapproachable, faceless, doctrinaire, working for special angles, lacking in sudden originality, and difficult to reach in a personal way. The Shadow tends to ignore broad communal needs, and works for angles, for special concessions. The mind of Shadow is so locked in ambivalence, you never know what gesture shows love and what shows hate.

This sense of Shadow in power exists today in most countries behind the Iron Curtain—Poland, Hungary, Czechoslovakia and Bulgaria. Most astonishingly, it is considerably true also of the Soviet Union. There, the politburos remain Shadows, having been imposed as an artificial Face by Stalin's occupying armies, clapped on like a mask, but not growing out of the people. The situation is a matter of historical development, not economics; Tito on the right and Mao Tse-tung on the left, having grown with their native movements, have an entirely different dynamic, whatever their policies.

We discuss here a bent in human nature, what happens to people as they get institutionalized. Our groups are therefore necessarily a bit loose. That is, a Shadow can become a Face, or sink below Shadow into a category we shall call Proletariat. Yet institutions have more continuity than individual human beings. Thus a labor government can function as a Face, whereas the unions that launched it into power remain a Shadow. This has bearing on our sense of Communist countries. Thus individuals from Soviet Russia can express the temperament of Face, while their government retains the temperament of Shadow, given the tenacity of institutions in their temperaments.

The most uncanny of ruling Shadows is the current leadership of Soviet Russia, who became a Shadow, not by imposition of an invading army but by crawling out of Stalin's massive political presence after his death. They know very well they survived by inconspicuous conformism while their more visible contemporaries were all exterminated. One need only see Kosygin on television, elaborately comparing Israel to the Nazi movement, his hands inert, his mouth moving like a lawnmower grinding back and forth over the same stretch of grass. Such a Shadow in power works in committee, answerable only to the Party. A mask, it cannot respond like skin, sensitive to irritations below, but responds like rubber, to rising pressures and the pull attached. Its decisions come dressed in doctrinal clothing like a space suit. It approaches problems, not by originality but by steady borrowings, getting a German firm to build a truck factory wholesale to resolve a lack of trucks, building standardized homes, standardized clothing, standardized kitchen appliances, always twenty years behind the times in style. So it works for special angles, slams a government on Czechoslovakia, courts the Arabs by its opposition to Israel. Shadows have more capacity than Faces to bide their time—America has the least patience of any major country today.

So Communist Party officials rule a country they only marginally inhabit, in a niggardly atmosphere that dulls their culture, dress conventionally, stop only at formal hotels, even in their own countries. Khrushchev showed some style and sparks of spontaneity; his successors do not repeat his mistakes. The Communist people have a capacity for Face beyond the grasp of their rulers. Thus the strange atmosphere of Budapest before the Soviet invasion, and even more the atmosphere of Prague, was that of a city waking from a hypnotic trance. Suddenly air flowed around their faces and bodies; they could make decisions, and the decisions held. They were embarrassingly naïve, like innocent children earnestly at work. Suddenly their own face was on their heads, a face that could laugh, cry, express things, not a mere party mask. The situation was too human to last. The Soviet tanks soon ground in, dragging an impenetrable shadow, and the Iron Curtain was back to its faceless normality.

This atmosphere of Shadow, this authority of an entrenched clique working by manipulation, is like that of the Indiana town whose clergyman talks with respect to his parishioners—he was ordained by God; whose banker talks with more respect to his depositors—he graduated from Indiana Finance; but whose undertaker talks with most respect to his corpses—he inherited the establishment from his father. Whatever their political aberrations, England, Canada, the United States, China, Yugoslavia, wear their faces on their heads. Soviet Russia, Poland, Czechoslovakia, Hungary and Bulgaria wear on their heads, not a face but a pair of clenched buttocks.

Indeed, the American aberration is the opposite, an excessive emphasis on Face. Thus, the American frontier, the line of settlement between Europe and the wilderness, had the quality of Face imposed on a recently discovered new Shadow. This Face is strident, pugnaciously optimistic; but its ambiance with its Shadow is tricky, nervous, and without rapport. Indeed, it expresses a kind of nervous concern, a self-consciousness about feeling responsible. So the Indians in more recent movies tend to be projections of a white man's guilt. In actual life, they still do not get a fair return; but it is the American face that is twitchy, not its conscience. This twitchiness is related to Americans' spasms of pacifism. Much pacifist feeling is triggered off by a hatred for war itself, for fighting itself; but in considerable part it comes from a revulsion at the idea of feeling guilty.

This quality of America as a new Face on a strange, rejected Shadow expresses itself in a sense of radical innocence—the guilts were left back there, in Europe. At the start, the Puritan movement had too tough a theology for such rapid seizures of innocence; but the instinct to shed an old skin was there. Thus the Puritans shed the English aristocracy for a more basic democracy; the Unitarian movement shed the divisions of God for a more basic divinity; the Midwest shed the financial aristocracy of Wall Street for a more basic agrarianism. Names were boiled down to a pablum of nomenclature, building to that mythic town Azusa, California, that offers you everything from A to Z in the U.S.A.

So America needs its face to shine and be expressive. The establishment of a brand name is the first big hurdle of a new American company—"What'll you have?" "Pabst Blue Ribbon." You buy a brand name as the Face of what America produces, the shiny handle its customer grabs. Faces communicate more immediately and obviously; to relate, to express, to communicate are strident hungers in our lonely crowd. Other countries too have their lonely crowd, but we have made it a way of life. In Miami Beach, eight hundred persons once sprawled in the main ballroom of the Deauville Hotel, silently touching each other with their eyes closed, to form one huge continuity of human beings, all with a single expression. One trusts they reached beatitude in the hotel ballroom, and not the next day, on the pages of *The New York Times*. Nudity is about as old as clothing; but American nudity therapy groups are an attempt not at body as body but at body as face, to be seen plainly and express all of yourself to another.

This view of society as contrasting Face and Shadow sounds fairly Hegelian—historic movement as a broad surge and countersurge of social energies. To justify our own terms, Face and Shadow, as preferable to the Hegelian terminology, we must see the Hegelian terms of thesis and antithesis as somewhat mechanical jargon, suited to a nineteenth-century physics of gravity and a clash of hard matter. So thesis and antithesis, by their verbal urgency, seem to gather social loyalties in opposition like static electricity machines. Fundamental nineteenth-century thought moved this way, toward simple basics of matter and force, bound by gravity and leaning together in building blocks.

To speak bluntly, that level of metaphysics, when used today, is worse than simply old-fashioned. Its function is purely pietistic. This is known not only in the West, but in the Soviet Union too: at the height of Stalin's power, the top physicists quietly dissociated themselves from any Hegelian dynamic of thesis and antithesis. They didn't call the dynamic right or wrong; it was simply cumbersome, time-consuming and irrelevant to the problems they were working on. They won their point because a government that wants a fast, usable atom bomb, cannot burden its scientists with metaphysical pieties. But if Communist physics can shrug off a dialectic of thesis and antithesis as an irrelevant language construct, then to approach social situations by such a metaphysical commitment is pietistic nonsense.

It is odd how old-fashioned styles of insight hang on. In the nineteenth century, Freud reduced all psychic energies to libido, and grasped libido as a flow of infantile rage and sexuality; Marx reduced social process to the process of production, grasping every assembly line as an atom of industry. Both were bravura attempts at rethinking the human process by a simplified structure of energy and process, and rebuilding it brick by brick. Of the two investigations, Freud's allowed more room for human aberration; in his old age, in *Civilization and Its Discontents,* he contemplated the poignancy of the human situation, of society trammeled in the processes that triggered it off. Freud seems somehow limited today, old-fashioned; and so even more basically does Marx. Work has changed in character; basic energy comes from unexpected sources. Society has become more fundamentally intertwined. In our jaded productive glut, our uneasiness at any clear metaphysics, we chafe at any single social dynamic.

Our own terms, *Face* and *Shadow,* do not pretend to characterize a firm system, but highlight a bent in human nature as it stirs in society; they are a way of clarifying some wayward persistencies in human behavior. But even taken on this level, the Hegelian terms thesis and antithesis are of exceedingly limited value. In the area of individual psychology, they are not wrong—they are just irrelevant almost all the time; and even when they are relevant, they are too abstract to clarify anything. For example, a widow who becomes a regular churchgoer may be filling in an empty week, or giving expression to an old repressed religious impulse, or be driven by sexual denial toward God, the minister, or the second choir boy from the left. Abstract patterns such as thesis and antithesis cannot grasp the energy transformations in the woman, her complex rearrangements of attitude and habit. A pattern that is not a concept about energy finally has no point. At times, in individual psychology, it can alert us to suggestive clues, keep us from being bland about a man's identity, but even when it is relevant, it becomes too verbal, too dogmatic, too either-or; it offers no key to the energies involved. On balance, then, the debits of the "thesis-antithesis" pattern outweigh its advantages. It should therefore be left strictly alone.

The terms thesis and antithesis seem more relevant to groups than to individual psychology. Thus, should we ask what is left of thesis and antithesis in society once the metaphysics has been taken out, the answer is, a surprising lot. Closed inside a particular human being, contrasts and oppositions adjust, clash neurotically, or go underground; but in the looser, more shadowy social world, they polarize without any compulsion to resolve themselves. So blacks define themselves against a white world, women against a man's world, Jews against a gentile world, workers against their employers.

And yet, though this tendency of a society to polarize in opposition is a strong one, the dynamic of thesis and antithesis applies only loosely and sporadically. A nation is not a steel spring in equilibrium, but looser and more open, with too many unexpected variables involved. How, for example, can a process like thesis and antithesis relate to the Czech government, slammed down by an invading Russian army, its slots then filled by native Czechs? One might as well call a wooden leg an antithesis to the thigh that walks it. But the terms *Face* and *Shadow* more closely describe the Czech poignancy, where a powerless culture that slipped off its mask and breathed fresh air a while is again ruled by doctrinaire party hacks.

Face properly emerges from a self-conscious and established élite, by careful steps or initiation rites loosely related to the training of Plato's philosopher kings or Milton's program of education. The Duke of Wellington had his point when he said the Battle of Waterloo was won on the playing fields of Eton. A country like England, with its tenacious continuity of government, maintains a surprisingly strong equilibrium of Face and Shadow, of clerks and policy-makers. A wrenched, twisted, or violated equilibrium tends to maintain itself in a neurotic way.

At the far extreme is the collective neurosis of a ruling Shadow, whether in countries, cities, corporations, clubs, universities, or any social group. Such a neurosis gets under way when a suspect Shadow seizes power or manipulates itself into authority. Not having aired its Face and been accepted by the populace at large, it rules facelessly, in committee, by administrative ukase, subverting the Faces without power, making them comic, ceremonial, trivial. Nor are such Shadows easily eliminated. Ruling Shadows will promote Shadow types like themselves. Thus Stalin seized power by administrative cabal, and then had his secret police kill the Face of the original revolution. This neurosis of Shadow-rule makes one pessimistic about government power. Clerks are Shadowy; they clog every government. A country ruled by clerks with no effective Face grows monstrous, as has now happened in Uruguay, which can produce only revolutionary violence.

As we noted earlier, America has the opposite aberration: it places too much emphasis on Face. Men in other countries may be tough; but here they come ostentatiously tough, pragmatically tough, television tough. In England, an election campaign lasts a few weeks and is over; its purpose is to clarify the issues and establish the bent of the nation's loyalties. But our law has locked in months of TV campaigning which cost cruel millions of dollars; aside from verifying the issues, the candidate has to establish his Face. One speculates it was his magnificent television Face that got

Goldwater nominated for president—it shone so radiantly above his other qualifications.

Perhaps the most poignant by-product of a ruling shadow is the paralysis of neighboring faces, uneasy alongside it. Face communicates with Face. They understand each other's balance of pride, ambition, guilt, rationalization, and silly dreams; but when confronted by Shadow, the illusion of the immutable, the eternal, gives Face an uncanny feel, as though it confronted the Great Stone Face. So, meeting Soviet Russia, a nation that formulates its past and future out of a party manual, the United States falls back on a neurotic confessional monologue. The material is always abundant for such a monologue; but the process is unmanly and degrading in front of a vast audience. The two countries talk past each other too much. America needs a more open dialogue with its power opposite; but it must filter through the language pablum of its rulers, and listen to the submerged Face of the Russian people, the difficulties of Soviet agriculture, the starved Russian market, its imitative designs, the controls it places on its intellectuals, its handling of wastes, its reality of crime and delinquency, its prisons. The answers would not be that incriminating; and their airing might give Russian reality a chance to breathe outside the party corset.

As between Face and Shadow, Face tends to think national, Shadow to think partisan and clannish. These are psychic inclinations, not historic inevitabilities. Indeed, the intransigent stubbornness of the human animal is slighted at one's peril. The tenacious clannish bent of Shadow makes one mistrust Marx's point of view as parochial, when he concentrates on economic forces and class structure, not on clan loyalties and tribal structure. So governments get more complicated, organizational controls more distant and alien, and clan instincts stir to illicit life.

The same process of depersonalization works in industry. As work grows more fragmentary, repetitive and imbecilic, the workers melt into an industrial team; but the thinner the organizational bonds, the more clan instincts and dream material well up. This occurs in any organization. Indeed, the absence of a team or clan produces a blur in human nature. So the current drug habit among busy corporate employees is, among other things, an attempt to synchronize with their environment. As a corporation grows too large, its identity blurs to a disfocus. Its employees thin their identities too, and blur their consciousness with drugs.

Herbert Marcuse is closer to the current scene than Karl Marx; and yet he has not noted the extent wayward clan instincts do the work he attributes to organizational thought control, melting corporate employees to docility in some clan or other in their work. Nobody manipulates this—nobody has to. To see this as a manipulation, whether instinctual or deliberate, is a misconception of the problem with traces of the paranoid. The bent of the human animal in a social group is to modify consciousness as it slips from Face to Shadow. Women's Lib to the contrary notwithstanding, the relative docility of women may or may not be inherent in the female consciousness; but it may also result from the deep bond of marriage and children, a bond even deeper than that of gang or clan. A free consciousness is exceedingly fragile. Erich Neumann's magnificent *Origins and History of Consciousness* finishes with a lame confession that several millennia of growth of consciousness can dissolve in smoke before the nearest TV set.

Those who move in the wake of Marx tend to reduce social structure to economic need; but man is also vehemently tribal and ego-oriented. For all the refreshing clarity of his analysis, Marcuse is essentially committed to a consumer-oriented government:

> The only needs that have an unqualified claim for satisfaction are the vital ones—nourishment, clothing, lodging at the attainable level of culture. The satisfaction of these needs is the prerequisite for the realization of *all* needs, of the unsublimated as well as the sublimated ones.

The reduction of all needs to "the vital ones"—food, clothing, and shelter—has a handsome, old-fashioned simplicity, even an anarchist tinge. Social engagements are always a means; the end remains the strong free individual. But when Marcuse subsumes *all* needs (his italics) to the basics of food, clothing and shelter, we ask, is his own need to write *One-Dimensional Man* a secondary personal satisfaction? No such reduction is possible. An unwritten book is there to be written, as an unbuilt bridge, an empty field, a wild pony, are there to be built, to be planted, to be tamed, as well as for the food, clothing and shelter they return. On the most fundamental level, a consumer society is a sick society. Basic as the need to eat, to be clothed and to be sheltered is the need to produce food, clothing and shelter—and also the need to produce truth. But this has consequences. One has not only to be a fine free man, the goal of the old-fashioned anarchist, but also to harness one's working capacities as an end in itself, not just as a means to an end. I eat, or I starve; I produce, or I become a parasite.

It is ungracious to confront simple, downright wholesomeness, and it calls in question one's own ever-flowing grandiosities. Nevertheless, one must ask Marcuse's admirers and those anarchist followers of Paul Goodman who have disengaged themselves from the establishment: How solid is their solidity? How final is their wholesomeness? To what extent is that wholesomeness a posture? —not that postures are bad, but they are never final. Anarchist life has much in it of eternal, idyllic pastoral. To the extent that its making pots, weaving, and enjoying life comes straight, it comes handsome. And yet simple living is a personal style as well as a moral gesture, an attitude of adult arrival, as well as the arrival itself. The style is handsome—so is the style of the concertmaster of the New York Philharmonic; but either registers as considerably less than final truth.

The thrust of personal fulfillment is always significant. What is wrong with the speculation that *Portnoy's Complaint* may have been autobiographical is the fact that Philip Roth wrote a smashing success—Portnoy couldn't have written himself a successful thank-you note after masturbating. So I personally sniff after the book you are reading as I write it, dance around it like a water-witch. The satisfaction is primary—in the fingers typing, the memory dancing, the brain formulating—because the work leans that way. I let it lean.

Years ago, I met Marcuse, a sane, dignified, aristocratic German refugee and philosopher of the German university tradition, a man brought up to intellectual inquiry in the philosophical establishment, and an exceedingly trenchant writer. Marcuse doesn't have to articulate his need to produce ideas; they come out like the air he breathes. Furthermore, he makes his living from the establishment; he publishes through the establishment. If one were paranoid about the establishment, one might call Marcuse its supremely insidious agent, giving hippie radicals an outlet. But brushing aside paranoia, one sees Marcuse is not dedicated either to the establishment or to its overthrow; he is dedicated to truth, with all the care, detachment and high achievement of the true German philosopher. The American hippie revolutionary dedicated to "openness," "freedom," "self-expression" is as rooted in this philosopher as a porno movie out of Denmark is in the work of Sigmund Freud.

The American hippie anarchists are suspect in their authenticity, quite simply because they are Shadow and not Face. Like all Shadows, their definition is to a considerable extent the negative of the society around them. For example, whatever it is today, the original Israeli kibbutz started as a Shadow of the *shtetl*, or Eastern European village it came from. Thus, the *shtetl* carefully distinguished the sexes, the man serving as a vessel of holiness, the woman as helpmate and housekeeper; the kibbutz leveled both to work hands. The *shtetl* valued the kosher in food, the kibbutz its utility. The *shtetl* respected privacy and learning, the kibbutz machinery and the capacity to live collectively. The *shtetl* raised chil-

Proletariat when the opportunity arises. Thus, the French Communists became a Shadow when they joined the machinery of the French government and participated in elections as a legal party. During the 1968 disturbances, the student agitators with Daniel Cohn-Bendit were a Proletariat, the Communist party a Shadow. Each behaved in a manner appropriate to its social role.

The blacks, at the beginning of the civil rights movement in the early Sixties, were a quiescent Proletariat suddenly come alive, with a romantic mystique. Specific and tangible steps elevated them to a Shadow: a black was elected to the Senate; another was appointed to the Supreme Court; the NAACP became legally active; SNCC got legal power as a movement; Martin Luther King legally broke elements of segregation; Charles Evers was elected a southern mayor; other blacks were elected to Congress; desegregation began to be enforced in southern schools. But the Proletarian mystique has profound attractions that not all the black community wants to give up. Quite simply, the Black Panther movement is that wing of black society that slights, ignores and mocks its channels to power as a sop, in order to maintain its Proletarian character. Thus, Malcolm X's distinction between the house Negro who accepts established authority and the field Negro who stands outside it effectively singles out the legal toady; but when Huey Newton extends Malcolm X's term "house Negro" to include any black who uses legal channels, he is fighting hard to stay Proletariat and avoid becoming a Shadow. Not reality is at stake here, but a gesture of soul.

Let us widen the spectrum of our term Proletariat a bit to include the southern black before the Civil War; the American laborer before the New Deal; the European laborer at the time of Karl Marx; the American hobo during the depression; the European Jew under the Czar, and in all Europe during the Second World War; the anarchist Loyalists during the Spanish Civil War. We may even include the hippies of a few years ago. Indeed, it was a momentous accident of history that made the European workers Karl Marx knew a Proletariat. Addressing himself to that Proletariat, and to that Proletariat alone, Marx gave a wholly economic bent to the Proletarian reverberations of the socialist movement, and grafted a Proletarian mysterium onto socialist labor. But then the unions consolidated their power, and labor parties entered various governments. Today, organized labor in Europe and America is in no sense a Proletariat; the opposite is true—organized labor has become Face. Indeed, Marx was himself a crucial factor in lifting the workingman out of the Proletariat.

No Proletariat can have an actual program, i.e., a proposed timetable of change in government machinery. A community afloat, altogether outside the machinery of government, it cannot even sense how such machinery moves. Government edicts come through as claps of thunder foretelling heavy rain. Instead of a program, the Proletariat draws up sweeping lists of demands, like the sweeping demands of the first black students at Ivy League universities, who worked from an embattled sense of Proletariat, not through accustomed channels to power.

Instead of specific political loyalties, such a Proletariat has a huge poignance, raw feelings without a vent, sweeps of emotion: rage, nostalgia, courage, sentimentality, hope and outraged memory. Beneath the sense of reality, trained and made habitual in human nature, there always lies a level of folklore and mythic adventure that adds color, a texture of validity, a grain of expectation. One particular mother becomes motherhood, acceptance, the being who will never reject you, or, contrariwise, some anti-motherhood of coldness, sterility and alienation. Real episodes come balanced against their mythic reverberations. Reality is a veil as well as an experience.

That veil of reality is much thinner in a Proletariat, which is closer to the level of folk tale and myth. Thus the Yemenite Jew, who had never ridden before even in a bus or an auto, climbed on board his first transport plane singing of his return to Israel on "wings of eagles." So many a southern black saw King as his own Martin Luther, preaching the sober Reformation truth to an ornate, decadent white church on Capitol Hill. This is the principal strength of a Proletariat: their word has a timbre of authenticity no Shadow can approach, and few Faces hope to equal. Their truths reverberate as elemental.

Proletarian sweeps of emotion, being reinforced on primitive levels of consciousness, are exceedingly seductive—their timbre has an underlying depth; yet that does not clinch their words as final, or even always relevant. Huey Newton has, for example, a deep sense of manly authenticity. Politically, he is a green boy, acting out fairy tales simplistic in their fanaticism. Sitting in a bamboo chair, holding a spear and a heavy gun, he will produce gallantry, heroism—and also a lot of corpses. Let us hope his hieratic posture, like a totem, produces a twinge of truth here and there. He wants what all people want—Face; but the passage to Face is through the vale of Shadow. Sooner or later, he will have to travel it, or end as a tale full of sound and fury, whatever it signifies. A generation ago, the American hobo went home when Roosevelt gave him a bus ticket. He had been a fairy tale long enough. Heroism makes for a draughty bedroom.

Proletariat also has scope. It may be pinched in circumstance; but it need not be pinched in spirit. On the contrary, it inhabits a continent, not just a room and a half; is employed by an entire race, not just one person. Its haunting sweep and movement suggest masses of people, with a broad geographical identity, and a vision national in scope. It shifts from country to country; its time is alive, pregnant with fresh, unknown outrages to be met with courage. Malcolm X, a Proletarian leader with such a sweep, visited Mecca, saw the blacks against their African origins, envisioned an address to the U.N. and the colors of the world united, all with a gritty Proletarian sweep and grasp. Paradoxically, a

Shadow occupies just a room. An outlaw on the run occupies all America; give him a lawyer to fight his rap, and he occupies one small hotel room, afraid to move.

Even more strangely, a true Proletariat taps deep wells of creativity in writing and musical composition. Some of our most cherished folk songs are Proletarian in origin—the cowboy song, the spiritual. Woody Guthrie was the great American Proletarian composer. So too "Song of the Volga Boatmen" grew out of the Russian Proletariat. Proletarian language comes raw, from the bowels. So slang wells up out of the slums, like Apache argot overflowing the French language. Writers with access to Proletarian movement tap deep sources of language, as Mark Twain did in *Huckleberry Finn*, and produced his masterpiece.

In a Proletariat, mythic and legendary heroes replace political leaders and organizers. The ancient oppressed Hebrews germinated a Samson, a hero of the sun—his name literally means "sun," as Delilah's name literally means "of the night." So too the old American Proletariat projected John Henry, a steel-driving man, to out-hammer the railroad machines. Without a Shadow hold on the government, the Proletariat sense their elemental humanity as outcasts of the earth. In the same tradition, *West Side Story* shifted *Romeo and Juliet* to a slum district of New York.

Once given legalized avenues to legitimate power, the Proletariat becomes a Shadow. Thus, the southern Black got SNCC; the hobo on the highway got the WPA; the depression worker got the AFL-CIO. The transaction brings staggering gains and losses: the former Proletarian stops marching and starts organizing, he stops composing songs and starts issuing manifestoes, stops writing folk parables and starts studying remedial English, stops camping out and starts collecting rent money. Programs replace his vision; the drab reality of slum improvement, the poignant sweep of his condition. A hopeless tripper, he sinks back in his own impoverished life. He now has a floor under his feet, but not the dirt that was porous to deeper, more elemental strata of human life. As Shadow, he now deals with government clerks who cannot be fired, speeded up, or gotten on the telephone, and have to be treated with respect. Dealing with most clerks is like writing a thank-you note for the correct time; it may be necessary, but one's stomach never works the same way again.

The shift from Proletariat to Shadow came with startling suddenness in the recent civil rights movement. When the first sit-ins began, and Martin Luther King led the Montgomery, Alabama, bus strike, the southern blacks were a Proletariat. Segregated behind impenetrable walls in stores, restaurants, jobs and applications to white schools, they found enigmatic doors all around them that led nowhere; they had no tested channels to power. As a Proletariat, the civil rights movement worked on some level of broad humanity, with a national sweep, poignance and fascination. Rumors spread from city to city, of cars that simply disappeared, of civil rights workers murdered by local sheriffs—and they were more than rumors. King himself, by his mythic name, his bearing, his patience under attack, his posture on specific issues, exemplified the Proletarian folk hero.

The leaders who led the blacks from Proletariat to Shadow, men like Martin Luther King, Malcolm X, and James Baldwin, sensed the price they would have to pay in Proletarian scope and depth, and struggled, each in his way, to retain an elemental immediacy. They differed enormously in complexity and bent of character, yet all had large intuitions of the possible and the destructive. It is no coincidence that each was an ordained minister.

Martin Luther King was the largest, simplest, and most elemental figure in the passage of the blacks out of the Proletarian murk. He avoided the pale cast of Shadow by remaining in steady rapport with the law of God, as he saw it, a law which accepted all men as one, recognizing no Face and no Shadow. Preëminently a man of law, he fought for substantial dignity, substantial self-respect, substantial human beings, step by step, insult by insult, and job by job. King avoided the imitative taint of Shadow by meeting all situations from the vantage point of eternity. His acts had the simple courage of a Gandhi, his speeches a Biblical cast. But as more blacks shifted from Proletariat to Shadow, and even to elements of Face, a simple Proletarian universality failed to solve all problems. One meets terminal cancer under the aspect of eternity, but not the First National Bank.

If Martin Luther King was unchangeable as a rock, Malcolm X lived a life of continuous change and growth beginning as a thief, a pimp, a drug-pusher, and then undergoing a conversion in prison to the Black Muslim faith. Its leading minister, he helped make the Muslims a national movement, but he was forced out after stumbling upon a reported scandal in the life of Elijah Mohammad, the founder of the movement. He made a pilgrimage to Mecca, where he shifted his sense of black-and-white relations to one of cultural indoctrination, and then returned to New York to launch his own Muslim movement. Soon after, he was murdered by other blacks, reportedly members of the Black Muslims, though they deny complicity in his murder.

Malcolm was the hinge on which the black community turned toward partisan confrontation. He related at once to the Proletarian scope and sweep of the movement, and to the legal relationships that could falsify it. The searing fire that made his talents the rallying point of black consciousness was not one of eternal law, but of righteous indignation, a towering sense that justice had been indecently violated. He shared a burning sense of God's justice with Martin Luther King, a man he deeply respected all his life, despite their different faiths; what he added as his gift to the blacks was the raw emotion of indignation. But that introduction of an emotion as a political factor is essentially romantic, a Proletarian gesture. This emotionality became crucial in the refusal of black extremists to allow that there was any justice in the American courts—once an element of justice is allowed as operating in the courts, the blacks become a Shadow, and their entire attitude changes. The same discrepancy in the breakdown of the rigid wall between white and black became increasingly apparent to Malcolm X before his death.

Malcolm himself had a charismatic presence, a carriage, a quick dignity, a dry, good-humored voice, an integrity of manner. He kept growing all his life, shooting up like the legendary beanstalk, hungry for sunlight and water. When his principles or his courage were at stake, he walked in the valley of death and had no fear. What he felt was not hate but righteous indignation, a towering sense that justice had been indecently violated. And yet the indignation he gave his followers too easily turned into a blank check for raw hate and self-indulgent destruction that led nowhere. It isn't for us to complain—he paid for one of those checks with his life.

What is fascinating, aside from its leadership, is the speed with which the black freedom movement, once under way, established channels to power in NAACP, CORE, SNCC, the Southern Christian Leadership Conference, the Free Democratic movement, and the American court system. Changing to Shadow (though not to Face) it gained organizational strength, but lost its romantic mystique. As a Proletariat, it attracted wide support and welcomed any helpful leadership; both white and black volunteers died at the hands of lynchers. But as the black leaders rose in the most fundamental way from Proletariat to Shadow, they shrugged off their broader white support. Shadows don't work that broadly; they rather consolidate organizational strength behind their own leadership, substituting party self-reliance for a mystique of national concern.

Indeed, not only has the black Proletariat now substantially become Shadow, but black elements are also becoming Face, first in sports, then in the graphic arts, and now in theater and literature.

The incursion of the blacks into sports and the arts has come in odd jumps, not just in who gets what role, but also in the very myth of arrival built into the movies. Sidney Poitier's movies are carefully planned as to his salary, his billing and how good his story is, and also, movie by movie, to enact the arrival of black as Face. So he will first protect a white woman, then flirt with her, then kiss her, then sleep with her, then marry her. Even his cool, masklike impenetrability is a function of his roles. In a vastly different way, Poitier is as mythic as Martin Luther King, enacting the arrival of the black to cinematic Face. A more individual register would be too real for his mythic role. You can meet Paul Newman on Madison Avenue; Sidney Poitier you meet in your dreams. His role as a northern detective investigating a southern murder is a fairy tale of an unexpected national Face, imposing on a local Face that had not known he existed. His engagement to a white girl of a prominent family says Hello to the national Face, its equal and partner.

Similarly in sports, the black has arrived at Face, one sport at a time. Long accepted in boxing, a sport of brute power, punishment and aggression, and also in basketball, a less public sport he almost dominates, the black took a vast step forward when Jackie Robinson signed on for the Brooklyn Dodgers; for baseball is a native American sport from the midwest cornfields, where men work as a coördinated team, not as solitary fighters. Indeed, blacks in old baseball often claimed to be Indians. It took still more time for the black to arrive at Face in tennis, a sport associated with England, the Wimbledon courts, the aristocracy, club rules, that tennis-ball speech of Shakespeare's Henry V. Yet eventually Arthur Ashe reached the top echelon of tennis players.

Indeed, with a heady excitement of arrival, the blacks are acting out the drama of Face in gestures and legal steps, slamming it down as a reality: Some black athletes raised their clenched fists at the Olympic parade. Arthur Ashe acted to force South Africa out of international tennis, making himself Face and them Shadow. The Afro hair-do has become fashionable in the cities, and is spreading through the army. A dream of Face even becomes a kind of festival. In the summer riots of '68 and '69, black rioters stole bulky appliances, often white ones—refrigerators, television sets, and washing machines—in broad daylight under newsreel cameras; their pictures were splashed across the papers. This stealing was not a reaching for money, but for Face, a festival of arrival, when the rules are all suspended. A week later, the Proletariat was back dragging behind its newly established Shadow.

All these influences, of course, shape black literature, as we see preëminently in the career of James Baldwin. Here my own position should be made clear as a white, American-Jewish writer, novelist and critic, with whatever specialized training I have. The agreement is at present fairly widespread among white critics to leave black literature alone. When I finish reading a review of a white novel or biography, I can usually guess what the book is about, and whether I want to read it. A review of a black novel only tells me some existential experience has taken place on paper; but I haven't the foggiest notion if the work is well-written, effective, talented, promising, truthful, profound, sexy—use your own adjective—who can judge an existential experience on paper?

Several reasons lie behind this paralysis of critical function. First, some black writers insist their experience is so intimately personal to the black experience, no white critic can grasp it. Second, the critic is burdened by a sense of guilt, feeling a group that has suffered so much should be left alone. Third, the work serves some mysterious, unnamed function to which conventional literary standards do not apply. Behind it all lies a ritual dance of Face: Shadow seizes Face, and Face sinks into Shadow and becomes mute. The arguments are oblique and somewhat murky. The autonomy of the black community of writers certainly must be respected. Nevertheless, when all is said and done, the reasons for a critical hands-off on black writing are, without exception, as cowardly as they are puerile. Let us consider each of them in turn.

The argument that the experience in a black novel is too intimately closeted in black experience to be grasped by whites is the opposite of the truth. I understand most black writers very well. Verbalisms sometimes bother me, but so does a heavy Irish accent. I feel closer to a strong black novelist than I do to John Updike, whose experience is also very different from mine. There is no such thing as a unique "black experience," any more or less than any other experience. No woman has ever forbidden men to criticize Jane Austen, who was a woman, though this may happen yet. When a critic understands, we respect him; when he responds like a presumptuous ass, we hang a feedbag on his head. Criticism is a partial, painful, fragmentary, personal activity; it works in fits and starts, often stupidly, sometimes arrogantly. To demand that a critic have the experience of a book before he tastes it is like demanding that a housewife lay a few eggs before you trust her to taste an omelet.

Two elements bring about the proscription. The legitimate one is that whites are so often patronizing in their treatment of blacks that the black writer cries quits. He doesn't want to be chided or patted on the head—he just wants to be let alone. The brutal truth is, however, that people too sensitive to take criticism should distribute mimeographed materials to their friends; they have no business publishing books. Madison Avenue is the Coney Island of the mind. Publication starts moving along the stand of sliding tin ducks to be shot at by any passing critic. But the prohibition of white critics has also an illegitimate basis. Quite simply, this is how a scared writer fends off critics. But surely the writer should trust his book to get through to the critics, or he had no business writing it.

The argument that critics feel a sense of guilt is even less worthy of consideration. The human race cannot lie on its back and wave its arms and legs in the air out of guilt. What is to Vietnam is to Vietnam, and what is to sloppy writing is to sloppy writing. On the contrary, the rare critic is the man who maintains his critical judgment no matter what moral stresses weigh on his spirit.

The last argument—that the writing of blacks serves some special mysterious function—is more intriguing than the others. Quality black writing is the verbal equivalent of blues music; it has a style and musical cadence like Bird, downbeat and hard. Black blues writing is soul writing, a limber bristle of words that get off their sleepy haunches and snarl in your face. The language is steadily inward, aggressive and withdrawn, flowing just below the surface, patient to shift and gather until the emotions grit in a quiet integrity. This is not the slow, inward dignity of Elizabethan English prose, building with solidity and structure, secure on its theological scaffolding, but a loose, unfolding soul-talk, cut away from land, adrift without an anchor, shifting with unsure currents down risky waterways over pools of hate and sudden treachery where the steady balance and elimination of phrase after phrase shifts about like poling a raft, half-repeating, changing direction, until it is located exactly right. And then it lands, as Malcolm X lands here:

The Mau Mau realized that the only thing that was standing in the way of the independence of the African in Kenya was another African. So they started getting them one by one, all those Toms. One after another, they'd find another Uncle Tom African by the roadside. Today they're free. The white man didn't get involved—he got out of the way. That's the same thing that will happen here. We've got too many of our own people who stand in the way. They're too squeamish. They want to be looked upon as respectable Uncle Toms. They want to be looked upon by the white man as respectable. They don't want to be classified by him as extremist, or violent, or you know, irresponsible. They want that good image. And nobody who's looking for a good image will ever be free. No, that kind of image doesn't get you free. You've got to take something in your hand

and say, "Look, it's you or me." And I guarantee you he'll give you freedom then. He'll say, "This man is ready for me." I said something in your hand—I won't define what I mean by "something in your hand." I don't mean bananas.

The critics hint darkly that this style serves some mysterious function. Let me guess what that function is. Such writing is a process of inner washing, scouring, correcting and establishing the soul with an anchor of integrity. Another writer wants to finish, his point made; the blues writer wants to finish, his tongue clean and his soul breathing air. His spirit is so coated with tarnish, he can hardly maneuver or connect. He begins writing somewhere inside his tarred soul, at the bottom of a pit, and slowly shifts about, gets his own feel: what his muscles are, how he moves, what false step can land him back in the muck; he has to find out what he wants, what he can say, and say it, and finish on the surface with air around him.

James Baldwin is no jar of crunchy peanut butter, like seventy others on the shelf, not with his complicated and colorful history. I personally have been twice in his company, once at a preview of his play, *Blues for Mr. Charlie,* and once at a black Catholic college he addressed in New Orleans. Both times, his nervous system rode hard, on trial and on the make, for laughs, for respect, to slam across his points. At each meeting, he was a different man. In New York he was mellow, quivering with gentility, shaking old friends' hands, his lips and eyes beaming quiet good will, but slightly too brightly. Cool velvet flapped in those cloistered interiors; a strange little boy was mellow with pleasure that we were all there. In New Orleans, he was tougher, a restless African animal and confident pagan, a throaty laugh half-asleep in his throat. He stood on that podium—he came very late—the center of black creation, his good will unfolding with a boyish whiplash.

Baldwin was turned on at both meetings, out of the blender, one hundred twenty proof, with shoulders so even and upright, he was part spine, part gall, and part fabric, all deeply textured sport clothes with emphatic lapels. His cheekbones poked up like broken teeth set solid in his burned, long, skinny face. Leathery litmus paper, he could swing hard at a party or gallop a meeting for three hours in a bravura performance, and never come within six light years of you, though his mood could change color with the music of your disposition.

To speak plainly as a critic, I found James Baldwin's first novel, *Go Tell It on the Mountain* a tough, tight, moving hunk of fiction and a small classic. After that—I looked at them all—I found each novel weaker than the one before. His characters grow steadily more stereotypic, his episodes more sentimentalized, his action more mechanical, his moral dilemmas a series of dream fulfillments. This has nothing to do with being white or black. In American fiction, talent after talent has begun with his best novel and gone steadily downhill. Hemingway wrote *The Sun Also Rises* as a young reporter in Paris and never equaled it. Similarly, Sinclair Lewis wrote himself steadily downhill. Though he has written book after book, James T. Farrell has never equaled the impact of *Studs Lonigan*. Ralph Ellison, Salinger, and Henry Roth have never published a second novel. Here, as in so many ways, William Faulkner is a rare exception. You judge a writer at his best, without carping over his every line; and at his best, Baldwin has carved an honest niche for himself in American letters. Furthermore, his essays have the moodiest, mellowest, most wicked ripple in the recent language.

As for his role in society, Baldwin broke out of Shadow and into Face as a black writer. Other black writers have come with talent; he had to be met not just as a performer, but as a conscience, an artist, and a citizen. Whatever quicksands sucked at his soul, while larger, smoother, easier men applauded, Baldwin laid his guts on the line with integrity.

The reviews of Eldridge Cleaver's book, *Soul on Ice,* as usual, told us only that some existential experience had taken place on paper. But then the stories followed. Cleaver was in and out of prison, and for heavy stuff—rape and violence, not just the pimping and thievery of Malcolm X's early career. Cleaver became a Black Panther leader, ran for president, slid out of sight after a gun battle, and showed up in Algiers with a government in exile. The stories made him sound like a latter-day Malcolm X, gone a bit closer toward the wall of fire. So I read *Soul on Ice*.

Cleaver has the rich, strong style of blues writing, with its shifting, repeating, eliminating, testing, to arrive at clarity and cleanliness of soul. In the hands of its masters, Baldwin, Malcolm X, and others, it holds a marvelous suspense, working around its goals, then finally landing on its target. Cleaver is looser. His book begins in a murky prison pit with no shores, only opaque waters—you never meet his family, as with Malcolm X. Malcolm X is flat honest about his earlier criminal record. You know exactly what he did because he tells you, and he also tells you what he now thinks of it. Cleaver's organ music flows with deeper soul music; but it isn't really in touch with what he does. There are no shallows, no shores, no anchor points, no plain talk to go with his soul talk, no simple moral slams, like "The truth is clean" or "Nobody pisses on me." You never know what he thinks finally about anything; there are only eddies of journal and reaction that lead nowhere.

The book is not a book, but a collection of fragments—the love letters leave unclear if Beverly Axelrod is white or black, or what finally came of it—just vignettes, episodes, moody prison music. Cleaver starts out fascinated with the white woman and ends up with a formal declaration to all black women; but is that a seduction, a solemn declaration, or just a prayer?—and what happened to the earlier lust for a white woman? You never learn. This isn't finished writing, but the product of a long term in prison, when you are offered soulful ambiguity.

All this is by way of comment on the whole book, but it is all beside the point after one essay. Strong in some spots, weak in others, the waters of the book rise to a head in the essay "Notes on a Native Son." This is an attack to the death on James Baldwin, an attack so empty of content and dense with triumph, you wonder what made Cleaver write it. Except that there is one obvious motive—and that motive is contemptible.

Cleaver says Baldwin hates blacks and loves whites. As evidence, he quotes a couple of Baldwin's lines out of context, ignoring his plots, ignoring his characters, ignoring millions of other lines Baldwin wrote. The quoted lines don't prove anything—they are quotes from characters, with ironic overtones that could lead anywhere. Cleaver makes insinuations about Baldwin's personal life that are none of his damn business. And is Cleaver's own sexual life so loving and inspirational? He brags about raping women, black and white. Doesn't he grasp what a sadistic perversion rape is? Nearly half his book is the mood-music of sex talk, to white women, to black women, soul talk about black eunuchs. Even his attack on Baldwin has the feel of a verbal rape. And he attacks head-on, in a book to establish political soul! The obvious motive is that Baldwin was a gifted writer and political leader of the blacks, and Cleaver wanted that role. Kids play that game of "king-of-the-hill," where you become the "king-of-the-hill" by throwing off the old king. Only kids don't play it to break a man's back. Cleaver's attack begins with a long statement of how much he got from Baldwin. The return he makes is ugly. There's an old folk proverb, "Don't piss into a well you drank out of." Writers like Cleaver should keep their piss to themselves. Their teachers deserve better.

Cleaver's Black Panthers are a somber group. I take them straight. They are black revolutionaries, related to Trotsky, Mao, Fanon and Castro, and they are committed to a revolutionary overthrow of our government. Their language dances a bit; but they say it, and say it flat. They are the black backlash, drawing back from becoming a Shadow. They sense the deep loss of the Proletarian mystique, the poignance, the continual movement, the world continuity, the elemental humanity. The romantic fringe of the black Proletariat refuses to pay that price, and becomes Black Panthers. Such a romantic mystique arouses much sympathy; but as a revolutionary movement, they have no power base in a black establishment that is more and more joining the middle class. What they are creating is not revolution, but an opting out, a sinking underground, a loose picking and choosing of when to use what agency, and to what purpose. The system will not be gotten rid of; it will only get more disjointed.

Going against the more usual drift of American blacks toward the middle class, the Black Panthers enforce tight discipline, paramilitary training and comradely élan. They spurn available channels to authority with absolute finality. They have to. Their wholly romantic fling shrinks in importance as an American black sits on the Supreme Court, in the Senate, at the UN, American blacks sit in mayoralty seats across the country. The Panthers label such officials house Negroes. They have to. Otherwise their revolution has lost most of its point. They have a food program for black children in schools, but only as a technique for building political support, as Tammany Hall gave neighborhood jobs, or the Republican Party television franchises.

The Black Panthers are bitter at their hostile press. Yes, their press is generally hostile, but not as universally so as they claim. The press at the New Haven trial was not hostile. Lonnie McLucas got a fair trial, to their embarrassed pleasure. What is more, they conducted the trial in a way to get him off, controlling his dress and behavior in court; the press and court then met them halfway. At other trials, they pursue other, more political purposes.

I personally respect the Black Panthers enough to be uneasy, not about revolution, but about a jaundiced wrench and disruption that can lead nowhere. I've met underground revolutionary groups before, members of the Irgun, gallant romantics, giddily disciplined to dying. Once, hitchhiking through Ireland, I smoked out a gunrunner for the IRA, and like a damn fool let him know it. We had one hell of a conversation. Last year, I heard a Black Panther address a student group, and got firsthand reports about another at Yale. The revolutionary is a breed unto himself, different from the Proletariat. He exaggerates to a stylized edge his romantic sweep, his intuition of underlying deep humanity, his mystique of creativity, but there is nothing simple about his commitment to revolution. In movies, novels, folklore, he comes through as supremely profound, simple, elemental. Such a creature may well exist; but I personally have never met any revolutionary that was not exceedingly complex, set in a high key. He has to be. He is a creature in part out of Genet, with a double focus of violence and tranquility, of open immediacy and hidden purpose. What he is after, however, is a very raw simple thing: revolution.

Always, the commitment to political violence, to assassination and its plotting, whatever its justifications, is a rancid fluid that changes the texture of a man's temperament. Living close to the ragged edge of desperation, sooner or later, he feels the violence turn him on until it never leaves his mind. He becomes its creature, like a nymphomaniac, who moves by fanatic rigidities, formulae of behavior, degradation and a steady fear of betrayal. After a while, he lusts after violence. Killings turn him on like Marilyn Monroe and the pages of *Playboy*. In Cleaver's new documentary movie, perhaps the longest sequence is the one in which Cleaver buys a long switchblade and then plays with it by throwing the blade in and out. He fingers that blade like a little boy his newly discovered prick, in complacent quiet, out of touch with place, people or any before or after, the prick of his blade the only reality he is in touch with.

The Black Panthers are a somber, but special group of revolutionary activists, today apparently thinning out. Much more important than their essential threat is the breadth of their appeal, the political support they mobilize among white liberal intellectuals. Such a liberal, if he supports an expansionist revolutionary party, must blind himself to the fanatic party controls that would follow a revolutionary seizure of power. He may gain their grudging thanks, as he digs the ground from under his own beliefs. The reason such liberals support the revolutionaries instead of other social programs among the blacks is quite simply that they are romantics who hunger for the breath and excitement of the Proletariat in a world too drab and mean for their spirits. Political five-year-olds, feeling their lives trivial after hearing their first Robin Hood story, they chase poignancy and national sweep. More constructive black programs are too drably real to turn them on.

I speak here not of true intellectuals, a rare and eccentric Proletariat of the human mind, with all the sweep and intuition they need, but rather of well-meaning intellectual professionals, most of them careerists and not true intellectuals at all. The essential problem of such a careerist is that he is a professional on paper, ignorant of action, yet feeling obligated to extend himself—an attitude-producer.

A charmingly trivial instance of the college professor as attitude-producer occurred about four years ago, when our English Department introduced a tutorial system for English majors. The entire department discussed the plan—tutorial systems are rare in large state universities, and we wanted ours to work. One clumsy feature was that each proposed tutorial unit was to have fifteen students. Since the unit replaces a single course, this might overload the system before it could prove itself. Professor after professor got up with quiet dignity, objected to the number fifteen, and sat down with respect. He had left the number fifteen there; but he had at least expressed his attitude.

I kept quiet at first; having had no experience with the tutorial system, I was uncertain how it operated. But when the project was coming to a vote with the number fifteen still there, I raised my hand. The department chairman called on me. I said, "I move that the word fifteen be removed from the tutorial plan, and the word ten be substituted for it."

The chairman caught his breath, then quietly asked for a second. After several moments of silence, five or six seconds came tumbling in. Before the amendment came to a vote, the chairman had the wording changed from "fifteen" to "a viable number of students," thus keeping his hand free. It seemed that professionally trained adults, in formal meeting, using democratic process, were about to vote in an unmanageable plan, once having registered their attitudes. Last spring, these same men voted to close the university in a protest strike against the Cambodian invasion and the Black Panther trial in New Haven.

The word had been quietly passed on the walk to the Senate meeting that we had to call a strike. There were reports of attempts to burn down the university—not an idle threat, it proved. A large storage building was soon burned down, and there were numbers of small brushfires. The meeting was packed and tumultuous. The strike was called in a locked approval of the original strike call from New Haven, to express opposition to the invasion of Cambodia and to the Black Panther trial in New Haven. There was a fair amount of open speech, given the large tumultuous crowd; but the actual strike call was essentially managed by the activist professors scattered around the hall, who regularly passed the floor to one another, not as a conspiratorial arrangement, but as a well-organized mutual cuing. When their wording was on the floor, the question was called, and the vote taken.

I personally read manipulation of faculty opinion in the linkage of Cambodia and the Black Panther trial. Why protest these two things at once more than the poisoning of Lake Erie, the outmoded seniority system in Congress, the logjam in the New York criminal courts, or the allocation system of Welfare? Why not strike for higher pay, while we were at it—that made sense! The answer seemed quite obvious. The New Haven trial was the trial of an activist revolutionary party; all other discrimination and legal malpractice simply oppressed the poor—their radical implications were tenuous, remote, and obscure. What that strike was establishing was not justice, but the public domain: that radical issues established the moral vocabulary of our university.

I raised my hand repeatedly, trying to add the murder of Martin Luther King to the itemized list of indignities we were striking against. At least King was at the receiving end of a bullet. We were closing our university in moral support of a man who by his own admission had fired a bullet into the face of a comrade, his excuse being that the man was dead already, so the bullet didn't count.

My entire maneuver became pointless when a colleague asked why a particular criminal trial in a distant city none of us knew firsthand should be prejudged in advance of court proceedings, when a murdered body had actually been found, and also why one murder indictment in another state should close an entire university. The activist leader told him that either we showed solidarity with the three-point strike call in New Haven, or our strike call would be meaningless and a waste of time. His argument was utterly specious—the papers report a strike, whatever the wording of the lower paragraphs. The point the radical was establishing was that the issues on which we were committing our consciences and striking our jobs were not open to individual decision, that an obscure radical assembly in New Haven determined the moral stance of our university, and not our own considered judgments.

My deep chagrin at that strike call increased on reflection. Why did only professors go on strike, and not the ethical and conscientious among tailors, shoemakers, writers and editors? The *Times* wasn't suspending publication. Torn pants were still getting fixed, garbage was being picked up in trucks. Long distance calls were still being transmitted. Did injustice pulverize only our professorial consciences? I suspected a simpler explanation: that editors, tailors, and garbage collectors take their work seriously, and serve a public that needs their services; our strike testified not to our deep moral worth, but only to our sense of triviality in what we do. The core of a strike is the interrupted encounter between two parties; but education has only the thinnest of encounters today. In a bitter mood, one might call our action a bargain. The faculty wanted to do research, the students to gain in social effectiveness. In a strike, the faculty has its research uninterrupted by the tedious classroom. The students can organize rallies, marches, and symposia, uninterrupted by the tedious classroom. Why didn't we think of it sooner?

At times, I dream of opening my own Protest College, on a large wooded estate in Westchester, a heroic undertaking. Singlehanded, I will undertake to teach the entire curriculum, with no excuses, no compromises for expediency—Colloquial Greek in the Age of Socrates, Suburban Identity Problems in California, the Hourly Wage behind the Iron Curtain, Eccentricities of Late Gothic Facades—that program will cover everything! On arrival, my students will go on strike against the curriculum; but I won't budge an inch. All winter, my students will conduct nightly sensitivity sessions over the meaning of purpose in education. We'll dovetail meaningfully: they'll pay their tuition; I'll give their lives direction. In May, I'll give "The Razzberry Statement" to Hollywood for a cool million. Half my students will marry and settle in Larchmont on the proceeds, having achieved social effectiveness; the rest will join a communal farm deep in the Rockies, having established meaninglessness. Will I have a registration my second year!

The sour residue of our choked laughter is the knowledge of the failed encounter between the educator and the student. It has made youth the basic Proletariat of today, not by their poverty—youth is very rich—and not by their suffering, which is a necessary accident, but Proletariat because they are choked off, without any channels to power. Indeed, youth today has the mysterious instincts of a Proletariat, from the tony rich in Las Vegas to the longhairs beaten up by skinheads, from the mindless finks out of sight to the quiet pacifists shot at by the National Guard. They have a national sweep—a strike in Berkeley touches off a strike in Columbia touches off a strike in Harvard or Yale. They shift about, hungry for contact with raw people, behind the walls of culture. Street people, they produce slang and generate their own folksingers. Rock festivals like Woodstock are latter-day secular pilgrimages that gather their devotees in the hundreds of thousands to hear their music. Even the names of rock groups—the Mothers of Invention, the Rolling Stones, the Mamas and Papas, the Grateful Dead—differ from the names of jazz groups as the Proletarian roots of rock differ from the aristocratic jazz élite. Their hunger for raw life gives them continuity with Vietnam, Cuba, China— with their own mythic heroes, Mao, Che, Danny the Red.

Yet they are an exceedingly muted Proletariat. To glorify them either as a blessing or a threat falsifies their first flickers of truth, their beginnings of self-consciousness. The whole strident consumer mentality, the turning on to music, pot, travel, is all a consolation prize, after they have lost out on the main chance. Essentially, they know they've been had. They study to learn to be effective; but their schools are not agencies of effectiveness. Yet what did youth ever have but distant, self-involved teachers and an indifferent adult world? And yet medieval students parsed their Aquinas without secretly celebrating the Black Plague. Why have collectives of students closed down entire universities? A fourth term in our survey must be explored: mystique.

3

MYSTIQUE

A MYSTIQUE is an intuition about ultimate life significance, what you do in a dry waste to find renewal and be yourself again. The intuition is entirely personal—anybody can have a mystique about anything; but it must be about an actual life experience. The mill-hand utterly committed to his open hearth has an open-hearth-furnace mystique. A veteran gamesman can have a duplicate-contract-bridge mystique, on first walking into a tournament room with all the players at their tables. Some women come mysteriously alive rocking a child to sleep; the mystiques of other women are less sentimental. There are men who step into a strange cocktail party, radiantly confident that within half an hour they will make friends with every person there, and find a partner for the night.

The experience of a mystique is generally repetitive, though it can come once in a lifetime, like a loss of virginity, or not at all; an overscrupulous addict can have a "some-day-I'll-die-of-an-overdose" mystique, a woman with a hysterectomy may live for her visionary baby, a virgin spinster wait to dissolve in her lover's arms. Other events pass like shadows; these, real or imagined, have a glow of ultimate meaning. The question of final validity is not relevant here. Karl Marx made a mystique of factory work, Pope John XXIII of priestly guidance, Huey Newton of black bodies and white minds. Whatever may be true under the aspect of eternity, in human experience all mystiques are created equal.

A mystique hides a strange element of paradox. On the one

hand, its vignette of action, the episode it repeats with such dedication, seems clearly narcissistic. The gratification comes, as it were, inside a picture frame, all its rewards spelled out in advance. A huge wash of pleasure is possible, but no radical openness, no innocent new thing, no really fresh air, only the familiar fulfillments of a settled ego. The weary mother will rock her child to sleep again, the cocktail-party veteran find another bed-partner, stir all night with shattering, ultimate love, and the next day wend his way to another cocktail party. He will never really meet anybody. And yet the experience in a mystique seems exceedingly hard-edge; people connect there as nowhere else. The supremely effective doctor has a mystique of healing the sick; his less narcissistic colleagues may never quite connect.

A mystique thus suggests a strange creature, the well-adjusted narcissist, completely self-contained, yet completely alive to the flow of reality. He is a well-adjusted dreamer, utterly involved, managing and enjoying with gusto a picture-postcard life.

This strange phenomenon of the well-adjusted dreamer is a sort of mirror phenomenon, a double reinforcement, where id and superego, conventionally in conflict, have momentarily joined forces and are one. The pleasure is approved from on high: the coach's eyes beam with approval as the boy's bat hits the ball; the voice teacher stirs with pleasure as the singer begins "Celeste Aida." Indeed, the fusion is closer. In a mystique, the person becomes his own approving superior. The little girl rocking her baby brother to sleep rocks all the infants of the world to sleep. God's word pours through the lips of the minister in the pulpit. Real or illusory, for a tough soldier in a minefield as for Walter Mitty dodging across an empty lot, the mythic reality is one.

This close overlap of enjoyment and approval would explain the simplicity of the activity. Motherhood in general is large, loose, and vague; but the mirroring, like a telescopic lens, brings to a focus a million sentimental memories, stories, advertisements in ladies' magazines. Mysteriously, suddenly, rocking that worn cradle, singing that old lullaby, a thousand diffuse energies collect to make cradling the act of motherhood.

The implications of all this for Marxism are straightforward and far-reaching. Marx, who believed in a mystique of labor, grasped the act of the laborer as a fundamental process of reality, as opposed, for example, to an exhilarating, but essentially trivial, game of polo. Such a process he saw working in nature and in man. His narrow, close metaphysics of process, though Germanic and nineteenth-centuryish, is of considerable historic importance, but it has no finality as truth. Human nature is too wayward to be reduced to the level of metaphysics.

The Marxist metaphysics today is academic, even in Soviet Russia. So its historic impact comes with a mixed response. It seems tolerably clear in the wake of the Hungarian and Czech revolts, and the mass flights that followed, that Marxism behind the Iron Curtain has at best a grudging and helpless acquiescence. Noam Chomsky, Susan Sontag, and other American visitors to North Vietnam may be correct in their view that the North Vietnamese enjoy a deeply truthful sense of arrival in socialism; yet the doubt remains whether a visit to Hungary, Czechoslovakia, or East Germany by these visitors would not produce a report from them of equal beatitude. Under an absolute state, human docility can be enormous. However sincere their attempt at a tabula rasa in reporting broad dedication in a socialist state, the fact remains that the Berlin Wall exists on the Marxist side of the Iron Curtain to prevent a mass flight from those utopian centers. At best, the Marxist record is, finally, spotty, like everything else on earth.

If Marxism is a live force today, a vision, a faith, a massive conversion experience, it is so by virtue of Marx's mystique of labor, by the fascinated intuition that here, in simple, constructive labor, lies health, truth, peace, fulfillment. Our core question must therefore be: what validity has Marx's mystique of labor? But the matter is so subject to personal impression, and so inherently resistant to hard evidence that I should put my own position forward as openly as possible:

The more one reads in history and literature, the more clear it becomes that man lives in two domains, the domain of matter and the domain of spirit. Technical discussions aside, in an utterly flat, operational way, whatever its grounds, the activity of the human temperament is its own domain, with laws, energies, rhythms, and moods that get violated when translated into laws of inorganic matter. The reduction of experimental psychology to electric twitches is hardly established in the laboratory; it offers no clue to historic behavior.

The practice of writers and thinkers who reduce actual social behavior to some material operation falsifies, muffles, imprisons and cheapens their subject. They may teach that way, but they do not live that way; and when they do, they are sick. Thus, considering the strange reinforcement and locking in of a mystique, I need not translate its terms into electric or chemical energy. It works by psychic energy, the energy of the world of spirit. This is not a religious commitment—the vale apart, the secret domain—with far-reaching philosophical implications; and yet I never met a rock with a mystique, I never met a lake with a mystique, nor even a telephone pole with a mystique—only people.

My problem with Marx is not his metaphysics per se, but how, since I regard his metaphysics of process as academic, I am to do justice to his impact on history. Indeed, let me go one step further and admit not only that I am a thorough pluralist about human history, but also that I believe any systematic operational monist who knows what he is talking about is biased, a liar or a political hack. The impulse to monism is certainly there, the imperative need to unify body and spirit, and somehow become a single whole person; but it is an impulse for harmony in an organic whole, not for a translation and elimination of one of the parts. The ploy of

Communist Poland and Czechoslovakia is to offer the open hearth furnace, not as a gesture of a free spirit—no freedom of spirit whatever is allowed—but as a sort of giant popsicle, to induce an impoverished submissiveness. Narrowly material fulfillment offers a suicide by smothering, as narrowly spiritual things offer a suicide of emptiness. The one produces aggressive self-degradation, the other wet dreams.

What is fascinating about the two large domains of matter and spirit is the equilibrium they maintain in social history, the way civilization has grown by a balance of "itness" and "thou-ness," by shifts toward concerns of spirit, and away. During the Renaissance, for example, the bent of civilization was to emancipate the hard material world, the world of "it's," from a controlling world of spirit. So the basic campaign of seventeenth century philosophers, Bacon, Descartes, Spinoza, Leibniz, Hobbes, and others, was a strategic mapping out of the domain of man's worldly experience, to clear the ground for a new thrust. At that time the scholastics were the enemy, most fundamentally, because they were the strategists of the domain of spirit, its general staff. The domain of things then aggressively demanded control of its own domain, to develop its own vocabulary, and even to reverse roles and rule over spirit, reduce spirit to its own terms.

The Olympian magnificence of Francis Bacon's style is not simply philosophical. His lofty asides, his magisterial presence, his strictures about language, method and personal behavior, all breathe an imperial Renaissance temperament. This was a latter-day Roman, a Francis Drake of the wilderness of nature, a frontier statesman negotiating with a decayed establishment, establishing borders for his brave new world, positioning for more favorable terms. When his negotiations are finished, the universe—the world of things—is in business for itself. We will shape, experience, and know it at our pleasure—let God be circumspect in His complaints. A generation later, Hobbes more aggressively projected a world of eternally bouncing mini-marbles, with no play of spirit at all, to be choreographed by Isaac Newton in the eternal dance of matter.

This establishment by Bacon and Hobbes of the domain of matter over the domain of spirit registered early among the poets. So Milton, in a turn that lasted throughout his life, steadily shrank back and withdrew into a dead universe, from the early flowering garden of *Comus*, to Adam an alien in a lost Paradise, to Christ confronting Satan in a dry desert, to Samson, "eyeless, in Gaza, at the mill with slaves." From Milton's first boyish opening in "On the Morning of Christ's Nativity" on, there is a steady loss of light, permeability, direction and divine influx. The still turning point occurred with the loss of Eden. Then the garden of spirit decayed to mechanical processes, and nature gave a death groan.

As the eighteenth century evolved, early eccentrics of the new age fought the scientific consensus in a head-on confrontation, as in William Blake's note-book poem sometimes called "The Scoffers":

Mock on, mock on, Voltaire, Rousseau:
Mock on, Mock on; 'tis all in vain!
You throw the sand against the wind
And the wind blows it back again.

And every sand becomes a Gem
Reflected in the beams divine;
Blown back, they blind the mocking Eye,
But still in Israel's paths they shine.

The atoms of Democritus
And Newton's Particles of light
Are sands upon the Red sea shore,
Where Israel's tents do shine so bright.

So Blake took his stand with the chosen visionary host who will follow the God-given path of light to the Promised Land, while

Democritus and Newton pile up the sand of atoms and ideas to mislead the unwary and drown the disbeliever. The demonic desperation of spirit, its defensive shifts for survival that underlie so much in the "Songs of Experience" come to a head in this notebook poem given the title "The Defiled Sanctuary":

I saw a chapel all of gold
That none did dare to enter in,
And many weeping stood without,
Weeping, mourning, worshipping.

I saw a serpent rise between
The white pillars of the door,
And he forced and forced and forced,
Down the golden hinges tore.

And along the pavement sweet,
Set with pearls and rubies white,
All his slimy length he drew,
Till upon the altar white

Vomiting his poison out
On the bread and on the wine.
So I turned into a sty,
And laid me down among the swine.

Throughout the nineteenth century, an increasingly common theme is the pilgrim quest of spirit in a choked dead world, the thrashing unto futility and death, whatever the intervening orgies of life and art: Ahab sailing in a whaling ship, Don Juan wandering all over Europe, Van Gogh in his journey to the Mistral country, Gauguin in his to the South Seas. More than artistic niceties are involved here. The sheer freight of things on the alien domain of spirit makes spirit turn demonic: we see the bulky expansion of manufacture, year by year and century by century, the contamination of the atmosphere, the poisoning of lake, river, and ocean.

The very bulk of objects versus people, as silently recorded in museums, grows steadily more embarrassing. Ancient lamps, that were tiny stone lumps or twists of metal, now have hanging in their place bulbs and beehives of lights. So six-stories become apartment blocks, then co-op cities, as our body-size loses all proportion to the size of the things around us.

This comparative diminution of body shrinks our sense of ourselves to a cipher, and induces radical fragmentation. As a result the "kick" has been substituted for taste in art; after the first kick, the object is phased out as a historic item or a sentimentality. A dance by the pulsing flicker of strobic lights gets rid of walls, of hard, continuous bodies. Gone strobic, the body becomes like the flicker of a bad movie projector, flashes of existence pulsing and disappearing in a growling kick universe.

So live entertainment comes in packages growing steadily larger in size of audience, of hall, of package, of take. Rock music has grown from underground clubs to fill Madison Square Garden. Fillmore East, a large movie house and the former New York outlet for rock music, had to be closed because of costs. The entertainment package steadily lengthens its list of items to attract a crowd to pay the overhead. Open-air festivals expand to Woodstock, with half a million in attendance. As the world grows more cluttered, we expand our dream of ourselves.

The body cannot be enlarged; but it can get amplified. Four hours in the darkening cool at Newport built up to Tina Turner, with three dancers behind her to amplify her motions, two praying mantises of cameras and sound men arching around, a full band slugging out the accompaniment, shell lights flashing and changing color in a pop earthquake, as she unlimbered and rolled to the music, then hunched up and murmured kisses into the loudspeaker to be amplified; the festival audience of tens of thousands stood on chairs, danced in the aisles, clumped around the refreshment stands, or sprawled on blankets on the lawns, making out. Over

them all, Tina gurgled cosmological kisses, Mmmm. Mmm-
mmmmhh!! Mmmmmmmmmmmmmhhhh!!! MMMMMMMMMM-
MMHHHHHHHHH!!!! God should promote relationships that
total!

Hunched up, belting out, waving, singing, and strutting, she set
my feet kicking. I headed out from a front row seat past block after
block of seats, packed with people standing, cakewalking on their
chairs, straining towards the stage, applauding to the rhythm of
the music. I then circled the broad, empty bleachers. Sometimes I
climbed a chair and watched the distant shells, shuffling in place,
then got off and meandered away some more. Smaller and smaller,
like a white wafer, three bodies behind her, Tina ducked, strutted,
and belted out the music, hunched up and bubbled out kisses.

As I passed the last row of seats, Tina started some husky soul-
talk about men walking out on women for a good time; and I knew
she meant me. I started to run. Couples were dancing on the lawn
and kissing on the meadow. The occasional refreshment tables on
the mall were shambles of mustard, ketchup, spilled Pepsi, and
plastic containers of sugar. Off to the right, in the parking lots, the
cars began to unhook and converge on the exits like Mississippi
barges, converging on the Louisiana delta. Festival police with
Mountie hats, swinging red flashlights, directed funnels of traffic
past the parked ice-cream trucks, the hot-dog stations, the bead
stands and racks of posters. The traffic flashed along the highway
ribbon below. A plane passed overhead.

As I climbed the back hill, Tina's talk cuddled in my ears; her
murmur glided up my arms and legs and around my chest. I took a
last look back from the top of the crest. Thumbnail Tina stomped
and cakewalked, three echoes cakewalking behind her, her husky,
coaxing voice up with the Great Bear. I marched steadily out of
sight, but the amplifier never weakened. Half a mile off, great
banks of stars caught in the wooded slopes; a few gas stations
pulsed below in the darkness. Tina's voice still hunched up. Her

thighs breathed it, her soft throat chiding, loving, forgiving, dropping kisses sweeter than wine, my Caroline, my Prue, my Ruth, my Rose, Oh my melancholy baby, rocked to a Mmmmm! Mmmmmmmm!! Mmmmmmmmmmmm!!! MMMMMMMMMMmmmmmmmmmmmmmmmmmmm . . .

This is the American mystique, bulky as a carton of Coca-Cola. Small as you are, you disappear in a tremendous thing, with the action though you're too small for the action. It lines up the crowds to glide up the Empire State Building, at the base of Boulder Dam, along the Cape Kennedy beaches as the count-down approaches zero. It has no sense of the substance of labor, only of its aura, its atmosphere of stupendous arrival. For labor itself, it cares nothing.

In Las Vegas recently, twenty thousand customers packed a hotel amphitheater to welcome Elvis Presley after a ten-year absence for a million dollar engagement. Twenty thousand gourmet dinners disappeared, course by course, around layers of tables, up a series of ramps, twenty thousand bottles of wine, cognac, gin, and vermouth, at twenty to sixty dollars a party, served by a band of waiters organized like a moon rocket takeoff at Cape Kennedy. After a ten-minute introduction of creamed soul, Elvis flipped out in a snow-white cowboy suit. Moving like a combination high school cheerleader and Robin Hood winning the Sherwood Forest archery meet, he belted out the vintage successes of yesteryear. Socko—he delivered love soured in white vinegar; wispy-wise, he sprinkled tenderness with brown sugar, and smoked it all night over a hickory fire. The applause was the same at the start and the finish of every number.

The stage was wide as Wrigley Field. Two or three times, to deafening applause, Elvis covered its entire length for a ten or fifteen minute walk, shook every upraised hand and kissed every pretty girl. A wave of people rose from below as he approached. The sighs stirred in a wind over the tiers of tables. My table, on the far right, back on the second tier, was too boxed in to make it in and back simply. And if I managed, could I fight through that forest of upraised hands and reach Elvis' hand? It was a problematical piece of Elvis or a rib steak rare with buttered asparagus on the side. As Elvis slowly walked, and the crowd rose to meet him, I glumly stuck to my rib steak rare, methodically sliced it, and sipped my wine. Elvis wasn't singing for me, not the way Tina kissed me from half a mile away.

That's how you register in America today, as the human equivalent of Kellogg's Corn Flakes, simple but amplified, with grit, but universal, all that homespun humility and downright honesty coming through like Tina's kisses, all over the hills along the shore. Me, I'm always spoiling it, being suddenly Jewish, or downbeat square, or too solidly intellectual, or scarily the writer. I zizz too fast, instead of responding to a crowd with amplified kisses.

But this American version of the vision of size—being you, just mythic you, like Tina's kisses or Elvis walking along the stage—has an old history, going back to the Pacific primordial statues, the boulevards before the pyramids of Egypt, the Sphinx as a beast-god. In the Renaissance, Leonardo sketched homunculus, the dim body of creation straddling the universe; and Bacon negotiated with the universe for terms. Michelangelo's Sistine Chapel then threw out the towering figures of its mythic spirit-men, become suddenly muscular, with ambitious bodies and moody strategies. The ideal woman's body was rediscovered from Greek sculpture—the distance of the breasts from one another, the ideal location of the nipples, the length and breadth of the hip, shoulder, thigh, and leg. Fifteenth century oils line up their people to stare at you as you stare at them; the sixteenth century began spiraling torso, drapery, buildings and landscapes in twists of flawless equilibrium.

America still has the bit between its teeth, though it has lost much of its nerve. We fish for our ideal type; but we want an extra something. We don't trust homunculus to make it any more. We need some machinery to put him in harness, amplify his delivery, package his soul in strobic lights—Richard Nixon making V for victory with hunched shoulders and glazed eyes. And yet, glamorized, pasteurized, homogenized, dry-cleaned, his tinted hair set in a permanent wave, Elvis remains a mystery, his heart as enigmatic as the heart of Nixon. Lichtenstein's comic-strip oils offer flawless but immobile gestures, Dick-Tracy bodies in polka dots, who blow up glazed balloons of talk that say nothing. So Oldenberg's idiotic hamburger rises over the city, ridiculous, monumental, an embarrassment. We glorify the package and wonder what's inside it.

How much currency can the Marxist superman still have in our century, even granted that he's more real than ours? Marx's visionary laborer was right for the nineteenth century, elemental, below the surface, producing the things of this world. A century ago, a human body was still relevant to the labor it did, somehow coördinated to its work. When a man lifted a stone, his hand held it—that was his lift. When he heaved up a shovelful of dirt, the shovel served as his big, broad, hard hand. When he worked a steam shovel, the cavernous steel jaw, hoisting a ton of dirt, was still his hoist, his lift. He was inside the machine, pulling the handle, turning the wheel, pressing his foot on the brake. The machine was the man's body extended, made bigger, harder, more tooled to its work. That was the mystique of labor.

But that rapport of a man with his machinery is tricky. For some reason, a man identifies with handles, not with buttons. So restaurant coffee machines have a long, stiff handle to start them. Then the cook makes the coffee: he pours in the ingredients, plunges in the cord, and pulls the handle. Machines with buttons keep the cook outside; they give no satisfaction and do not sell. So, for some reason, driving blends the driver with the machine, anonymous, a nomad, on the hunt, on the move, attuned to two tons of steel that heave, turn, lunge forward, brake and never tire. This nomad's steel carpet isn't a machine to accomplish labor, but a sudden, huge insect body out of steel he blends with for a while.

But the professional truck driver, whose truck is his laboring body, is the most trustworthy thing on the road.

When Marx wrote, work was mechanical work, powered by steam and coal, driven by massive factory machinery the worker stayed inside. Machinery was still the extension of a man's body. The body in overalls simply grew bigger and more powerful inside the steam hoist. Labor then had a cleansing, objectifying ambiance. Work was a mysterious dialogue of spirit with matter, where something not there before was made or something that existed was changed. His new table, his building, his farm, his school: by that he tested his worth.

But Marx added an unnecessary complexity when he read the work of destiny in the machinery of labor; man's body, amplified and extended through factory machinery, became the body of God in a monistic universe. The metaphor of divinity is not trivial. Marx came from a converted and estranged German Jewish family —his father became a Lutheran in 1817, a year before he was born; and yet, despite the family estrangement, the classless society might well keep a Messianic echo. Living in a world of estrangement behind estrangement, Marx dug for essentials, the here and now in the very tissue of common life, as established in labor.

Marx recognized only the overriding mystique of labor, as a self-actualizing, inherent natural force. Hence he envisioned the dictatorship of the proletariat as leading to a withering away of government and a society of the blessed. He had no grasp of independent human will, shaping and controlling labor for itself, no sense of the tenacity of bureaucracy, the sheer vested interest of human wills in power. He therefore saw a revolutionary committee as fulfillment of a natural process, like the flowering of a plant, not as a concentration of ambitious, frustrated, dedicated, politically instinctual, kinky egos, who get along in order to survive.

Marx's blindness to ego overriding labor, to the sheer clank of party machinery in action, made him the innocent visionary who enabled the Bolshevik Revolution. His metaphysic tied him to material production with a built-in dialectic of employers and employees; but his mystique of labor has profound merit. Honest labor and gestures of love are the two genuine encounters of spirit with material existence. In a mysterious way, the workless are maimed and parasitic. A man grows up, shaping the world he inhabits.

But Marx's monolithic metaphysic of process muffled the Marxist party machinery and silenced its talk. Essentially, spirit works by dialogue, as common ground opens between two free individuals where surprising connections can take place. But verbal as many Marxists are, their brains, their symbols and memories busily establish process instead of meeting people. They live knotted in process and encounter no one. They make one claustrophobic. As a result, Russian political pronouncements work like cosmetics, to announce the season's colors, but they never betray what the lips and eyes are doing.

These reserves shape the texture of Soviet Russia. Russia today is an entrenched power entity, like any monolithic state, an empire, with a history of proud achievements, and an investment in treachery. It starved the Ukrainian farmers in the hundreds of thousands; it exterminated a million in the Siberian labor camps under Stalin; it forcibly overthrew the free governments of Hungary and Czechoslovakia; and yet the Russians hang on hard as they slug out. Silent, muffled, primitive, indoctrinated, they beat Hitler to his knees. The working people make a quiet go of it. It is a going concern. But locked and closeted within their steady chew of process, Marxists avoid simple, blunt, factual truths about Soviet Russia. Plain realities behind the Iron Curtain are always swallowed up and disappear. It's not that lies are told; some lies—many!— are told, but that's not what's under discussion here. There simply is no encounter to begin with. You talk through Marxists, not to them. They are psychic mufflers and evaders, steadily selective about what is up for discussion. The core members long knew about Stalin's slave camps, but they kept shrugging off the evidence until Khrushchev made its existence official, whereupon it became a part of process, and could be handled in context. They talk like divine process discussing itself—say the twitch of God's toenail gossiping about His orgasm. It simply isn't done.

This temperamental bent lasts even after the commitment disappears. Estranged Marxists relate to Soviet Russia as aging virgins, intellectually emancipated, relate to sex. You occasionally get muffled chokings of genuine integrity, but never flat, simple, spontaneous reactions to things as they are.

For example, it is reasonable to say that no one in the Soviet Union knows today how many Russians Stalin's secret police killed, that no historian, no census-keeper has a stubborn enough grasp of truth to keep his own history from going down the drain. These were their own countrymen, their relatives, innocent poets, dedicated patriots, exterminated by their own secret police; but their memory disappears like car exhaust. In America, things happen; in Russia, processes take place. There, truth is a bar of plutonium. Using tongs, behind a lead shield, on a state occasion, you move it from here to here, informing the authorities in advance what you are doing; but touch the truth with your bare hands, and you will soon be put into an isolation ward for decontamination.

It is good to call a spade a spade. It is a simple economic fact today that West Germany can manufacture cheaper, stronger, more useful and more attractive goods than can Soviet Russia, where state-controlled manufacture is sluggish, massive, unimaginative and inefficient. Were Eastern Europe an open market, the Iron Curtain would turn westward. For all the pontification about socialist solidarity, historic process, the evils of capitalism—in the Russian invasions of Hungary and Czechoslovakia, a government with a good army and bad factories blocked out a government with good factories and a bad army. The Iron Curtain will significantly relax its hold on its captive market when the Russians can build a Mercedes-Benz.

But even taken with full respect, Marx's mystique of labor as factory work was changed by the work of an American, Thomas Edison, when he made electric power effective. With electric power you pull no handle or valve, but simply turn the circuit on and off, thus making electric systems an extension of the nervous system, not of the whole body. Labor today, serious labor, is an engineered trigger to a network of forces. The present mystique of industry is a mystique of force, not a mystique of labor, embodied in the engineer, not the laborer.

But the western radical today does not know his own mystique. For all his theoretical professions, he deals with and dreams about power, not labor. His only possible contact is the *Lumpenproletariat*, also a loose, powerless group. For the Weathermen to riot in Chicago, smash windows and destroy property in order to wake up workers merely exposes their dream world. So the French radicals rioted in 1968 to wake up the French worker. The French worker woke up, demanded a salary increase, and went back to sleep.

To call the Soviet Union a dictatorship of the proletariat is a pietistic euphemism. Labor has no power whatever in the Soviet Union. Any labor leader or worker who actually demanded a salary increase would disappear within hours. All political power is in party hands, a carefully organized, self-perpetuating piece of social engineering that is sane, tenacious, and gives limited support to consumer interests, to soften unrest and broaden its national support. It regards labor as a form of national wealth, like oil or corn. For a time, Russia proclaimed Gold-Star workers, as we proclaim Gold-Star mothers.

Indeed, today, in the United States, in Russia and in Europe as a whole, labor has been absorbed into the establishment. The leveling has been operational, not a matter of dialectics. Fifty or a hundred years ago, labor was proletarian. The unions were grudgingly tolerated; they were often simultaneously fought to death by hired teams of strikebreakers. This established the laborer as a tolerated outcast. The coal mines circulated evangelists through the mountain areas to distract the miners. A Department of Labor was as conceivable as a Department of Sexual Freedom or a Minister of Social Unrest. Class warfare along economic lines then made sense; the worker had economic freight, but no political power. In the largest sense, labor was a proletariat. The mystique of labor also made sense—a man's machine was his body writ large. It was slavery for another to run it.

Today, labor periodically rules England. In France, the Communist Party candidates run for public office. Communist papers sell on the open market. The government enforces party contracts. Far from being a force for revolution, the French Communist Party is a pillar of the establishment, a force for security and inertia. In America, George Meany relates to the government as a cardinal to the government of Spain. So the executive of the Construction Workers Union announced for Rockefeller for governor—Rockefeller had handled their party right. In America, as in France, the unions are bridges of stability from the government to labor unrest; they are wealthy, strongly organized, with venerable traditions—built into the government.

The Weatherman claim that the American worker has been bribed by the establishment is inane wish-fulfillment. Even James Burnham's talk of a managerial class focuses a bit narrowly on the élite power decisions. The establishment has a body as well as a brain; the labor unions are that body. The organized worker hasn't been bribed by the establishment; he is the establishment, by his will, his organizations, his vote, and even the hard hat on his head.

The Proletariat of today has nothing to do with labor. It is a rich, angry, spoiled, persecuted, contented, tumultuous, ignorant, bitchy-happy Proletariat, an ocean of mass-educated youth. It is a Proletariat because it has common goals and no regular channels to power. It kept quiet before because it was learning how to work and how to rule and accepted its Proletarian status in order to learn effectiveness. The dynamic of the last century has largely passed it by, though its instincts vibrate with the knowledge that decision also has passed it by. This Proletariat wants to become effective, not to be revolutionary. So it limps forward with a hobbled chafe, bubbles up as hippie, as street people, then adjusts to mediocrity, muffled, subdued, turned on, periodically virulent.

Typically, as a Proletariat, mass-educated youth have a mystique of their own. They have pathos, but no demands; a sense of outrage, but no program; folksongs, but no manifestoes. Their underground news service passes messages across country. They gather in hordes, and feel the sweep of history. Yet necessarily, their position steadily crumbles around them. Temporaries, ignorant of their own dynamic, essentially insecure, they sniff out lines of personal development and pass in masses into the labor market. Insufficient threads bind them together in jobs, community organizations, political parties.

Their issues are national; but their fronts are local, a campus here, a candidate there. And even on a local level, their venerable institutions, the established universities, are surrounded by permanent street communities who usurp their name, participate in their riots, champion their demands, and do everything but study, graduate, and leave. Steadily coddled by movie adulation, that commercialized sales pitch to the young, they are bribed to forget their effectiveness has been castrated. As a result, they kindle to life at a crisis, then settle back for further study. They want live communities, and get instead the cover of *Time* and the face of Agnew on a Mickey Mouse watch. This Proletariat lacks political experience or effective adult models in their teachers close at hand; so it remains a vast hunk of life, a band of brothers, serious, unsure, seeking self-respect and a purpose to live by.

Their blindly old-fashioned left fringe, the current generation of radicals, is a sentimental antique. All anger and righteous ideology, they publish, commune together, gather in conventions, flexing for a relevant position. Blind as lemmings, having vaguely inherited the labor mystique from the Marx of a hundred years ago, they grope toward labor for support both in France and here in the United States. Vaguely, they cultivate home crafts, loom fabrics in the living room on store-bought looms, tinker with motorcycles, wear white Ophelia dresses, and parrot the Victorian sentiments of William Morris to feel at one with the steel industry. An occasional American Trotskyite speaks with nostalgic excitement of making contact with a migrant worker, his first bus stop on the journey to his Holy Spirit.

In a mucky way, the contemporary revolutionary senses the contradiction. He avoids the labor union establishment, the tough unions like the Steel Workers which have a clear political definition, trust funds, big housing developments and a hard international line; too many of their jobs are at stake in the war effort for a speedy withdrawal from South Vietnam. He concentrates rather on fringe workers, Chicanos, migrant farmworkers, unemployed blacks, the dropouts of technical high schools in our cities. But such marginal workers are the rejects and misfits of society, without the mystique of deep worth that can bring off a revolution.

The radical senses this, but hopes to use that *Lumpenproletariat* as a key to the unorganized American worker. But what mystique has unorganized labor in America? That they are now exploited? Let them get jobs through better training, and they will cease to be exploited. And the establishment opens a few avenues to keep quiet the few corners of real discrimination. In Marx's day, society moved by a dialectic; today it moves by an accommodation. All governments now have hunks of socialism built into them.

The old dies hard. In Europe and America, the blind lead the blind across the pages of history in a revolutionary Marxist program. Against a consolidated establishment, the American radical treasures century-old ideas of class warfare, and sings ballads that say "It's better with a union man." So Soviet Russia issues papers grounding song and meter in Stone-Age work rhythms. The hoary Anglo-Saxon poem, "The Seafarer," becomes a document of the life of a working sailor, *Piers Plowman* a proto-revolutionary document of exploited labor. In the thirties, Marcel Pagnol's trilogy, *Fanny, Marius,* and *César,* gave us a panorama of the ways of labor, the work, the dignity, the exploitation, the humor, the deep loyalties of comradeship in labor. So too Jean Renoir's *Toni* set forth the somber tenacity of the exploited immigrant worker in southern France.

All this is today a sentimental distraction. The laborer of Pagnol and Renoir could not have produced the atom bomb or the moon rocket. Indeed, America has already shifted to a mystique of force, of singing power lines, jet planes, and steam turbines. But this force is no longer human, as labor was in Marx's day. It has no rapport with our bodies and our wills, and produces a strange world of paradox, a personality split of simultaneous force and impotence. We grow limp in our national drive, sluggish in our atomic reactors, bystanders to our rocket kick. Our youth sees movies about power, but does not have available the one key that can unlock all doors, a sense of effectiveness.

Walled in and alienated from Russia as from the United States, the contemporary radical turns full circle from the mystique of labor to the mystique of force, whatever his manifesto says. The tangle of machinery, foremen, specialists, overseers, consultants and power cells is too complex to parcel out meaningfully as manager and managed. It has rather consolidated into a power block a military-industrial establishment the radicals would confront with force of their own. The radical vision, to Jean Luc Godard and his circle in France as to the American Weathermen, is to arrive at miraculous effectiveness, to throw bombs that are in harmony with the bombs of the establishment.

This mystique of force is apparent in Godard's first revolutionary films, *Pravda* and *See You at Mao*. It is as though, breaking into revolutionary films, Godard diminished any continuity of human life, carefully rendering people as ingredients in a process, a somber collage of the symbols of exploitation and the force of industry itself. The laborer, as a struggling human being, does not come through. How can he, with his union membership card?

Godard can be exceedingly suave; but when he renders a nude pelvis without the rest of the woman's body, his camera acts to splinter the human body. This is not simply an aesthetic decision, rendering a stylized body in semi-abstract, for Godard has repudiated aesthetic purpose. His purpose could be to suggest exploitation, to make a satiric comment on the parts of man turned into parts of machinery. But the film renders it otherwise. Godard's female body is too attractive, her pose too casual and relaxed, to suggest any exploitation whatever. Godard is here splintering the human being to make whole human beings mere clichés. But surely the mystique of labor requires the person of the laborer. Godard's is not Pagnol's gesture, nor Marx's, for both finally remain humanists. No such humanism is apparent in Godard. On the contrary, in his development, he has cut out as sentimentality the humanity his earlier films suggested.

Furthermore, even Godard's concern with labor is not with the making, the end, which is the shaped thing, but rather with the mood music of machine force and movement. His open-hearth furnace ignores its functional dynamic and the workers directing it to express hypnotic fascination with its own rhythm, its awesome content, the shock of its impact. It communicates not a mystique of labor, but an idolatry of the machine, a mystic identity with industrial force—the open hearth rendered like the Wafer of the Eucharist. Godard's loyalties have no humanist direction. He has rather turned into a Jansenist of industrial force.

The shift makes good sense. Godard has no continuity with the

Citroën factory, as its workers become bourgeoisified; nor can he grasp the extent to which the union worker has settled into a working partnership with capital, simply moving a turbine in a vast combine for money. Godard's identification is not with the worker, but with force itself. So his movie ends with a fist repeatedly smashing through a British flag, the gesture repeated like a visual incantation, a collision of a superior force with an inferior control, a hypnotic rendering of force, to convert the audience to a dynamic of force against impotent restraints.

In his obscure shift from a mystique of labor toward a mystique of force, from the workingman toward the *Lumpenproletariat,* from Soviet Russia toward anarchism, Maoism and revolution, the old loyalties of the modern revolutionary keep a tenacious hold. He has a loose continuity with the Proletariat of youth, sharing youth's rootless ambiguity—but not with the worker, for whom he has no program. Both intransigent and without a vision, youth and the revolutionary share a lot to bitch about. This is not necessarily bad; but a grind mated with a bitch only produces mongrel dissent.

So the revolutionary fishes for a base of operation, amid revolutionary blacks, in South America, in Africa, among women, migrant farm workers, disenfranchised students, the gay, Maoists, in Buddhist meditation, free speech, and the Vietcong. He identifies with Cuba, struggling against odds, but not with Castro, for he is already established. His mystique of force has a history as venerable as the human species. So, in ancient Rome, Spartacus did not rebel because he championed gladiators as a Proletariat. He rebelled because his powerful body was in chains, because guards no stronger than he could lead him to his death with impunity. Indeed, Marx's mystique of labor was exposed as too narrow when the Russian revolutionaries approached him for support, and he brushed them aside because Russian society lacked a mass industrial proletariat to work with. Other modes of proletariat his economic concepts could not handle.

The present world has hideous exploitation in it; but it has had exploitation since the beginning of time. The acute plague peculiar to the present temper is the vast expansion of force, the sheer volume of production and population, the shrinkage of empty space, the poisoning of the environment. The murky pressure for power that makes the revolutionary work the antiquated machinery of class warfare finally simmers down to triviality. However he complicates his power base, the modern revolutionary lives in rapport with incalculable force, with atom bombs and electronic computers. His throwing of bombs identifies with that force rather than with labor, with which he has no continuity. Indeed, his gesture is an imitative attack of force on force, sentimentalized by the pathos of his helplessness. His revolutionary gesture in a heavily industrial society is only a romantic gesture of empty explosion that will accomplish nothing but local emasculation, since he has no real dialectic to begin with.

Force can work to subdue an undefined murky area, to control and organize it. This we may see in some of the more wobbly countries in South America, at least as a sniff of coming chaos, when the terror of urban guerrillas demoralizes and paralyzes the country. In the United States all the revolutionary will achieve is a more cranky Fascist regime, Athens-style. Mao didn't proceed that way, nor did Castro; both of them began with a viable working group. The Western revolutionary engages not in actions, but in gestures—violent, destructive, giving vent to the romantic pathos of grown men, frustrated at being without power and throwing bombs to prove it isn't so. Their gesture is to awaken, not the worker, but the frustrated, the young, the impotent and the bored.

This gap of continuity makes grotesque the jockeying between the Communist labor unions and the youthful rebels at the Sorbonne in 1968. The students closed the university; the Party proclaimed the rebellion ephemeral, and cut off all communication. The students took to the streets and enlisted workers directly. As momentum gathered, the Party calmly waded into the middle, thrust aside the student leaders, and took over the revolt. The student leaders sighed—organized labor, their true French Proletariat, was finally stepping into the picture. God's in His heaven! all's right with the Revolution! The Party then accepted de Gaulle's terms for an election. Cohn-Bendit felt the Party had betrayed the Revolution. What did he expect, given the stake of the Party in the establishment? And had the Party won, what had Cohn-Bendit to look forward to? A French Bulgaria, where he could lead another university revolt in five years, and then be locked up in a mental hospital for extended examination? Furthermore, this grotesque miscalculation is repeated every time revolutionaries approach workmen by outdated mystiques. If the American revolutionary wants a wider base of support, let him peddle class warfare to the Mafia, who complain the Italians are discriminated against.

And these are the remains of class warfare. Once a Proletariat, the working classes today are a tough vested interest, conservative, anti-intellectual, their work fundamentally impersonal. Factories move their workers in shifts, not in teams. They want substance, not gallantry, better wages, paid vacations, etc. A production group, they will not shape policy on either side of the Iron Curtain. Indeed, the militant anticommunism of American labor stems finally from tough self-interest; the historical record testifies that after a communist takeover, organized labor is exceedingly vulnerable.

So Marxism today is a carefully shaped collective mentality, retaining power in the Party. When successful, it produces, not a militant working class, but general docility. The price of the docility is the open market—a bitter price to pay. Low-key Fascism produces the same docility. No wonder Nasser and Brezhnev got along so well! They spoke the same language, and wanted the same things.

Radicalized youth with a mystique of labor must imitate the Amish and Hutterites, who left an establishment they could not overthrow and founded independent work colonies. Our grass-roots anarchists are our most adult radical youth, withdrawing with persuasive integrity from the drug-infested caldron of Haight-Ashbury and the East Village, and establishing communes in the Rockies, Arizona, and Oregon. This is what the first Israeli kibbutzim did, echoing the Dead Sea Scroll communities of centuries ago. The poet Gary Snyder is doing this—a beautiful nut if ever I saw one—hewing himself a wooden cabin in northern California.

The gesture is handsome, but leaves me feeling cheated. The gesture of withdrawal leaves America scary with power, chewing up the earth, and abandoned to imbeciles. It also shrugs off its half-asleep Proletariat of America, its rich, noisy, spoiled, go-down youth.

It's my country.

We have to dig a little deeper.

PART II

THE DIALOGUE BETWEEN RUSSIA AND THE JEW

4

THE CZARIST FOUNDATION

GROUPS FIT oddly into one another. However they relate, their symbols drag on—stubborn pockets of hate, blackouts, old schizophrenias, like a nervous spot on the skin where the scratching goes on long after the scar has fallen away. Little can be predicted long-range. In any location, during any particular period, certain tenacious forces come into operation; but only after a situation is settled, does their blueprint become apparent. Why those forces first came alive, what made them overlap in that way can be most obscure. In fact, the true political struggle is to decide not which contestant will seize power, but which one will impose his blueprint of plans, issues and ritual crises on the others.

Back in the fourteenth, fifteenth and sixteenth centuries, for example, Jews circulated among the landed Polish gentry in a venturesome, piecemeal fashion. Those petty landlords, dukes, counts and princes, needed reliable craftsmen and docile managers. What with Germany choking him eastward out of its cities, old expulsions in the west, and his own rising native population, the Jew had no choice but to push toward Russia. From princedom to duchy, he gave what services were needed; without these services, he had no illusions about his security. But the Czar acquired his Jews en masse in the great partitions of Poland, not piecemeal but as a blurry adjunct to an enormous land grab. The vital issue the Czar concentrated on in the Polish partition was ground. It would be straightened out later who inhabited it.

Jewish life in Holy Russia was thus from the beginning tentative and nightmarish. The Jew was confined to the borderland acquired from Poland, now named the Pale; but he was not to live in Holy Russia proper. He thus was and at the same time was not in Russia. He and the native Russian were like two people thrown together on a no-exit train. Russia had never invited him. His residence was an unsure accident, a happenstance of imperial expansion; yet hundreds of thousands of Jews were there to stay, short of extermination, exile, or forced conversion. Oh, a Jew could get a temporary permit to move off the few annexed western provinces and onto the body of Russia itself; but like a deep sea diver without a helmet, he got back fast to the Pale or the sea drowned him. So the Jew trod water on the fringes of Russia for over a century. There on the border he was tolerated; but on the territory of the local pack, the Russians didn't want an alien smell.

Anti-Semitism in Czarist Russia had the same tentative abstraction as Jewish residence rights. The Poles were superstitious enough landlords, sullen, unpredictable, listening to the priest, the pocketbook and the local weather. When a national enclave around Warsaw mobilized for defense after Napoleon withdrew before an overwhelming Russian army, the Poles allowed no Jews in their ranks, so as not to mingle Jewish blood with the noble blood of Poland on the battlefield. The Jews persisted in volunteering. The Poles then relented, but on condition they shave their beards, so that they should at least fight looking like Poles. Then, finally, they allowed a separate troop of authentic Jews to fight; as long as they kept distinct and separate, they could die with their beards on. The episode is perversely funny—the Poles always arrange to be crushed masterfully. Today, the Poles are ruled by a Communist party nailed on their backs by an invading Russian occupation army, and productions of Dostoevsky's *Crime and Punishment* appear regularly on the Warsaw stage. It expresses their temperament like a British production of *The Pickwick Papers*.

Russian anti-Semitism never came through as a simple, cranky emotion, a hate, or a village superstition. Actual Jewish life in Russia was a makeshift local phenomenon—in this town, in that group of provinces, the Jew made a living by certain trades; but his political relationship was above the village to a national authority. Detached continental schemes were always being formulated for him in large policy decisions, but there was no human being there for him to encounter afterwards. As a result, the Jew never knew a local outburst from a trial balloon, a political theory from a scribal error, not even what political formula established the meaning of his words after he said them, or how final any law was.

In Poland, the difficulty of communication between Jew and gentile was obnoxious, but utterly comprehensible, as in the story of the Jewish beggar who, miracle of miracles, got the ear of the local Polish count in a moment of boredom, and told him such a heartrending story, that the count began to listen. The beggar stepped it up—his daily routine, the hours he worked, the hoodlums and dogs who attacked him, his unmarried daughters, his vows to his family, his lack of money even for food, let alone coal and clothes for the winter, his oncoming old age, nothing finished, nothing settled. A tear rose to the eye of the count. The beggar stopped, breathless with suspense. The count rang for his major-domo and said, "Throw the man out; he's breaking my heart." Communication in the Russian provinces is murkier—like a meandering trip that runs out of money and peters to a stop in a train station at the desk of an indifferent clerk.

In St. Petersburg, there were always matters in hand to be settled that involved the entire Pale. Tentative plans for assimilation and segregation were simultaneously considered in different ministries; sudden decisions were promulgated on the spot as to how Jews should be named, schooled, employed, shifted about. A name like Rosenfeld of Silverberg involved a political decision. The Jew was an odd political entity, like the Indian in this country, who belongs and yet does not belong, for whom theoretical arguments about what is and what is not a native have terrifying consequences.

Early in the nineteenth century, the Czarist army forcibly inducted young boys for twenty years of military service. Provinces had their quotas: towns and villages were taxed for their quota of boys. Boys were seized at gunpoint, kidnapped, exchanged, bought and sold, shipped off on guarded trains; eight, nine and ten-year-olds equipped with a muffler and gloves to protect them against the Siberian winter. Families hid their sons against the seasonal kidnapper or saw them lost forever. The draft was planned ambiguously for recruitment and forced conversion; in operation, it attacked the poor and made rich families vulnerable to a huge new source of legal extortion. The government just wanted its quota of boys; its agents arranged who should be seized. Once collected in troops and herded off on trains, mufflers or no mufflers, the younger boys all soon died, speedily and without apparent reason. Taken after ten, they could survive; but they then resisted conversion. So after years of trial, the plan was dropped—the technique didn't work.

Later in the century, two rabbis were imposed on every community, a Talmudist, to satisfy the conservative community, and a Russian-speaking rabbi as a balance. Once again, the plan was ambiguous: it would promote administrative efficiency by advancing a leader the Russians could talk to, and it would also break up the community by dividing the leadership between two men who would act against each other. Sholem Aleichem, the noted Yiddish short-story writer, served briefly as such a "Russian" rabbi. But in practice, administration remained just as cumbersome, and the two rabbis quietly coöperated. Only, another set of official mouths was added to the list for the public exchequer to support. So, after years of trial, that plan was dropped, too.

The anti-Semitism of Russia did not stem from the local bour-

geoisie—the gesture of a businessman knifing out a strange com-
petitor. It was rather the more celestial reaction of a country with
a holy mission to an alien presence that had somehow to be put in
its place or gotten rid of altogether. Indeed, the Czarist government
would have denied it was anti-Semitic at all, just as the Soviet
government denies it today. An odd ethnic group simply had to be
fitted into its place. If the results had not been so cruel, the procedure would have seemed perversely funny. In the outer provinces,
the Jew clung to the body of Holy Mother Russia like a piece of
tight underwear. Russia squirmed and improvised, refusing to accept a bad fit that was there to stay. When such a celestial presence
talks policy, you never know how raw are the emotions underneath
it.

National bents, once established, persist through the centuries,
overleaping war and revolution. I recall opening a discussion of
Soviet anti-Semitism with a political scholar by asking to what
extent Stalin's mistrust of his Jewish doctors before his death was
an anti-Semitic whim, and to what extent an established policy was
suddenly surfacing. He told me with bland finality that my alterna-
tives were false and artificial. Stalin's emotions, however whimsi-
cal, became national policy upon utterance. No distinction was
even thinkable. Puzzled, I pressed the question: that point of view
might suit a common clerk; but when Stalin's top lieutenants
obeyed a sudden gesture, surely, as sane, experienced men, they
knew an emotional whim when they saw one. He shrugged. Anyone
in the Russian state apparatus automatically read as policy any impulse whatever of Stalin's. One must evidently devise a special term
—"celestial anti-Semitism"—to distinguish the Kafka-esque Russian form of anti-Semitism from the more direct Polish variety.
Such celestial anti-Semitism pervades the Soviet Union today, not
as an emotion—the official journals are completely bland on the
subject—but as an automatic control of every twitch of policy. Soviet Russia vis-à-vis the Jews is like an ameba with a foreign body

deep inside its cell wall; the ameba quietly shifts and adjusts until the foreign body completely disappears.

In our terms of Face and Shadow, Russia is a country with a long history of solitary withdrawal and patient arrest. The Russians have bided their time through too many centuries of arrest and withdrawal not to have a deep and resilient shadow when in defeat. Quietly pervasive emotions now mingle with their silences and their patriotism. Their national memories go back over black walls of oppressive silence, extended invasions and conquests. So their face is a resistant blank. Their instinct for survival is deeper than language; their myths are a refrain of survival and resurging growth. Khrushchev was too noisy, too public an adventurer, to fit the role of Russian ruler. His temperament didn't blend into the foliage and the wallpaper, as Stalin's had done, or as Brezhnev's and Kosygin's do now. Khrushchev's anti-Semitism was a gusty emotion, not an oblique inference. His attack on Stalin was too bald a revelation of truth, suggesting choice, decision and a spark of communal awareness, rather than simply a vegetable growth. His adventure in Cuba was too risky, too open, too far from home. Moreover, the loss was too public.

There is a bitterly amusing report from Canada of the official visit of the Canadian Communist Executive, many of them Jewish, to Khrushchev, upon his accession to power. When, during that visit, the subject of Israel came up, Khrushchev unloaded himself of filthy peasant anti-Semitism, caricaturing the Jews, their international weakness, their untrustworthy character, their cosmopolitanism, their hunger to move, the difficulties of assimilating them. He knew who he was talking to. Then why was he doing it? To test their loyalty? To enjoy himself? To get rid of them? To establish his word as law? Whatever the reason, on their return to Canada, about half the Executive resigned from the Canadian Communist Party.

This psychology has deep social roots. Family and patriotism, childhood and countryside, army and state mysteriously grow and tangle together, with no careful threading out of the civil and the personal. Hence the deep Russian mystique of the land. One can call any European country one's motherland; but one hardly says Mother Germany, Mother Switzerland, or Mother Belgium, as one invokes Mother Russia. Indeed, the family metaphor gives political attitudes an emotional thrust. The very presence of the Jew on the body of Mother Russia stirred a primitive sense of rape or adultery. It was not to be tolerated. *La Belle France* is looser, younger, more enterprising and more available; but the body of Mother Russia belongs to the Russian people. It had to be cleaned of its tick.

Styles in infant care are related to national temperament. Thus, the Japanese custom of extreme indulgence the first years of life followed by a regime of careful discipline and training, gives the average Japanese citizen a tranquil docility of temperament. In this area, Russia has perfected a system of body massage by trained nurses in day-care centers that, according to report, gives the infant a deep security in a position of potential loneliness and abandonment by working over his body, caressing, reassuring and blending the child into official society. The child's sense of a mother dissolves into Mother Russia, without the sense of abandonment of an American orphan asylum. By report, when the Russian army was steadily driving Hitler back out of Russia, a foot soldier who was shot as he advanced died flinging his bayonet forward at the enemy. The experience of ego growth that psychoanalysis stresses is too autonomous for psychoanalysis to take root in Russia, nor would the Soviet government allow it.

The enormous sense of healing and biological renewal in the Russian countryside works through the scenes of hunting in *War and Peace* and *Anna Karenina*. Indeed, it is supreme over all else. Pierre remains dislodged, unsettled, exploited, until he returns to his estates, where he regains his equilibrium and becomes a man.

After his loss and abandonment in the city, Levin fairly drinks in the fresh air of swamp and countryside like milk to renew his spirits. Anna Karenina lives with her lover on his estate; but the place is too formally organized, too dryly efficient to allow a healing continuity with the soil. The countryside suggests a vast motherly body, like the most primitive paleolithic sculpture of sleeping women, all rock, all womb, all fertility, with no features but a swelling torso.

Western countries were polarized in a more secular way between Face and Shadow; but the Russian Face was holy, mystical with a divine mission. To it, the wandering Jew was a distant shadow, a borderline proletariat, suggesting a depraved, and not just a foreign, body. Outside ordinary morality, cut off from all continuity, an eternal wanderer and spiritual criminal, rootless in body and soul, the Jew under the Czar was trivial in the deepest sense, to be improvised on like a Tinkertoy set. A spiritual pervert who had rejected Jesus, uncanny, neither to be lived with nor gotten rid of, the Jew could lend money on interest, scurry about, and engage in all petit-bourgeois activities, but only in the border-regions of the Pale. He thus fulfilled a preordained function in the divine scheme, an entire community hung on the walls of a holy city like Saul's mutilated corpse after battle, to point up the effect of losing the grace of God.

Jewish life in Czarist Russia gave him a strange Siamese-twin quality. The Jew was too tentatively accepted to be a Shadow; he had too long a written history to fade away comfortably as Proletariat. So Jewish and Czarist culture shared one country, but had two different heads, each strong and well-defined, each with a Face of character to whom the other hung alien, murky, in double shadow. Yet the two communities grew so strongly together that each reinforced the other's sense of authenticity, and canceled out its long-range purposes. The Jew was more a Jew, seeing the Russian over his head; the Russian was more a Russian, seeing the

Jew all along his borders. A century and a half after the Russian occupation of the Pale began, nothing was essentially changed; only, the ground was more crowded, every alternative had been repeatedly tested, and the choices were uglier. Indeed, the tensions between the Jew and Russian officialdoms bridged over the shift in Soviet power. For all its mask of silence, and in spite of an ephemeral break during the revolution, the relations of the Soviet Union to its Jewish minority and to Israel are rooted in Czarist attitudes it inherited wholesale. Only, put into the crucible of the Revolution, the Jewish Face disappeared.

Thus, in the weaving of the Russian spirit, the broadly dominant strand, the approved Face, was native, traditional, Slavic, rooted in the past, with a mystical bond to the Russian soil, a tough sense of survival, and a landed familial aristocracy in an organic relationship to the peasantry. It adopted its Christianity from Constantinople, not Rome; when the Byzantine Empire fell before the Turks, Russia inherited its mantle of destiny and the blessing of God. Like Rome, it was the center of its world. Its instinctual decisions came as from a touchstone of authenticity; its skin had the very texture of the Russian soil. Its voice used the Russian tongue. Slavic turrets rose over its villages, native as turnips; and ikon after ikon in its peasant homes engendered worship.

Its great historic myth was that of succumbing before an enemy, falling back, absorbing him, going underground, but then vomiting him up from its very bowels and springing up, more powerful than before. The nation was a tough, undefined mass of growth, with a seed of life and roots in the soil, more primitive and elemental than even a tree. Other great empires, Rome and Byzantium, died forever once they were decisively defeated, but Russia had the seed of life within her, and could not be killed.

Tolstoy tells the folk myth of the living seed, in the tale of a village tournament between a master potter and a gardener to decide who could produce the most flawless piece of craftsmanship.

On the festive day, the entire village gathered for the trial before a table of judges. The potter first stepped forward, holding an exquisite new pot; behind him stepped the gardener with a new hybrid flower. But the potter stumbled in his anxiety, fell down and smashed his pot to pieces. In a rage of frustration, he rushed back, tore the flowerpot from the gardener's hand, and smashed it on the cobblestones. The gardener knelt down, and fingered through the soil spilling through the broken pieces of clay for his bulb. He found it, held it close and looked up at the potter. "Your pot is made of dead material—once destroyed, it is lost forever; but my flower grows from a living bulb, and will take root and flower once more." That flower is, among other things, the flower of Russia, which fell before the Mongols, the Poles, the Lithuanians, the Teutonic Knights—but always sprang back to life again. The potter, I daresay, used a French design.

History strangely follows the choreography of its controlling myth. In the Second World War, victory over Nazi Germany was a national project to the United States, a vast undertaking like crossing the great plains to Oregon or digging the Panama Canal, a project to be finished successfully so one could get back to normal. To Russia, Nazi Germany was another depraved foreigner, who had invaded the heartland, and was to be chewed up, digested, and vomited out. Mother Russia would then spring up, rejuvenated and grabbing at more land than before.

We have described the Face of Czarist Russia. Its tolerated Shadow was the bourgeois middle class that, cosmopolitan, capitalistic, with international money, preyed parasitically off a landed aristocracy. That Shadow, long alien and mistrusted, grew virulent with the bourgeois French Revolution. This was not merely another expanding nation, but a change in class dominance. In France, the middle class had usurped the powers of government, changed borders at will, deified progress, played peoples against peoples, and threatened all law and order. So the Napoleonic invasion of Russia was not merely a desperate war, but the resolution of an elemental national myth. The struggle of classes came to an absolute head, as the French bourgeois fist punched deep into the body of Mother Russia. Indeed, to the Russians, this was a national epiphany. Not just her soldiers and guerrillas, but Russia herself swallowed Napoleon and chewed him up. Moscow burned; no foreign body could be allowed to rest there. And when Napoleon was finally vomited up, Russia felt its myth of history supremely vindicated. Russian soil was stronger than its bourgeois invader. Indeed, as becomes apparent in Tolstoy, a fresh element then entered the myth of the invisible landed aristocracy, and that was the essential sterility, indeed the triviality, of the bourgeoisie. They are characteristically approached in Tolstoy with patronizing mistrust and contempt. They lost in their great surge under Napoleon; their shadow was never again as virulent.

No wonder the largest movie ever made, a movie made with no thought of its colossal cost, was the magnificent Russian *War and Peace*. The western critics who rejected it as lacking in personal stamp failed to grasp the movie's function; their rejection was like judging mime by the criteria of method-acting or ballet by those of modern dance. The movie was a national not a personal creation, a vast, seamless tapestry of Russia overcoming its invaders. It called for exquisite acting, but not distinct characters; mythic types, not individualized human beings. Thus, Napoleon foreshadows Adolph Hitler and echoes the Teutonic Knights. Pierre is the Russian Bear writ large—untrained, clumsy, taken advantage of—who sank deep into the Russian people and was rejuvenated. Indeed, *War and Peace* itself is underestimated if it is taken simply as a novel. As it tells a story, it renders a national triumph, the vindication of the Russian ethos. In this respect, it resembles the *Iliad*, which renders the triumph of the Hellenes and vindicates their ethos.

I personally respond to the Russian myth with uneasy wonder. It vibrates with such deep authenticity as to suggest absolute finality;

yet that slam of life, indestructibly rooted in real soil, is not my myth. Its sense of deep-rootedness shrugs off communication—vegetables dig for water and fight for sunlight; but they do not talk to one another. I personally have an entirely different, essentially Jewish myth, one based on and rooted in the living word, as exemplified in the old ghetto folkway of smearing honey on the pages of an alphabet book, so a beginning reader can lick the honey off his first letters, and find them sweet and nourishing.

But the Czarist dialectic of landed aristocracy and bourgeois challenge was complicated by historic change. The expansion of industry, late in the nineteenth century, buoyed up a second, deeper Shadow. That first, bourgeois Shadow—international, egalitarian, free-thinking, interested in money and trade—reached its zenith in Napoleon and was overcome. Once that supreme test was passed, the bourgeois class could be tolerated for its usefulness in trade and patronized for its ineffectiveness in seizing power. But with the rise of Marxism in the West, a more extreme ideology loomed behind it, ominous because not yet fully tested—the Shadow of socialism, the overthrow of private property and violent revolution. The factory worker had his craft as the peasant had his land; but no natural aristocrat stood over his head to direct him, only a bourgeois manager-owner. But this situation developed in a murky obscurity. That bourgeois Shadow, which had somehow earned the stamp of sterility and impotence in Napoleon's defeat, was the traditional antagonist.

So *War and Peace* finishes with the two surviving landed aristocrats, Nicholas Rostov and Pierre Bezukhov, raising a new generation on guard against changes in Russian life, against international trade, cosmopolitan tendencies, and bourgeois immoralities. They are the Face of Russia, secure over its bourgeois Shadow so long as they stay on guard.

But the intellectual wing of the Russian bourgeois Shadow lost its sense of destiny. Imitative, international, without a strong sense of rootedness at home, it loosened its religious ties and became disintegrative. So Alexander Herzen, a type-cast native intellectual, became a religious free-thinker, loosened his ties to the land, wandered through western Europe, and was finally left behind by the sweep of history. Herzen's life can be shaped into a pilgrim's progress; but to Russian tradition, it was a progress toward triviality and damnation. There is a way in which a "Rake's Progress" and a "Pilgrim's Progress" are mirror opposites to one another. So, as one moves ever deeper below the Shadow bordering official Russian culture, one finds demons of libertinism looming up—atheism, revolution, chaos and finally suicide. This sort of "Rake's Progress" became the writer's myth of the Slavic soul gone astray, the myth that possessed the traditional Russian soul.

Indeed, Dostoevsky and Tolstoy, the more conservative masters of the last century, were so persuasive in their novels that as we read them we lose sight of the special bent of their plots, a movement into ever deeper shadow, each step more sinister and threatening than the last. Thus, Dostoevsky's *The Brothers Karamazov* begins as Fyodor Karamazov attaches himself to the landed gentry, to whom he ambiguously belongs. He becomes a landowner, marrying into the gentry by an unexpected coup, and lives by affairs, put-on marriages, questionable arrangements, always on the borderline of legality, and by sharp business practices, never committing himself, yet never letting anything go. He even seduces an idiot wandering beggar, who then bears a son. All his life, he plays hanky-panky with religious ideas as he does with his obligations to his family, indulging in paradox and unanswerable puzzles; visiting Father Zossima, ostensibly to settle a family quarrel, he tests and presses him irritably, forever jarring, teasing, exasperating, but never actually locking horns.

Each of his sons picks up a thread of the father's weakness and pushes it a step further. Dmitry is even more unstable than his father, unable to establish his inheritance, unable to marry the girl who loves him, unable to settle down in a home, unable to stop frightening and irritating people. Forever, he rushes about to no purpose. Ivan pushes Fyodor's religious paradox to a head-on indictment of divine justice and a complete break with tradition. Alyosha, the nominal hero, even more enigmatic than his father, never quite becomes a reality on the human scene. And Smerdyakov, the bastard son, shows an extreme of cultural perversity, adulating bourgeois France, where he plans one day to visit. He calls on a lady friend, not to plan a home, but to show off his clothing and brag of his plans to emigrate.

All these disintegrative, cosmopolitan, atheistic and shadowy sons are windy intuitions derived from an unstable father. Alyosha remains muted and insubstantial as he slips about the city. Ivan runs away from home, cuts himself from human contact, has a conversation with the devil and slips into insanity. Dmitry thrashes about ever more wildly, dragging an old hanger-on veteran in disgrace through the streets. Then he tears off on meaningless pilgrimages after money and finally returns to his father, armed to kill him. As for Smerdyakov, his parricide is emblematic of revolution; in a far extension of succumbing to French culture, he violently eliminates the head of the family. Having murdered Fyodor, his father, and been rejected by Ivan, his half-brother, he commits suicide. Against a background of constant, thrashing possibility of mystic conversion, of sinking into the depths and finding redemption there, this is an elaborate, familiar progression, a sort of "Slavic Progress," where old family ties are loosened to allow demons to enter: the hypnosis of money, degenerative violence, homeless wandering, atheism, capricious revolution and violent death.

Against the dynamic of breakdown, a counter-dynamic is offered that is native, pietistic, rooted in the soil, instinct with holiness, healing by redemptive humility. Father Zossima, its crown and source, a former army officer, has wandered all over Russia.

Everywhere, he communed with the peasants and became part of the Russian soil. On finding the true path, he prostrates himself on his face before a servant. Receiving a group of peasant women, he always sits at their level, never to loom above them. A saintly older brother converted him, a natural saint, who died radiantly happy, at home, loving all people, gazing out his window at the landscape of Russian earth. Each person Father Zossima meets, he persuades to go home and make peace with his family.

The story of Dostoevsky's *The Possessed* is another such step-by-step progression of a landed, traditional family through secret marital arrangements, flight from home, revolutionary cabal, increasingly deranged personal entanglements, public defilement of social sancta, to a final suicide—once again the progress of a Slavic Everyman to revolution and sudden death. Here, as elsewhere, this "progress" in Dostoevsky moves from landed families, the Russian soil, and Slavic mystical religions, through exile, estrangement, repressed violence, and isolation, to insanity, exhibitionism, murder, and sudden death, except as penance and humility interrupt and redeem it.

Dostoevsky offered no clear redemption through labor, nor did he sense an independent workers' dynamic. His path to spiritual healing is essentially mystical and religious. Raskolnikov in *Crime and Punishment* will of course labor in Siberia; but it is the experience of penance that will redeem him, not the hard work—indeed, he is already redeemed, sunk on the Russian soil, resolved to surrender and go. The social Face of Russia here is the conservative landed gentry, its force the force of mystic love. The social Shadow, its bourgeoisie, is characteristically dishonest, grasping, inadequate, with hideous mannerisms. But a third class is beginning to loom on the horizon—not the class of workingmen, who remain shadowy blobs of labor, faith, the Russian soil—but the revolutionaries, who fascinated and terrified Dostoevsky. In this, he had extraordinary prescience; the party officials of that class rule Russia today, the descendants of those revolutionary organizers whom Dostoevsky first saw rising in *The Possessed*.

Dostoevsky's compelling psychology reads not as his own bent, but as the law of human life, a decline from landed religious gentry through bourgeois irregularity, sterility and cosmopolitanism, to suicide, insanity, murder and revolution. And yet, the breakdown of any boyhood morale can lead to disaster. Indeed, to take the bull by the horns, I can envision just as likely a progress the reverse of Dostoevsky's, beginning with a Manhattan progressive-education school, avant-garde art, John Cage, international camping trips across Switzerland and Yugoslavia, a brush with liberal politics, folk festivals in the Canadian woods, through a middle ground of business success, Wall Street investments, marriage, a Madison Avenue executive job, a piece of the firm, leading to a life increasingly sterile and pointless among the landed Episcopalian gentry in northern Westchester, with suicide, adultery, drug addiction, neurotic perversions, the breakdown of family ties, and revolution to follow, with the landed family at the bottom of the sink. But then I never did feel at home in Scarsdale.

Dostoevsky had a gift for psychological intimacy; but what he feared most was cosmopolitanism, which he saw as killing intimacy and bringing sterility and psychic death. The Soviets have so solemnized the threat of cosmopolitanism, rooted both in Dostoevsky and Tolstoy, that it should be faced head-on. What they fear is a real possibility: cosmopolitanism can indeed turn demonic, empty a writer of passion, anger, and love, and reduce his creativity to a bland taste that savors everything and digests nothing. But what of that? Anything can turn parasitic and destroy creativity—cosmopolitanism, villagism, industrialism, nihilism, eating starches, dieting, loneliness, mobs, Mozart piano concerts, Brezhnev's speeches to the Supreme Soviet, or random noise. No metaphysical absolute will deliver the last word about the wholesomeness of village life.

A creative artist escapes parasitic sterility, not by a neat synthesis, but by straddling both poles of antithesis, and shaping the consequences to his own creative purposes. He lives loosely free, by his creative process and by the immediacy, size, and force of his grasp of truth. He must accept all his mystic mommas, his poppas, his brothers and comrades, but only until they start to smother him; then he has to cut loose. If he goes sterile, what does that prove but that life is hazardous, creativity wayward, and people sticky chickens? Neither the Communist Party nor the Rand Corporation offers a guaranteed path to survival or success. An elegant presence —a classic composer, say—can accept a neat mental receptacle; more clumsy and befuddled presences require more spacious surroundings and irregular furnishings. Land is handsome, but so is movement; traditions are glorious, but so is radical growth. One can take the regular ferry to the isle of sunshine, or sail there in the belly of a yellow submarine, just so long as one gets there.

As a writer, I personally mistrust all my mystic mommas; thank God, they snitch on one another, so I have an inkling of what they are about. If they are too decorous, I kick a little Jewish; if they are too self-indulgent, I grope for a little touch of Harvard in the night. But I take all my mystic mommas seriously, however they disagree among themselves. Only when they try to define my essential life, do the logical contradictions become a problem. Indeed, to speak to the issue, as I see it, the accusation of cosmopolitanism in the Soviet Union is an administrative technique for blocking off all radical creativity, all fundamental originality, all eccentric personal truth, with a mechanical clerkly twitch. The purpose of opposing cosmopolitanism, like that of all formulae of political censorship, is to reduce all art to sentimentality more neatly. The motives are blatantly apparent, and they are rotten to the core. An accusation of cosmopolitanism is an automatic tic, a label slapped on presences too large for the local constabulary—it is what Khrushchev barked at Shostakovich to shut off his "Babij Yar" sym-

given his station, it is fraught with implications. Tolstoy's novels celebrate not a landed gentry, but a landed aristocracy. He displays the same progression of alienation, and shares the mistrust of the ruling landed class for bourgeois internationalism; but Tolstoy's Slavic progress is not driven or thrashing, as in Dostoevsky. It comes through as a broad panoramic landscape, not as a river storming to eternity in floodtime. It likewise has a countermovement; but its redemptive turn hinges on natural growth, on family, labor and humility as in Levin's retreat to his country estate, not on an orgiastic mystical experience of penance and humility. And yet the process of degeneration is essentially the same as in Dostoevsky, from landed Mother Russia, with her conservative families, through cosmopolitanism, internationalism, bourgeois trends, the loss of the family bond, to insanity and suicide.

Indeed, Tolstoy should be found more congenial in the Soviet Union than Dostoevsky. He wrote with elegant, linear precision. His pages have the large, careful scope and balance of Poussin, yet their figures are rendered with the vigor of Rubens. His horse races, his hunts, his dances, his political cabals, his battles and army movements unfold like a large finished tapestry; yet the events shift from moment to moment with a stamp of actuality. His sense of the economic classes was much clearer than Dostoevsky's; he knew their resources, their lines of power. His aristocrats are aristocrats, his merchants merchants and his peasants peasants; each knew his resources, his style, and his station. Dostoevsky had a more virulent sense of intellectual repression, a more murky ambiguity of petit-bourgeoisie blending into laborers and seething with revolutionary fever, a thick stew laced with criminal and revolutionary gangs at the bottom of the social pot. These characters are too quirky and individualized to exemplify their social station, but they churn with religious impulse and animal, cranky oddities. Tolstoy's figures might be rendered as classic Greek sculpture, Dostoevsky's never.

Tolstoy should also be more congenial to Soviet readers than Dostoevsky because he loved physical labor. He wanted his workers kept in their place; and yet he loved them, and hated the bourgeoisie. His sense of joyous fulfillment in physical movement, at work, in the dance and in war, has easy familiarity and amplitude. His characters gesture with an air of finality and mythic grandeur. At the start of *Anna Karenina*, Levin, visiting the skating pond in Moscow, takes a skating jump down the icy stair, half falls, rights himself with his hand, and is away in the icy air. So too, later, angered by a stupidity in his laborers, he seizes a scythe and mows a field before speaking—a control of anger Tolstoy himself exercised on his estate. The sense of labor as healing, steadying, redeeming, is constant in Tolstoy. His peasants are natural men, organic to the soil they till. Walking behind a pair of peasant lovers at harvest season, Levin is physically aroused by the girl, she is so at home on the earth. Indeed, Tolstoy's own frustrated love for a peasant girl helped trigger the wreck of his marriage.

Tolstoy's peasants are a natural, healing growth. They are organic to the estates they work on; but they need an aristocratic authority imposed on them. In *War and Peace*, on the Bolkonsky estate, old Prince Nicholas dies during the Napoleonic invasion. With the aristocrats away, a strange vacuum sets in. The peasants gradually join in an anarchist herd which rises to take over the estate and finally are about to assault Mary Bolkonsky. Luckily, Count Nicholas Rostov, on a scouting foray for the Russian army, meets the peasant mob, knocks out its leader, and restores rightful authority. All this, needless to say, is as emblematic as *Pilgrim's Progress*, for all its realism. Substitute an experienced party member for Count Nicholas, and a collective for the landed estate, and the scene would be congenial to contemporary Russia. Indeed, the fear of a steady decline into an amoral herd lies behind the Soviet compulsion to have party members scattered everywhere, even attached to the regular army.

Tolstoy knew his workers, but he had no inkling of the revolutionary dynamic Dostoevsky exposed with such terrifying immediacy in *The Possessed*; Tolstoy offers no entrée to the Bolshevik mentality. In *Anna Karenina*, Levin's older, revolutionary brother lives through a typical Slavic progress, such as we have described. Leaving the land, he becomes an intellectual, a revolutionary; he never marries and drifts into a pathetic limbo. Finally, he comes home to die, of course prematurely. Once he is in home surroundings, Kitty's loving care, giving him family affection and good linen, clean air and nourishing food, eases his last days. Thus the landed, conservative family, settled on the soil, welcomes back its revolutionary prodigal son, though too late to save his life.

Curious here is not the familiar stepladder progression from land to death, but the portrayal of Levin's brother himself—pathetic, wistful, well-meaning, but lacking in any coarse power, any tough grasp of his life-choices and of the consequences of living them out. No defiance is left in the man; he is chastened, withdrawn inside himself. Tolstoy's spirit had a catholicity of scope; but he knew nothing about revolutionaries. The last thing a revolutionary should do is die in such yielding fragility. But Tolstoy's blindness to the revolutionary dynamic made him a most classical writer. The author of *Notes from Underground* could never have designed the Parthenon.

As for Tolstoy's rejection of the middle class, his very unfamiliarity with them marks him off radically from the essentially middle-class French novelists. Tolstoy identified with his aristocrats, he enjoyed his peasants, he was blind to his revolutionaries; the middle class he rarely touched upon, but when he did, he did so with savagery, caricature and blind rejection. Thus, in *War and Peace*, the outbreak of the Napoleonic wars brings processional pageants, spontaneous demonstrations of patriotism, in Moscow: from the workers with innocent ardor, from the aristocrats with gallant abandon, from the bankers in a hollow show, giving what they cannot keep back. Pierre Bezukhov wins back the peasants on his landed estates by curbing his parasitic managers and thus ending the nightmare of rapacious bourgeois administrators which had spread over his holdings like an economic cancer. The middle class in Tolstoy, as in Dostoevsky, is an unnecessary parasitic growth, sandwiched between landed aristocracy and the peasants.

Tolstoy's novels unfold like Chinese scroll paintings. They are neither *fin de siècle*, nor novels of early dawn, but surge to a full burst of the mainstream of living. They recall Poussin and Rubens, as we have noted, but they are too strongly lined to recall Botticelli. *War and Peace* unfolds with a trumpet blast of noon; *Anna Karenina* recalls an afternoon adultery, bending toward night. Each city and locale is carefully delineated, each class and each individual; their vignette episodes unfold with magisterial finality in a broad tableau of human affairs. As in Shakespeare's *Antony and Cleopatra*, a large, permissive inevitability, unfolding the processes of nature itself, replaces any radical free will.

And yet, the inevitability in Shakespeare's *Antony and Cleopatra* is easier and more relaxed. In a large, loose suspense, ambiguous layers of significance are suspended above one another with no attempted resolution. W. H. Auden has admired *Antony and Cleopatra* most among Shakespeare's plays because, as he put it, it is a play about two middle-aged people who must keep speaking glorious poetry to one another, for otherwise they have nothing to do but sit at home and watch television. So *Antony and Cleopatra* is simultaneously a surfeit of permissive pleasures, a grand tableau of Olympian inevitability, and a platform for soaring radiance of language. It closes with a vision of eternal majesty and fertility. Cleopatra dresses for death as for a coronation:

> Give me my robe, put on my crown; I have
> Immortal longings in me . . .

Her words are a strange blend of wifely obedience, self-transcendence and girlish flirtation:

> Husband, I come:
> Now to that name my courage prove my title!
> I am fire and air; my other elements
> I give to baser life. . . .
> If she first meet the curled Antony,
> He'll make demand of her, and spend that kiss
> Which is my heaven to have.

She dies nursing her infant of eternal life, her womanly instincts drifting across her vision of Olympian inevitability and coloring it to sheer wonder:

> Peace, peace!
> Dost thou not see my baby at my breast,
> That sucks the nurse asleep?

In Tolstoy, the careful precision of inevitability, for all its broad scope and breath of human immediacy, becomes glazed to the texture of porcelain. One misses the voice and being of Cleopatra on Tolstoy's Olympian heights. I have always balked at the inevitable spinsterhood of poor Sonya in *War and Peace*. Murky, bland, and withdrawn as is her temperament, in the course of 1,200 pages there is many a male nut who could have complicated her destiny.

And yet, for all his breadth of vision, as one grasps the familiar surge of life-and-death energies in Tolstoy, one realizes how judgmental is this most Olympian of novelists. Indeed, the antinomies in his work press upon us. Thus, this most universal novelist is also the most parochial—finally no health seems possible except on landed Russian estates like those of Levin, Rostov, and Bezukhov, estates like those Tolstoy was familiar with. All else in Europe, all else in Russia, is suspect. Tolstoy, like Dostoevsky, sketches in a progress of moral degeneration through wandering, triviality, cosmopolitanism, marital dissolution, revolution, and suicide, as one leaves the conservative landed estates; but Tolstoy's progress is a leisurely tableau of social process, a moral landscape of Europe, rather than an urgent will storming to completion. The stages are pieced out in frozen attitudes and small, specific steps, endlessly repeated and arrested in a round as circular as the cycles of the moon. In a single person, the entire process is present only in the person of Anna Karenina, and even her we meet only after her marriage has begun to go awry.

Indeed, the process is so finely graded, we can locate our diminution of health by our degree of distance from the estates of the landed gentry, where the life force operates most strongly. As we move away, it dissipates into sterile futility. Thus, on the estates of Levin in *Anna Karenina* and of the Rostovs in *War and Peace*, life is most wholesome and elemental; and loving families raise the noble children of the earth. In its dewy young aristocrats is the secret grace of life. There Levin goes bird-hunting in the still morning, with the magical evocation of wood and marsh. Vast teams of sleighs ride through the winter, old Slavic dances stir in the summer, serving to unite rich and poor, aristocrat and peasant, as one. There the women are raised who will marry and bring forth a new generation to rule Russia.

Among the Russian cities, only Moscow is close enough to the estates to be their capital and market. It has ice-skating, native architecture, and a surge of Russian folkways. There Levin meets the sweetheart whom he eventually marries. The patriotic Muscovite population burn their city, rather give it to Napoleon. St. Petersburg, at a greater distance from the landed estates, is subject to meaningless political gestures, odd religious fads, eccentric cabals, factions of European cosmopolitanism. There, the Kuragins trap Pierre, an inexperienced new landed aristocrat, into marriage with

Helena, who sets up house in St. Petersburg, joins a French faction, takes a lover, and mysteriously sinks into sickness—anemia of the spirit, as it were. Her last doctor is an exotic international specialist—trained in France, no doubt. Far from the Russian soil, her life energy thins dangerously until she succumbs.

Farthest from health are France and western Europe. There Kitty idles her time in convalescence, and entangles a married man in a fruitless and dangerous infatuation. There Anna Karenina flees with Vronsky, her lover, upon first abandoning her husband. Her rootless wandering from country to country, nowhere sinking roots, registers her estrangement from life, her sterility, pointlessness, and coming death.

Tolstoy's panorama of the expanse of Europe, a tableau of sickness and health, comes to its climax on the aristocratic landed estate. If Mars and Apollo, Venus and Hera, could enjoy an earthly incarnation, they would grow up with the Rostovs. There is an enormous freight of support for such a view in western literature. This is the aristocracy of the Renaissance and of ancient Greece, the setting of Plato's *Symposium*, the Belmont of *The Merchant of Venice*, the estates of George Washington and Thomas Jefferson during the American Revolution. Steadily pressing for health and continuity, Tolstoy mistrusts large, loose sweeps of vision, but keeps a tenacious bond in family and soil, an equilibrium between city and wilderness. His aristocratic landed spirit might have grasped the world of *The Merchant of Venice*, though Shylock's stubborn dignified continuity would have given Tolstoy problems; and the "patens of bright gold" in the floor of heaven might have smacked too much of the music of the spheres and too little of the soil of the steppes. The esoteric magic and visionary spirits of *The Tempest* Tolstoy could not cope with at all.

The cohesion and finality of Tolstoy's moral judgment take on a glaze of inevitability. I shrink, awed, before his panoramic vision of man, the spread of Europe under his steady microscope, but in the end I become enraged. The human spirit is a bit more mercurial than Tolstoy allows. His glaze has a suggestion of static suspension; his life process has an undertow of sterility and despair. His sense that health emerges from the soil and apparently is not to be attained anywhere else is finally stubbornly parochial. There are many avenues to Jerusalem. I grew up as Shylock's neighbor; and I will bear witness that Shylock for one would not have died like Levin's older brother.

5

THE PLAY OF FACE AND SHADOW
IN THE JEWISH COMMUNITY

WE LIKENED England earlier to an elm tree, Russia to a huge winter bush. The Jews have a more uncanny feel—they are less vegetation than flying spores of yeast that land, root fast, then break away fresh families of spores. They land oddly, on distant shores, in Amsterdam, Brazil, Odessa, the Bronx, Louisville, Kentucky, and Biro-Bidjan; they take hold, find the coloration and shape of the land, and begin to multiply. Soon they ferment hot local intensities of trade and thought. Fists of yeast puff up, clusters of mushrooms that swell the local economy, producing rich wild tastes. A hand smears them away, and they are gone.

The medieval Jew lived by what he could produce, collecting, finishing, and distributing money and needed goods. He improvised in local starvations. When banking was sinful and clumsy, he kept a bank; when a backwoods town needed local craftsmen, he opened a shop. A useful exile, he made things happen to the local settlers, lifting their dry, flat villages into communities. Yet he had no home base, only a position of bitter paradox. So his colonies blew across northern Europe like spores of yeast, a catalyst to a sluggish economy, a trigger to bourgeois change, fructifying land provinces.

To this medieval world of landed communities, the Jew was an eternally landless wanderer. A creature of craft, he was full of un-

111

canny talents, at once indispensable and damned. Indeed, the medieval person added a metaphysical twist to his stubborn sense of his own rootedness. To the scholastic philosopher, all movement is vertical, body to earth and spirit to heaven, toward hell for sin and depravity, toward God for hope and faith. Land journeys, whether of commerce, diplomacy, war or pilgrimage, were crooked turns on the winding path toward God. This paradox controls Donne's poem, "Good Friday, 1613. Riding Westward:"

> Hence is 't, that I am carried towards the west
> This day, when my soul's form bends towards the east.

Traveling westward on business on Good Friday, Donne bends against the grain, like a gargoyle.

So the long Gothic cathedrals throw up thin, bunched vertical thrusts, their heavy stones heaving up, the clusters rising impossibly, like communities of believers, their flying arches soaring like the leaps of individual souls, all conjoined among rising spires and towers; their stony weights remain immovably massed on earth to harbor through centuries the saints they enshrine. Around their arched entranceways, elongated saints stretch out and dissolve, the clench gone from their bodies, coursing up stone grooves to where gargoyles, gnomes and meditative insects lean out over the earth. The high rose window hangs in the air, an enormous glass blossom, to echo the stain of Paradise in the heavenly rose, swarming with millions of souls, elect, in bliss. You turn away, descend a wispy alley, pass a low roof, approach an open fountain: a boulevard of turrets rises in an eternal march.

This simultaneous grab of the chunky earth and thrust toward the circle of the moon, the sun, star beyond star, a shell of fire, the primum mobile and paradise, each celestial sphere with its intelligence, its guardian angel, had nothing casual about it. The medieval temperament had little Cleopatra in it, to brag of an Antony, whose "delights" rose "dolphin-like, and show'd his back above /The element they liv'd in." Horizontal movement, by contrast, was essentially bizarre—secular, penitential, the entertainment of *jongleurs*, the self-correction of pilgrims. Even if it were successful, where could pre-Crusade voyaging lead? Travel far enough in any direction, and you literally fell off the earth and disappeared. To this mentality, the Jew was a perverse sport, moving, as he did, everywhere, without a center, a direction or a home.

The expanding bourgeois economy of the Renaissance made free geographical movement legitimate and serious. Thus a man might be:

> . . . borne to strange sights,
>   Things invisible to see,
> Ride ten thousand daies and nights,
>   Till age snow white haires on thee . . .

A climbing cloud, the appearance of a speck, a mast, then gradually an entire ship, over the horizon, had already suggested circular motion in the classical age. Now Columbus approached the Indies —the East Indies—by sailing westward, thus moving toward a rounding of the earth. The gesture was the first step toward the voyage of Magellan. But a movement in arches, around spheres, made the vertical an illusion. So Giordano Bruno, by proclaiming that space is infinite, made position a mere matter of convenience and attitude. When the sky is infinitely extended, any direction is up.

The possibility of random movement in infinite space without any necessary goal made motion morally random. Space became scary, empty, secular and pointless, full of clumsy mysteries, like Milton's chaos. It now even became a problem where to locate heaven and hell. So Milton, with infinite space to play in, struck out in celestial travel, through hell, heaven and all creation, and

finally landed on a flat, abrupt "Paradise within thee, happier far."
Astronomy had become a problem in engineering, not an emblem
of perfection. The final cause was soon dropped in physics—a little
less direction to move in, a little more profit on the way.

All this introduced a curious ambivalence in the view held of the
Jew in the next two centuries. The Jew still had the Faustian taint
of the Wanderer, the mark of Cain, with all the uncanny mistrust
this stirred; but a heady new bourgeois age was dissolving old
fixed patterns. The Jew of Malta, a villain to Marlowe, was still a
cousin to his Tamburlaine, one of the great Elizabethan heroes, an
over-reacher like Tamburlaine, with a world to take possession of.
So, in Holland and England, the Jew was steadily accommodated
with more and more respect as an equal.

In a more pedestrian way, to conservative governments of central Europe like Germany and Poland, with their feudal heritage,
the Jew was economic yeast, a skillful alien, a catalyst of unpredictable change. All this had a bearing on the spotty treatment of
the Jew through Central Europe, where the balance sheet of love
and hate for the Jew changed from country to country. Thus, both
Germany and Poland, ruled by a strong landed class, at first tolerated a working middle class which might include the bourgeois
Jew. During hard times, however, competing merchants, fighting
for a dwindling local market, were likely to become virulently anti-
Semitic in order to drive out Jewish competition. Thus, anti-
Semitism came from relatively local bourgeois elements, not from
the native élite.

As we move steadily eastward, the ambivalence becomes grim-
mer and more earthy, the tentative acceptance becomes a wall
against contact. In Czarist Russia, as we have seen, the approach to
the Jew was nationalistic and administrative, and never fixed with
finality. As a result the Jewish masses were permanent dwellers in
limbo. Their government communications took place through a
translation process that canceled out any human touch as it was

uttered. The Czarist establishment sat between them and the Russian masses; only cramps of denial and twitches of frustration got through. As a result, the Bolshevik Revolution registered in both groups; but no shaft of common understanding passed through. The new Soviet structure absorbed old Czarist attitudes; and the Jewish community disappeared behind a slam of silence.

The Jewish community in Russia, massive and isolated from the beginning, had for a time had a remarkable degree of self-sufficiency. The Jew's enormous religious heritage, with its elaboration of legend and history, reduced any mishap to its own terms, and made the temper of the Pale formidable. With only the thinnest legal connection with the authorities, the Russian Jew became a Proletariat of school, village and open field. Though resented with a patronizing awe by the German Jew, the masses of Jewish population had a continuity across the continent—indeed, reached to God and His armies of angels. Yet for all the air of magic exaltation of the Chassidic movement, the Proletariat condition became increasingly degraded to a cheapening confusion, until, under Hitler, all Lithuanians, Poles, Galicians, Chassidim, Proletariat, and all else vanished in the gas chambers, or onto the pages of books in the library.

Sholem Aleichem's open naïve style is no distortion; it closely renders the persona of the Pale, a timeless innocent who has scrambled about the Bible and historic legend over a span of centuries. Blocked outside history, without Face or Shadow, he lived in legend, rumors, fitful good luck and enduring degradations. Other peoples decorated their history with legend; the Jew shot his legend through with history. He said Pharaoh and meant the Czar—except that to him the Czar was Pharaoh. If Moses wandered with the Hebrews only forty years in the desert, and he was still in Russia after a hundred years, it only showed God didn't count; but maybe history was just running downhill. The way things were deteriorating, Gog and Magog were probably enrolling in the Moscow Imperial Academy. But then, Reb Levi Yitzchak of Berditchev had a secret tunnel to Jerusalem, and could get the Jew out in a hurry. The present exile was certainly worse than back in Egypt, where seven fat years had preceded the seven lean years, and Joseph, the prime minister, had been one of the sons of Israel; here in Russia, the seven fat years were fat with dreams, the seven lean years lean with starvation, and Rasputin was no Theodor Herzl in a monk's outfit. It didn't add up. God's prosecuting and defense attorneys should agree on a verdict. Otherwise, the defense attorney will have the Jew singing hosannahs while the prosecuting attorney whips him running day and night over burning coal fields; and both will think they won their case.

Those who describe eastern European Jewry as intensely religious are correct, yet they entirely miss the mark. These were not the Presbyters of Scotland or the Jesuits of Spain, but a religious Proletariat, with a sweep, poignance and grasp of legend intimate as the nails in their shoes. Indeed, their loss of historic time reinforced a peculiar element in their religion, the unconditional present tense of holidays and festivals, each a dramatic reënactment of a supreme historic moment. On Rosh Hashanah, the cantor thunders with the conviction, "On this day the world was created."

So the Passover Seder, at which men and women participated together, was an emphatic landslide in time, bringing them flush with the moment of Exodus from Egypt. There is no nonsense about a table of bearded men, dressed in white cotton robes, fur hats on and staffs in their hands, leaning back on a pillow for the last feast, ready at midnight to begin marching out of Egypt-Russia, let Elijah only give the call. So they endlessly elaborated, "And thou narrate to thy son on that day saying, because of this, God did this to me in Egypt; that not our ancestors alone did God redeem from Egypt; but also us with them, to bring us to the land we swore to our ancestors."

This religious drama was taken quite literally. In the seventeenth century, Shabbatai Zevi, the most successful of the false Messiahs, spread word across Europe to get ready to come. Entire German communities, tough veterans of commerce and trade, sold their belongings and camped by the wharves, waiting for the word to set sail. The moral dictum for a Jew to feel the birthpangs of the Messiah touched off in every generation its hysterical, dangerous and pathetic crop of false Messiahs, most of whom went to early deaths.

Legend and rumor, plot and analogy were no dream world, but hot and immediate as the next ritual bath. Political events came alive as they touched the fabric and tissue of legend. Thus, an early Zionist memoir tells of a secret assembly of the revolutionary socialists in a Polish Academy. The revolutionaries were more popular with the girls, since they took more chances. The main speaker, a starved runt in an oversize hand-me-down coat, built up to a pitch, crying, "See this coat—its sheepskin is from Siberia, its lining from Bulgaria, its cotton thread from Egypt, its buttons from Australia; yet it is one coat covering this one body of mine, one . . ." Rising on his toes in excitement, he swung up his arms. The entire right sleeve tore loose and began sliding back on his body; and a young Zionist leaped to his feet. "Yes, that tear comes from the Warsaw pogroms; and the dirt on your backside is off the boots of a hundred Cossack anti-Semites." In the nearby synagogue, the drowning waters of the Red Sea were recalled with the same immediacy and fervor.

The 1902 quarrel between Herzl and the Fifth Zionist Congress over whether they should make a Zionist settlement in Uganda must be understood in these terms. Great Britain offered to allow a Zionist state in Uganda, then under their control. Herzl, a Viennese Jew, was inclined to accept; but the eastern European delegates, religious and atheist alike, as one rejected the offer. Their minds had a framework and tissue of legend, historic sweep and internalized drama that had room for only one country, Palestine, then still under the Turks.

For all its Proletarian sweep, there were elements of schizophrenia in the Jewish community, of a timeless mythic innocent, reinforced by Proletarian isolation, side by side with a tough historic sense. Both vehemently worked. Thus, for all its Sholem Aleichem eternity, the Jewish community developed its own thin, but durable internal Face and Shadow, that developed its own internal dynamic. Its Face, inherited from pre-Czarist days, was bourgeois in economics and traditional in ideology. Its last large gesture was to accept the Chassidic movement, thus bringing hundreds of thousands of families into the Pale of the community. Thereafter, throughout the nineteenth century, it suffered a steady decline, for all its communal tenacity. Its historic view had no relationship with the ruling powers of the world, and gradually hardened into a social schizophrenia. The Zionist movement, which might have mobilized Jewish energies, came after the religious establishment was too ossified to respond. The emigration, first of individuals, then of entire communities, to America spread word of a better world close at hand, yet too far away. Poverty and the steady, insecure competition unmanned the Jew of the Pale, all in slow and easy stages, against winds of rumor, a panoply of festivals, and obscure reports from the West. So the communal body aged in its dreams, and scarcely knew how close the knife was to its throat.

Its Face remained thus bourgeois and traditional; but the community gradually declined during the nineteenth century to develop its own Shadow, a working class with a socialist ideology. Late in the century came yet another, more extremist Shadow, a Proletariat within a Proletariat, as it were, in the revolutionary movement. The deep-rootedness of the Jew in the bourgeoisie was based on Talmudic law, essentially a bourgeois code. As the old saying went, every Vilna water-carrier was a banker in the making; all he lacked was money, connections and a brain for business. The turn toward socialism, especially in the large cities, where early trade unions developed in Krakow and Warsaw, was deeply Jewish, with humane concerns and a displaced Messianic hunger, though without the religious practices of Judaism. Both Face and Shadow worked to maintain the community. Its revolutionaries set out from the beginning to destroy it.

This mixed community landed on Ellis Island. Since America is a bourgeois country, the bourgeois Face got enormous emphasis, and essentially founded the Jewish community of the United States; but the strong communal Shadow, working class and socialistic, helped establish organized labor in the United States. The ILGWU had its basis in Warsaw and Bialystok, not in Birmingham and Manchester; the huge housing and communal developments of the garment workers' unions are rooted in European socialist habits adapted to the American scene. The revolutionary fringe joined the American Communist Party, and harbored Trotsky for a while.

The mind of the eastern European Jew was an intellectual, emphatically this-worldly Proletariat, caught up in myth, sinking under poverty, contempt and oppression, who scrambled to make a living. Its core and touchstone was not the occasional Zionist *chalutz*, building a new life, but the mind of the Yeshiva, the advanced religious school that trained young men in the tens of thousands. I recall a Talmudic proverb from my own Yeshiva: "He who assigns hours to study is an idol-worshipper." We joked good-naturedly that all classrooms were idolatrous, having their hours fixed in time; but the proverb had a mystical meaning: a life God encompasses is religious; a life encompassing God is idolatrous. Like God Himself, Who is everywhere, God's Word can be assigned no place. So the Talmud was at once a library and a forest, with commentaries on the page, commentaries in back, commentaries on the commentaries, a living, spreading wilderness, with us as the latest nutty crop of acorns. To assign an hour to the Word, which should speak everywhere, is to make it a thing, an idol.

This was a strange growth, the tough, traditional mind of eastern Europe, economically bourgeois, religiously an exalted aristocracy, temperamentally a Proletariat, politically in touch only with legend, surviving by sheer instinct and tenacity. The Yeshiva that trained its religious élite cut itself loose from practicalities to pursue investigations like those of the pure mathematician. And yet, being divorced from practicalities, Yeshiva study produced a sense of frustration, of rigid ritual observance, choked helplessness, lethargy, unreality, and also an exalted detachment from all earthly affairs, a stubborn retreat to the holiness of the Word. A despised minority, it stubbornly insisted on its election. Recently, the Lubavitcher Rebbeh was asked by reporters in an interview, "Isn't it arrogant of you to see yourself as God's Chosen people?" The Rebbeh answered in bewilderment, "Where does the arrogance come in? I did the choosing? God did the choosing. I didn't do the choosing. How should I know why He chose us? He did it; I had nothing to do with it."

So the creative spirit floundered in a mystic beatitude, amid unkempt, aimless ghetto poverty—vast, floundering Yeshivas, endlessly re-chewing the Talmudic cud, as the fiber of their community weakened and floundered in ignorance and poverty. Afloat in a stagnant pool of holiness, the men became ritual objects; and society gradually became a matriarchate. Its women lacked their share of official holiness; but every anthropologist knows that holiness is a dubious blessing. Primitive tribes straitjacket their ritual king with taboos, while a second, practical king moves freely and rules the tribe. In the eastern European Jewish family, as manhood grew emasculated, the father became increasingly the ritual king, the mother the practical ruler. The man spent years over religious texts, sharpening his theoretical brain and habituating himself to study; then, religious credentials in hand, he married into an established business family. Synagogue, community and his rabbi's needs absorbed him. His wife, unencumbered by lengthy prayers and the mantle of holiness, raised her children, maintained her household, and made sure her family survived. She, not her husband, kept the family store.

Indeed, the combination of emasculated holiness and matriarchal family power suffered a traumatic reversal of role of man and woman, as masses of eastern European Jews funneled through Ellis Island onto the Lower East Side. Quite simply, in eastern Europe the woman had maintained the family, by her dowry, family, education, home maintenance, budget, and supplies, and even by earning the family living; her husband was her ritual object. But in America, the husband sloughed off his ritual role and entered the garment industry; the wife steadily became the ritual object. This reversal neurotically rigidified the American Jewish family; but the man got back his economic and political virility as compensation. All the woman got was Mother's Day, in her honor.

The eastern European Jewish community, then, a floundering Proletariat numbering in the millions, was a decaying community, with old traditions and mellow decencies, a community that welled with oceanic stirrings of hope, mistrust, superstition, mysticism and outrage. Its folk songs were like the folk songs of the blacks, another large unstructured Proletariat with deep feeling and broad yearnings but no established status. With grumbling exaltation, the East European Jews made their education straddle law, history, and the scaffolding of the universe—and never solved a problem. Their sense of destiny reverberated with a continental shift of people—pilgrimages to a distant Rebbeh, flights from pogroms, emigration to America, Germany, England, Palestine, memories of wanderings to Spain, Italy, Egypt, Babylon, a wash of Biblical tale and anguished prayerful history. Ideologies struggled to the surface against a deep poignance: mythology and folklore, socialism, territorialism, Zionism, Messianism, revolution, vegetarianism, money, modernity, and frustrated spiritual power. Large washes of rage, self-contempt, faith, joy, grim ambition—images of the Messiah and the end of days—were reënacted in the synagogue; rumors of pogroms whispered down every alley.

Zionism was no major factor in the East European picture. That community crumbled westward; it did not organize southward. Zionism came very late and very thin, as a desperate analogy to European nationalism, out of an assimilated Viennese playwright and journalist who attended the Dreyfus trial and converted a scattering of eccentric individuals in the Pale. The Jewish community mistrusted Zionism as harebrained and irreligious, a long detour from their actual plans and hopes. Only the Kishinev pogrom of 1905 stirred a quiver of desperate awareness through their torpor, seeing the Czarist police remain quiescent as in home after home families were raped and tortured. That pogrom exposed the shameful enervation of Jewish manhood after a century of erosion, the settled varnish of anti-Semitic rancor, the indifferent brutality of gentile neighbors. It brought a prophetic quiver of coming horrors, of the Nazi radical solution. Then Bialik, the Hebrew poet, first stirred some broad support for the Zionist movement when his poem "The City of Slaughter" was read aloud at assemblies of the first self-defense units in the entire Pale.

Zionism, a panic reaction of national desperation, was a late eccentricity that happened to be right, flailing out for survival in a torpor of malevolence; but the settled drama of the Pale shifted westward. The web of companies organizing to arrange for American passports, passage and care on the way undermined the sense of the here and now—the sluggish had an out, the energetic were soon gone. My own great-grandfather, youngest son of an old Kovno family, at about seventeen, followed all his older brothers and sisters to Chicago; mistrusting the religion of the new community, he took a ship back to Kovno; then he migrated a second time to Jerusalem, now accompanied by a wife and eight-year-old son, my grandfather.

The remaining community scrambled for a living. Self-indulgent in bourgeois ways, it marked time, warmly communal, but enervated by endless prejudice. It maintained traditions by sentimentality and superstitious instinct. The growing labor community was strongly secular and socialistic, with vision as much out of Messianic synagogue manuals as out of western philosophers. A growing population in a shrinking, shifting community that threatened to disintegrate under their feet, they needed bridges anywhere; but their strongest bridges were only paper. The rest were words that died in the air.

Sigmund Freud, who happened to be an early Zionist supporter while Zionism was still frowned upon in his community, viewed the entire Jewish religion as a collective superego for western man, a superego that generated hatred in gentiles. This view, which has strongly influenced modern thinking, should be seen for what it was: a parochial reading of German Reform Jewry, with little relevance to East European Jews. Thus the Viennese community had no Proletarian elements about it, but was programmatically German Reform or rigidified German Orthodoxy. Freud's formulation of the Mosaic code closely approximates the formulae of German Reform theology, reducing the Mosaic code to a demand for clear devotion and moral self-control, all suggesting superego factors:

I thus believe that the idea of an *only* God, as well as the emphasis laid on ethical demands in the name of that God and the rejection of all magic ceremonial, was indeed Mosaic doctrine.

Hence, Freud could say, "The Mosaic religion has been a Father religion; Christianity became a son religion." He then goes on to explain anti-Semitism as a late, imperfect accommodation of an obstreperous pagan id balking at a newly acquired Christian-Judaic superego:

> We must not forget that all the peoples who now excell in the practice of anti-Semitism became Christians only in relatively recent times, sometimes forced to it by bloody compulsion. One might say they all are "badly Christianed;" under the thin veneer of Christianity they have remained what their ancestors were, barbarically polytheistic. They have not yet overcome their grudge against the new religion which was forced on them, and they have projected it on to the source from which Christianity came to them. The hatred for Judaism is at bottom hatred for Christianity, and it is not surprising that in the German National Socialist revolution this close connection of the two monotheistic religions finds such clear expression in the hostile treatment of both.

Freud's finding a resentful id in the German community that rejected the Christian moral superego has suggestive echoes in Nazi folklore and propaganda and a philosophical basis in Nietzsche, but his dynamic applies to German Jewry only. Thus, hundreds of thousands of Chassidim visited their Rebbeh, not for moral instruction but for the fulfillments embodied in an id religion for a festive overflow of blessing, an illumination of holy spirit. The Lithuanian Talmudic aristocracy struggled for a tough, autonomous ego, not a melting of self into an imperious code; theirs was strongly an ego religion. It finds its highest illumination when the Biblical Moses demanded equity from God after the episode of the Golden Calf: "And the Lord spake unto Moses face to face, as a man speaketh unto his friend." This was an adult ego gesture, not a well-intentioned superego.

This characteristic attitude stamped the rabbinic aristocracy of the Pale. Hence the Talmudic parable of the rabbinic court whom God's angels of judgment found in error. Each time protesting

sheets of fire, flood and earthquake rose against the pronouncements of judgment, the chief justice called out that judgment was
in the hands of his court, and not in the hands of flood and earthquake. So, for all its arbitrary fiats, the Talmud contains enough
equity principles to justify it as a tough ego religion. Whatever
eccentricities were conditioned into their temperaments, those
rabbis were hard-working judges and communal diplomats, and
not instructors in ethical constraint.

Freud's concept of the eternal Jewish superego as its cause
rather romanticizes Russian anti-Semitism. A simpler explanation
lies in the primitive dynamic hit upon by modern biology, the
principle of the pack smell. Apparently, only rats and human beings wantonly kill their own species. Thus, each rat pack has its
territory, that other packs enter at their peril. Such foreign rats, as
we now know, are distinguished by their smell. In the crucial experiment, a rat was removed from its pack and chemically cleaned
of any smell whatever. An alien pack then tolerated it, since it had
no strange smell. When it had acquired the smell of the new pack,
it was put back on its own pack ground. Seeing rats all around
with an old familiar smell, it approached them happily, whereupon
the entire pack pounced upon it, tore it limb from limb, and ate up
its every fleck of meat in a matter of seconds.

The home in the border regions of the Pale, the exaggerated
Slavic love of Mother Russia, the mythic biological continuity with
the land, all suggest some such dynamic. Furthermore, Russia,
which regarded its Orthodox Christianity as its native faith, to be
vindicated against Roman Christianity, traced its religion back to
Byzantium, not to its Jewish origins. A simpler explanation of Russian anti-Semitism is that the Jews of the Pale lacked the smell of
Czarist Russia, and were therefore kept out of the heartland.

This East European community was larger, looser, more aimless
and more pathetic than our usual formulations make it—a tentative
bourgeois element in a country whose mythology regarded the

bourgeois as alien and enfeebled. Its myth figure, the Sam Houston and Buffalo Bill of *shtetl* folklore, was not Theodor Herzl or King David, but Rothschild, who came out of the Frankfort ghetto to entrench his family in every European capital by well-tooled business brains. Hadn't the English Rothschilds mobilized the financial resources of the West to overthrow Napoleon? Hadn't the Rothschilds dug the Suez Canal, built the Railroads of Europe? They financed the first wine press in Palestine, a small local gesture entwined in the fabric of Jewish history. So the legendary brag of the virtuous but penniless Yeshiva boy was that if he and Rothschild changed places, he would be richer than Rothschild, because he would give Hebrew lessons on the side!

The literary masters of this impoverished, shifting and culture-laden community knew its temperament, but were cramped by its limitations. Its masters, Mendeleh, Sholem Aleichem, Peretz and Bialik, tumbled from the same barrel, all with intensive Orthodox training. All could be called Writers of the Bridge, their work to mark the bridge out of the Pale, to set up signposts, warn against pitfalls and suggest what constitutes arrival. All knew both Hebrew and Yiddish intimately. Sholem Aleichem began writing in Hebrew; Bialik translated his own poems into Yiddish. Indeed, Bialik's Hebrew was so local that he stumbled on Hebrew free verse by the eccentricities of a Galician accent. Their choice of language was a matter of vision and direction, not of original language skill.

Relevant here is the strange mode of fiction of these writers, one found more often in movies than in written stories. This might be called pre-pubertal fiction. Of this genre are the classical movie-comedies of Charlie Chaplin, Buster Keaton and the Marx Brothers, where mythic boys, sturdy, well-meaning nuts and indestructible imps, with boy-emotions, exuberant self-assertion, precision, truth, and directness, struggle to establish themselves in an adult world overloaded with authority figures and constant movement from place to place. Adolescent emotions of love and brooding passion are simply not to be found in their pages. The establishment is always being called into question, as a nobler, cleaner, simpler justice comes into play, one at once serious and not serious. These are boys, not men, radical innocents, who demand a boy's truth. Their outrage is even conventional—boys that young should be obstreperous. Like Puck, they love their world; they would find it delicious, if only it would make some sense!

Pre-pubertal fiction generally embodies much hard, erratic movement, topsy-turvy situations, sudden about-faces. The irrepressible imps will not stay down. Nothing in their world has finality. Groucho and Harpo Marx zip around a department store on roller-skates, conveyor belts, and one-wheeled bicycles, chased by the local cops, who it turns out are robbers. In *Zéro de Conduite*, a fatherly midget with a long beard runs a boys' boarding school. His feet kicking under his chair because they can't reach the floor, he leans forward and murmurs to a boy larger than he, "Why do you find it hard to accept me as your father?" So, by a series of misadventures, Bialik lands a pious rabbi before his congregation in the most outrageous Sabbath violations. In Sholem Aleichem, who knows where a traveler will land, or what will greet him at the train station? Sholem Aleichem himself, welcomed to America at a mass meeting in Cooper Union, told the audience, "I come to America for the second time. I was first here in 1905, on the outbreak of the Russo-Japanese War. I now come in 1914, at the outbreak of a World War. God help the universe, should I visit this country a third time." These master writers of the Pale, proletarian writers without anchors of security or channels to power, yell in boyish outrage at an imbecile disoriented world.

Indeed, their lives parallel the topsy-turvy fiction world. Mendeleh (pen name for Sholem Jacob Abramovich) came of Talmudic stock; but upon his father's death in his native Minsk, he plunged off from his Yeshiva studies and became a wandering beggar through Lithuania and the southern Pale, mingling with vagabonds, gangs of thieves, the beggars and the disinherited. Finally, he began to write—typical pre-pubertal writing, with racy satire and pungent detail, spelling out the degenerate atrocity of the Pale communities, exposing their ignorance, dislike of manual labor, superstitious conceit, injustices to the poor. His stories are militant, outraged, unpredictable, as they jounce from place to place: *Fischke der Krumer* (*Crippled Fischke*) is the story of a wandering beggar; *Die Klatchke* (*The Nag*) makes a worn-out drayhorse emblem of the Jewish people in exile; *Masaot Binyamin Hashlishi* (*The Travels of Benjamin the Third*) tells how two exuberant small-town innocents set out to live in the style of Don Quixote. Eventually Abramovitch became a school administrator in Odessa, stopped writing, and fathered the next generation of writers.

Sholem Aleichem ("How do you do"—pen name for Solomon Rabinowitz) was born to Nachum Vevik Rabinowitz, literateur, amateur philosopher, and Chassid, a man whose wife raised over a dozen children and kept the family store. Sholem Aleichem got a modern religious education at an advanced school; but poppa lost his business, and took a miserable inn. The family intellectual won a school prize for scholarship, and was nicknamed the Bible Boy; but the family did badly. Momma pawned her jewelry and silverware, and finally died in a cholera epidemic. The family said kaddish, and Nachum Vevik soon remarried; the new wife was a hot-tempered Berditchev woman, whose racy curses Sholem Aleichem compiled in a dictionary. Impartiality was her saving grace; her own children, her stepchildren—she cursed them all with impartial dedication. She mobilized Sholem Aleichem to hustle in the streets and attract travelers to their inn. At night, in the attic, he read Hebrew and Russian novels and journals. At sixteen, he bought a pad of paper and secretly began a Hebrew novel, *The Daughter of Zion;* but his stepmother cried scandal at the wasted kerosene, and ordered Nachum Vevik to destroy the confiscated novel. Nachum

Vevik showed it to a confidant, and Sholem Aleichem was elected to the local tea-and-cheese club, a genius in the making.

Scratching seventeen and launched into a series of tutoring jobs, with baby-sitting and household chores on call, Sholem Aleichem became private tutor to Olga Loieff, the thirteen-year-old daughter of Reb Elimelech Loieff, a wealthy Sofievka merchant and litera-teur; he was to train her in Russian, Hebrew, Bible, mathematics, history and literature. Sholem Aleichem moved onto the estate; Reb Elimelech's son died, leaving Olga an only child. Reb Elime-lech constantly traveled on business. Overnight, our itinerant tutor and baby-sitter became visiting scholar and the available bachelor at a wealthy estate in storyland.

Sholem Aleichem soon informed Olga of her good fortune in being private student to a literary master; she was to study enough to keep Reb Elimelech happy, as they pursued their mission in life: to advance his literary career. Olga agreed with ardor. For several years, they read Shakespeare, Goethe, the French and Russian nov-elists. Sholem Aleichem wrote fiction in the style of each, Olga hailed each a masterpiece, and Sholem Aleichem threw it in the fire and began a fresh project. Then one day Reb Elimelech came home unexpectedly and threw Sholem Aleichem out on the road, penni-less.

A virginal scholar and vagabond, Sholem Aleichem wandered the highway to Kiev—that was the Left Bank of the Ukraine—where else? and stole into the city without a residence permit. That night, the police raided his beggars' inn. He shrank into an attic packed with Jews without permits, starveling innocents like him-self. Kiev multiplied tutors like roaches—they crawled out of the walls and from under the beds—all with literary genius; it had no interest in any of them. He took to the road as a wandering beggar, then landed a job as Russian rabbi of a Ukrainian village. Like any good Jewish intellectual of the Pale, the one talent he had su-premely was the ability to pass a language test.

Meanwhile, back in Sofievka, Olga began a series of hunger strikes. She kept it up week after week, month after month, until Reb Elimelech, in despair, set off to find his former tutor. After all, what did he have against him as a son-in-law, except that he was penniless, a dreamer, a liar, and a professional failure who would never make a living? He finally tracked him down—it wasn't easy —brought him back to Sofievka, married him to Olga, and then died, leaving them a quarter of a million rubles. Sholem Aleichem sold his Sofievka estate and moved to Kiev in 1885—it now made him no difficulties about a residence permit—to become a speculator on the stock exchange.

His life now moved into high gear as his wife began producing babies. For years, he had published literary and educational material in Hebrew and Russian journals. The meteoric success of Mendeleh in Yiddish inspired Sholem Aleichem to try his hand at a few Yiddish stories of good-humored satire and compassion. He immediately found publishers. He founded his own journal, *Yiddishes Folksblat*, where he first published Peretz in Yiddish; Peretz then became his lifelong friend. In five years, he established himself as a Kiev literary prince, and lost all his money.

Sholem Aleichem moved to Odessa, and joined the circle around Mendeleh, whom he called grandfather; he won praise from Gorki, and even from Tolstoy, but he felt shy about not writing novels. He finally wrote his first, and rushed the manuscript into Mendeleh's hands. Mendeleh lay down on the couch and read in silence; Sholem Aleichem sat on a chair and waited. After an hour's silent reading, Mendeleh looked up. "Is the oven on?" "Yes, certainly," came the author's eager reply, "We'll soon have hot coffee, food, a *lechayim*." Mendeleh calmly returned the manuscript. "If the oven is on, throw this in; novels are not for you."

Sholem Aleichem continued writing, in Odessa, in Kiev, elsewhere, barely able to support his family, but knowing no other craft. Sometimes he lacked rent money. He fell ill with tuberculosis, and later with diabetes, of which he died in 1916. Indignant at the 1905 pogroms, he visited America to work as a lecturer, small, dapper, long-haired, in a velvet coat and flowing black tie. And he, not Herzl, was the chief figure of the nineteenth century Pale. All his life he kept on the move, climbing on milk trains, chatting with the travelers, hearing their stories, getting off and rushing to the nearest desk to write. So his great bridge reached from *shtetl* to New York City, with all its indignities and jostling stops, giving the Pale of a voice of outrage, of loving indignation, and a sense of how to get out.

The sprawling Jewish Proletariat of Eastern Europe had two heads that kept shifting Face and Shadow: an aging bourgeois Face, traditional, rational, struggling for unkempt survival; and its socialist Shadow, non-religious, deeply involved in labor unions. Indeed, Isaac Bashevis Singer is the emblematic Yiddish writer with two heads; he has testified with rueful good humor that while ordinary adults outgrow one father, he had two, his biological father, a fanatic Ukrainian rabbi, who sent him to study in a Yeshiva, and his older brother, I. J. Singer, author of *The Brothers Ashkenazi* and a card-carrying Party member, who, at the time of the revolution, yanked him out of the Yeshiva and slapped him into a proofreading job on a new Communist Yiddish press.

But as the century wore on, that socialist Shadow cast a more fanatic shadow; completely alienated revolutionaries, stark fanatics and dialecticians bent all their energies to achieve the overthrow of society and the government, picked up the slack social energies of the Pale that were there for the asking and coiled them into whips of violent action. These men were of Trotsky's bent, men who saw as one Russian folkways and the Jewish community they disowned, and were dedicated to digesting them both in the revolution.

Hitler exterminated the Jewish Pale in the Second World War; but the 1917 Revolution had already broken its back. Its own fringe Shadow of revolutionaries did the deed. Empowered by the Soviet authorities, they invaded the Jewish community, administered, reorganized, spied upon and eliminated its institutions in cannibalistic fashion, exterminating indigenous leaders whenever they expressed any independence. Thus Bialik, the distinguished Hebrew poet, was invited in Odessa by his brother-in-law, a Bolshevik general, Jan Gamarnik, to join the Bolshevik regime. Bialik told him to his face that his own comrades would someday shamefully murder him, a prophecy fulfilled in the thirties, when almost to a man, Stalin exterminated that class of revolutionary fanatics and dialecticians. But their work was done. The Russian Jews are still alive; but their culture has been steadily smothered and eliminated by bland, administrative asphyxiation.

Indeed, the American Jew is, absurdly, the polar opposite of his Russian counterpart. If the Russian Jew is a century-old Proletariat, the American Jew is all Face. He has always felt at home in America. He should. His traditional bourgeois head found a thoroughly bourgeois country; and later his socialist head also managed to find its American counterpart. During the depression, it surfaced with the labor movement under the New Deal. The unions then joined the establishment as Face; and class warfare became negotiation between two industrial powers, labor and management. With this change, the last great social revolution in America, the poignance of labor firmed up to a sense of organization. Its humanity found a base of power, its outrage an itemized program. It sentimentalized old labor hymns like "Joe Hill" and "Which Side Are You On?" sung like Negro spirituals or songs of the Spanish Civil War; but it stopped writing fresh songs of that caliber—how soulfully can you sing for a third week of vacation with pay? As the unions got established, the industrial wasteland faded; continental sweep narrowed to a bargaining table in the middle of the room, with the same kind of chairs on either side. Steadily, man by man, and issue by issue, the Jewish socialists gave up their socialist doctrine and became liberal activists. Typically, Abraham Cahan met Roosevelt halfway, and the *Vorwärts*, the great Yiddish daily, changed from a socialist organ to a New Deal supporter.

Once both its heads became legitimate, the American Jewish community became all Face, without a Shadow. A literary, deeply familial, historic and ambitious people, suddenly, on arriving at Ellis Island and receiving an immigration certificate, jumped from deep Proletariat to pure Face to produce a euphoric ease such as the world has seldom known. The legendary Hyman Kaplan, writing his name in school, put a star between each pair of letters. Those stars were the stars of arrival on Delancey Street, a shining neon Garden of Eden.

Sholem Aleichem's story is relevant here, the story of a starved unemployable Yeshiva boy, without money, family or a way of making a living, jogging an immigration official at Ellis Island about United States policy in China, pulling at his sidecurls, chafing in his long black gaberdine at the unsatisfactory answers and pressing the questions until the official let him pass to escape. So a relative of mine, a seventeen-year-old stitcher, fresh-arrived from Poland and half an hour over a sewing machine in his first sweat-shop job in a noisy, steaming loft, nudged the next stitcher and asked in Yiddish, "Please, exactly how much money will buy this entire establishment?"

I must confess to something of this "my-soul-is-not-just-a-raisin" complex that puts the outsider in a chafe to arrive. At fourteen, I read that Coleridge had envisioned the poem "Kubla Khan" in an opium dream. I knew no more about opium than about the men's room of the Taj Mahal—a dream was a dream. If Coleridge could do it, then why not I? To make myself dream a poem, for a week, night after night, as the duller sort lie in bed counting sheep, I lay in bed setting my hand to paper and starting to write. I calculated that sooner or later, I would doze off as my hand hit the paper, and wake up with my own "Kubla Khan." And it worked! I dreamed myself writing a poem! I woke and wrote it down fast—I had a pen and pad at my bedside for just that emergency. Finished, I breathed a sigh of relief; no accident was fragmenting my poem, no unexpected ring at my doorbell—I had it cold! And then I read the poem. I read it again. I read it a third time more slowly, and carefully threw it away. Dedication is not enough; you also need talent. I switched to planning ways of irrigating the Negev in southern Palestine. I had a scheme for tapping the Gulf of Aqaba, complete with power generators for the plunge to the Dead Sea and using the Jordan for irrigation, that would have made a commissar green with envy. All I needed was money, connections, and some training in engineering.

To this immigrant instinct, all things were possible. Doesn't the Declaration of Independence say: All men are created equal? Well, that includes me. And that our Creator has endowed us with certain inalienable rights, including life, liberty, and the pursuit of happiness? That's some advance in goals—in Russia, you pursue the American consul; in this country, you pursue happiness. Well, I know just what happiness is; it's a decent, well-paying job, a loving wife, a home for my family, rubber grippers under my feet in the shower, an air-flush, a vote, and a chance for my son to get into Harvard. The Declaration of Independence—that's my equalizer. For a hundred years under the Czar, I had squirmed around starving in a hand-me-down coat; and now a bunch of us were here together, all free to pursue happiness! Well, count me in on this treasure hunt!

In a bulky arrival, with civics classes for immigrants, wagon trains of pushcarts, the garment trades, the clans advanced themselves, upward-mobile and outward-bound—go west, mein Yiddishe mameh, go west! As an electron suddenly jumps from ring to ring around its nucleus, so the Jew jumped en masse from Proletariat to Face in America. This produced strange aberrations, an enormous self-consciousness about keeping a clean Face. There was a time when the arrest of a Communist spy sent every New York Jew to check the spy's national origins in the *Times*. The first Jew arrested for murder in New York shamed the entire community. The Jew organized charity drives, served on public bodies, pushed liberal causes. He also took out heavy insurance—nothing could now be left to chance.

Indeed, this sudden arrival at Face exploded into the American entertainment industry. That's what Faces do, perform. They clown, mug, cry, laugh, yell, and establish themselves. So crop after crop of actors, comedians, singers, producers, impresarios, psychopaths, cantors, clowns, and fixated babies grew up and scattered from the Chicago and New York ghettoes. The ghetto Jew wasn't there to shut up and be invisible, but to be enjoyed, looked at, and accepted, over and over and over. The Yiddish stage produced Paul Muni and the late John Garfield, the London ghetto and the music-hall tradition, Charlie Chaplin. Sam Goldwyn and Louis B. Mayer built gauzy empires. Their troopers had a sense of explosive arrival in the entertainment world.

There was a similar explosion in the arts, as a new Face struggled to express itself. The Jewish immigrant had a deep religious tradition, a synagogue training in seeking to communicate with God across wastes of exile. Arrived in New York, and become Face in a sudden clap, he found all this hunger for spiritual expression released to produce a tidal wave of creative expression. I have no hard statistics, but my sense is that most serious composers of a few years ago in this country were Jewish. The statistics as to painters were also outrageously disproportional. Not only was this community finding a voice, but in a country that associated creativity with neurotic perversions, an exotic community appeared, which found it manly to create.

It was in Odessa, the Wild West of Russian Jewry, that that timberwolf, Mendeleh, had settled as school principal and patron of writers. A catchphrase of music critics of thirty and forty years

ago was that every great world violinist was a Jew from Odessa.
My mother's family originated in Kovno, Lithuania; but I know
the Odessa temperament. A few years ago, a Soviet journal ad-
versely reviewed the unabridged edition of Mark Twain and then
ignored the editor's reply. After repeated letters, he wrote personally to Khrushchev, denouncing the pretended objectivity of the
journal and its lack of scholarly integrity in denying space to his
reply. Khrushchev then made the journal print the editor's reply.
Reading the story, it struck me that only one from Odessa would
have had the gall to write that letter and make it work. To my
pleasant surprise, the *Times* carried a brief biography of the editor. I checked—the editor was originally from Odessa.

Yiddish has had a strong influence in this country, in slang
words like *ganev* and *shlemiel,* and in phraseology and word order.
In English many German-sounding barbarisms, like postponing
the verb, are really Yiddishisms. Indeed, many of Bernard Mala-
mud's sentences follow a fairly strict Yiddish word order, as if his
characters were shaping Yiddish phrases, and delivering them in
English, one word at a time; so too when the most important word,
whatever its syntax, begins a sentence, as "Money he'll get from
me? Advice he'll get from me. Heart he'll get from me. A hit-in-the-
head he'll get from me. But money he'll get from his old lady. It's
her job to give with the money."

The Yiddish style is one of cultured chatter, of easy stab and
distracted withdrawal, as in Saul Bellow's work. Bellow is a master
stylist thoroughly grounded in Yiddish literature, he has worked in
Yiddish editing and translation. Its point of view is pickled in a
mellow, learned skepticism, not in an innocent naïveté, as in
Huckleberry Finn. All the Yiddish writers have it, Sholem
Aleichem preëminently. So, for example, the opening pages of *The
Adventures of Augie March* digest and ruminate on a rush of personal experience. Hemingway had a more astringent quality, the
clean, dry precision of a Manet painting. In contrast, Bellow ren-

ders not a wash of experience, but an overripe soul, chewing, digesting and settling its experience into place:

> In the bathroom, Herzog turned his tie to the back of his neck to keep it from drooping into the basin. This was a luxurious little room, with indirect lighting (kindness to haggard faces). The long tap glittered, the water gushed forth. He sniffed the soap. *Muguet.* The water felt very cold on his nails. He recalled the old Jewish ritual of nail water, and the words in the Haggadah, *Rachatz!* "Thou shalt wash." It was obligatory also to wash when you returned from the cemetery (*Beth Olam*—the Dwelling of the Multitude). But why think of cemeteries, of funerals, now? Unless . . . the old joke about the Shakespearean actor in the brothel. When he took off his pants, the whore in bed gave a whistle. He said, "Madam, we come to bury Caesar, not to praise him." How schoolboy jokes clung to you!
>
> He opened his mouth under the tap and let the current run also into his shut eyes, gasping with satisfaction.

This explosion of the American Jew in the arts was not a permanent self-discovery—the community as artist—but a celebration of euphoric arrival. Once the shock of Face had passed, quite simply, anything could happen.

The nuclear Jewish plot in this country is the sale of one's soul to arrive at a spiritual wasteland. Whatever one's new program, there is an uneasiness at having lost or bartered away one's soul. Thus, Abraham Cahan's *The Rise of David Levinsky* is the pilgrim's progress of a newly arrived Orthodox immigrant, decent and well-mannered enough, who begins in the garment industry, invests, and gradually becomes a successful operator. All his life, he has love affairs, some even with married women, yet he experiences no great lift of soul, only a patient conformism. Chapter by chapter, his beard diminishes and his bank account gets longer. At the end of the book, he stands, a permanent male spinster and well-tailored millionaire whom life has passed by. If we may mix our metaphors, he has sold his soul for a golden calf; but that calf was dead and it staled to a mess of pottage. So Ludwig Lewisohn saw an American wasteland of smug superiority, glazed with ersatz so-phistication, and an abysmal ignorance of all previous culture, as though, in some strange way, Ellis Island filtered out soul.

The gentile myths of the American Jew scarcely touch his haunt-ing fear of cultural failure, of the loss of his authenticity, the eter-nal fear of the wanderer, in a quiver of uneasiness that he has found a home at last, and that it is just a hotel bedroom. He had it on arrival in America, then on arrival in the suburbs. A late set-tler, he needs strong roots; but the American bourgeois class, to which he belongs, is losing its cool under the mystique of imper-sonal power. When the Jew stops cherishing himself as a human being, he is dead.

Other aberrations affected the slippery shift of ground as the Jew arrived in America, like the reversal of role of men and women mentioned earlier, that evolved in stages. Among the first immi-grants, the woman stood side by side with her husband, caring for the candy store, the corner grocery, the tailor shop. In this first flush of immigration, boundaries blurred, and new relationships opened up. So the man eased his role as a holy vessel, and came to a humbler partnership with his wife, two immigrants, partners in a new land. But as the man improved his status, he soon became the exclusive bread-winner; the woman bent her energies toward mastering avenues toward culture and status.

In this development, the woman's blessings became gilt-edge cas-trations, in the hothouse atmosphere of an immigrant home; as in the classic novel of the Ellis Island generation, Henry Roth's *Call It Sleep*. But as the family got established, as the generation advanced a notch, every gadget in momma's pantry, every number on her private phone list, diapers, baby-sitters, caterers, house maids, dog-walkers, took away a service and made her expendable. The man now earned the family living. Steadily the street, her children's peer groups and a general loose independence thinned her spiritual authority. As a result, she retrenched into a creature of leisure who didn't like her leisure. Jewish exaggerated penis-envy comes not because the woman lost her penis at the beginning of time, but because she lost her pants at Ellis Island. So the equilibrium set in of entrenched authority and diminished function. Momma broods and watches restlessly, and rules her family—it's a bore just to lounge around and decorate.

I recall visiting the old Rappaport's Restaurant on Second Avenue on a family night of garment industry executives. At each table in the deep, wide room, like a made-over basement shop, with a low ceiling and row after row of tables, the family totem pole sits swathed in yards of fabric, bulky hair hanging over her shoulders or piled on top of her head, an oversized fur coat tossed back on her chair, a diamond watch pinned on her shoulder, carats sprayed across her fingers, her children stiff around her, upright with respect—respect for momma! It's the family night out!—yards of corset immobilize her dignified poundage, her two quiet battleships hanging over the table, their bulk camouflaged in flowery orlon, so buttressed, shrouded, folded around, weighed down, lifted up, on exhibition, shiny and imposing, you wondered what was flesh, what was buttress, what was trapped air, and what your euphoric imagination. That woman may not have had much freedom; but she ruled her family—and that is more important.

As the years went by, from this changing role emerged a female will, the matriarch, ruling a diminished estate. D. H. Lawrence wrote with too much metaphysics about the frustrated female bull that will have her stubborn way, somberly aware, with a hopeless determination, that she is not free and happy. The metaphysics in Lawrence's coaling villages became sociology in second-generation Jewish New York. The rules of the game were changing too fast to make it on culture—your momma's *pupik* won't train you to understand the New York Philharmonic. So she encouraged culture, and made it on family participation. The equilibrium was still maintained.

Clifford Odets' Jewish momma is the granddaughter of the Jewish momma of eastern Europe, the edge of hysteria in her disposition masked as sentimentality. Too much is slipping away from such a woman. The equilibrium is thinning out. Her older sister had seven or eight children; she has three. She married as a virgin, but times are getting looser; her daughters will out. She doesn't believe in the hereafter; this life is it, and it is too stark. She can't control her husband or his business, only admonish him not to make mistakes; she can't control how her children will do in school, only lay down demands; she can't control their religious observance, only drag them with her to synagogue on occasion. Up from Grand Street, she has made Jewish cooking an art to be enjoyed: her *kugel* the pride of the neighborhood, her *tsimmes* you lick the fingers from, her gefilte fish will float out over the street unless the windows are closed. She is advancing nervously in the world.

Her husband won't give much help. He sits over the Passover table, and makes *Kiddush* on Friday night; but in Europe, he was the *batlan* with the book. Here, the world is his domain; what is more, he has seized that domain from her. His loss of holiness, his loss of education, and his new money-making role produce the sadistic business bully and escapee who refuses to answer questions, refuses to plan his business with his wife, insists that it is his domain, and that he plans to keep it that way.

He has a sour-sweet investment in a jaded, gingerly establishment, whose authority is thinning out. He can divorce her, make her a rejected, yet also a free woman; but the process involves complicated sparring and negotiation, and even divorced, she still has her home. Married, he has to come home each night to her domain, do the chores, and take the children roller-skating; but the children are an extension of him. He can be free, but may turn into

a male stud. The equilibrium is now at its thinnest. Should he fail
to bring home his pay-check, or lose his job, something inside him
crumbles, and he turns into the Jewish masochist and shnook, who
comes to his wife for reassurance and support, or does chores
around the house as compensation. She then mothers him like her
other children, and turns into the Gold-Star Jewish mother.

The breaking point in this equilibrium comes when the husband's bond thins and snaps, and he begins having affairs. With so
much idealized adolescence around, this need not break up the
marriage—more than one marriage with growing children has the
wife as mother, the mistress as sweetheart of the same husband and
father. But the wife now has a blank check in morals in her hand,
and can begin acting out. Subtly, she begins playing the child
against the father. As for the children, who mesh and interact in a
scramble of parental energies, they suddenly discover authority is
in their hands and all clear functions are gone. They turn the wheel
in a brave new world. Indeed, they can now teach momma how to
live.

It is a botch. This brave new world has too many overpopulated
slums. The current language about freedom and self-discovery
turns too easily into an evasive brag, an excuse for narcissism or
the consolation prize for a life of triviality. Finally, freedom is the
freedom to do substantial things; self-discovery is the arrival of an
oceanic being in whom large mythic roles are effectively acted out.
The test of freedom is its arrival at a self, doing substantial good
things.

Our language grows circular, and must have a stop.

The kick of life is the only burning bush left in this wilderness.
We see it, take off our shoes, and keep walking.

6

THE FREEZE OF FACE IN SOVIET RUSSIA

THE SOVIET Revolution of 1917 was a double shift of figure and ground. The Russian landed Face was overthrown, and its extreme Shadow, its revolutionary Proletariat, took power. Its bourgeois Shadow was bypassed like the eye of the storm, and retained an image of being dependent, weak, and unworthy. The reversal was too extreme. As we shall see, elements of the old Russian spirit absorbed the revolution into a familiar Slavic mould.

In the Russian Jewish community, the outcast revolutionary Proletariat eliminated both its heads, the bourgeois and the labor-socialist. In an hour, Leon Trotsky replaced the Gaon of Vilna as the supremely arrived Jew. The results were catastrophic and irreversible. In a process internal, savage and total as digestion, the artificially imposed Face set out to absorb its usurped community. Activist Jews programmed Jewish affairs with the anatomical knowledge of dedicated surgeons, set up bureaus, infiltrated the organizations, separated out the two Jewish heads, and severed them one by one from their body.

Distinctions were piled up, one behind the other, and then slammed down: Yiddish was glorified, Hebrew excoriated; anecdotes glorified, prayer excoriated; labor glorified, Zionism excoriated. All definitions of Jewry were simplified, rarefied and eliminated by a process of administrative redefinition, from nation to religion, to ethnic folkways, to language culture. Existence was by administrative fiat. If no definition held administratively, there was nothing to administer; once there was nothing to administer, nothing existed. Synagogue visitors and conversations in the lobby were checked by Jewish activists. As attendance declined under spying and denunciations, synagogues changed to factories, warehouses, rest-homes, cows' barns. Nationalism was eliminated shekel by shekel, religious practice matzo by matzo.

The explosion of dance and celebration in the Moscow streets on the arrival of Golda Meir, the first Israeli ambassador, the march of tens of thousands in her honor, suggest that the two Shadow heads had sunk deep underground into the body of the community. What Moscow Jewry celebrated on the arrival of the Israeli flag was Hebrew, not Yiddish; nationalism, not folkways; historical vicissitudes, not a theoretical dialectic. Indeed, both underground Jewish heads joined in that celebration, the bourgeois head, Hebraic, nationalistic, religiously observant, with a financial and technical investment in Israel, and the socialist head, honoring a state ruled by socialist labor.

The celebration was gallant, but intolerable to the Soviet Union. Its brute and ponderous hostility to the State of Israel, while using Israel as a stepping stone to Cairo and Damascus, is also a furious dialectic of multiple rejection. Whatever the programmed patter of its diplomats, the settled cultural anti-Semitism of the Soviet Union would preclude any Jewish resurgence. The Jewish bourgeoisie and its labor-socialist community were both caught between the millstones, mistrusted, regarded as ineffectual, and finally chewed up by both the Czarist and Soviet authorities. And even the Jewish revolutionaries were eliminated as Soviet society grew more nationalistic in the Thirties. Did the raising of the Israeli flag stir a flicker of life? That flag was dropped into the Soviet air-tight room for a steady process of asphyxiation.

As for the Revolution itself, there was a brief, aggressively open period, when rampant experiment prevailed in the arts and in society. Kandinsky, Chagall, Gabo and Pevsner were invited back from western Europe to direct revolutionary art schools. New forms of art were explored; exotic varieties of opera meshed and flowered in drama and dance. Stanislavsky briefly expanded his theater. Constructionists and Suprematists worked in extremely simple abstract painting and sculpture. Isadora Duncan came to Russia by invitation, and founded a school to advance modern dance.

This flowering ground to a halt in a series of bureaucratic controls and shifts of policy around the Party Congress of 1922. The death of Lenin in 1924 and the rapid rise of Stalin to power slammed the door finally shut. Stalin's struggle with Trotsky, aside from a sheer brute competition for control over the party apparatus, the army and the national economy, embodied deep bents in the Russian character. Thus, Trotsky, the loser, conceived the revolution as an essential process of class warfare, Russia as the aroused mailed fist that would smash open a revolution around the world. A theoretician of process, who had roamed Russia and overseas and been repeatedly exiled to Siberia, he saw history as unfolding energies buried in society. He cherished no mystique of the Russian soil. His *The Russian Revolution* pours out adulation only for the process of revolution. Thus, his diagnosis of Czar Nicholas II is not simply personal; it sees the Czar's loss of energy as a manifestation of the lethargy of his class:

> We hope to show in what follows, partially at least, just where in a personality the strictly personal ends—often much sooner than we think—and how frequently the "distinguishing traits" of a person are merely individual scratches made by a higher law of development.

Trotsky then goes on to write a revolution whose plot-line resembles the plots of Tolstoy and Dostoevsky; but its touchstone of truth is not landed aristocracy, but revolutionary process. To him, the line of health that keeps a society alive, its prime energy, is the dialectic process of history. Once Nicholas lost contact with the flow of history, a steady process followed like the progress described earlier—perversity, marital irregularity, rootlessness and loose wanderings; an influx of sterile and exotic figures; corruptions and symbolic suicide. The final healing redemption is the victorious revolution and the manifestation of Lenin, where the energy of history emerges triumphant.

Thus, Trotsky finds Nicholas II fundamentally apathetic, a case of more extreme failure of life force than Dostoevsky's Smerdyakov or Tolstoy's Helena Kuragina. Hence Trotsky's initial diagnosis:

> The so-called "breeding" of the czar . . . cannot be explained by a mere external training; its essence was an inner indifference, a poverty of spiritual forces, a weakness of the impulses of the will. The mask, an indifference which was called breeding in certain circles, was a natural part of Nicholas at birth.

So Trotsky's czarina suffered exotic corruptions; with a hysterical or perverted energy, she seized power from the weak czar:

> In order to justify her new situation, this German woman adopted with a kind of cold fury all the traditions and nuances of Russian medievalisms, the most meager and crude of all medievalisms, in that very period when the people were making mighty efforts to free themselves from it. This Hessian princess was possessed by the demon of autocracy. . . . In the Orthodox religion she found a mysticism and a magic adapted to her new lot. She believed the more inflexibly in her new vocation, the more naked became the foulness of the old regime. With a strong character and a gift for dry and hard exultations, the tzarina supplemented the weak-willed tzar, ruling over him.

So Nicholas' court undergoes a Dostoevskeian deterioration, stemming from the perverse weakness of a king without the energy to rule:

Nicholas recoiled in hostility before everything gifted and significant. He felt at ease only among completely mediocre and brainless people, saintly fakirs, holy men, on whom he was rather keen. But it was not active, not possessed of a grain of initiative, enviously defensive. He selected his ministers on a principle of continual deterioration. Men of brain and character he summoned only in extreme situations when there was no other way out, just as we call in a surgeon to save our lives.

No wonder Trotsky felt, "The dynasty fell by shaking, like rotten fruit, before the revolution even had time to approach its first problems."

As in the novels, inner decay brings a wandering and loss of control. Lines of communication are lost; authority shifts from general to general; Rasputin, a Slavic Macbeth, is assassinated and refuses to die. Nicholas' actual death is a sort of degenerative suicide, like the deaths of Anna Karenina or Smerdyakov.

Trotsky saw the moment of truth of the Russian Revolution as occurring on February 23, 1917, when the workers and the Cossacks gingerly felt each other out. The workers were steadily and energetically moving toward them. Like restless atoms in a vacuum tube, the people pressed toward every opening with revolutionary urgency. Their nominal leaders straggled behind, rendering as policy what their wills had already effected. Then, on February 23, the military Cossacks sent to beat back the strikers, moved through the crowds in orderly files, not as a wall of hooves and bullets. In this moment of truth, a contagion of communication joined czarist power to the will of the workers. The revolutionary synthesis began on the streets of Leningrad:

The workers of the Erikson, one of the foremost mills in the Vyborg district, after a morning meeting came out of the Sampsonievsky Prospect, a whole mass, 2,500 of them, and in a narrow place ran into the Cossacks. Cutting their way with the breasts of their horses, the officers first charged through the crowd. Behind them, filling the whole width of the Prospect, galloped the Cossacks. Decisive moment! But the horsemen, cautiously, in a long ribbon, rode through the corridor just made by the officers. "Some of them smiled," Kayurov recalls, "and one of them gave the workers a good wink." That wink was not without meaning. The workers were emboldened with a friendly, not hostile, kind of assurance, and slightly infected the Cossacks with it. The one who winked found imitators. In spite of renewed efforts from the officers, the Cossacks, without openly breaking discipline, failed to force the crowd to disperse, but flowed through it in streams. This was repeated three or four times and brought the two sides ever closer together. Individual Cossacks began to reply to the workers' questions and even to enter into momentary conversations with them. Of discipline there remained but a thin transparent shell that threatened to break through any second. The officers hastened to separate their patrol from the workers, and, abandoning the idea of dispersing them, lined the Cossacks out across the street as a barrier to prevent the demonstrators from getting to the center. But even this did not help: standing stockstill in perfect discipline, the Cossacks did not hinder the workers from diving under their horses. The revolution does not choose its paths; it made its first steps towards victory under the belly of a Cossack horse. A remarkable incident!

With that break in the class wall, the army became porous to communication. Not power, but the will of the people became decisive. Pressured by history, the workers, like raw oxygen, sought a compound. That first Cossack wink to a worker closed the revolution in a fusing synthesis. Thus, Trotsky's mind saw the revolution moving with the patterned inevitability of interstellar dust, first mastering Russia, then engulfing Europe, and then the world.

But Stalin won, not Trotsky; and the machinery of bureaucracy gradually log-jammed the state apparatus. The dictatorship of the proletariat had been established; what need more of process?

Ideological confrontation had been programmed into the Communist Party during its earlier period; that ideological confrontation was now programmed out of it, by labor camps and political trials, if necessary. From now on, discussion and debate would move with ideological unanimity, like a Soviet election, where millions of people vote ballots with one candidate per office. The function of a Russian election is to allow millions of atheists to say "Amen" with conviction to their inevitable destiny.

For the next twenty years, Russia would work to consolidate its industrial base, building a protective wall against outside contamination, while holding the world at arm's length. The changes were so steady and slight nothing registered except as a five-year-plan statistic. Thus, a scientific fraud like Lysenko is finally eliminated; the Russian Face stiffens on the subject. The dictatorship of the proletariat allows no dialectic changes, only a blackjack to eliminate an unreliable assistant. Stalin steadily caught potential opponents in administrative nets and in webs of legal apparatus, entangled them with secret police provocateurs, and sent them straitjacketed to their graves.

Russia's present rulers, Brezhnev and Kosygin, will never react in public to any material on Stalin. They carry themselves like a Madison Avenue firm representing an international cartel—Sweet-Breath Toothpaste, after tests have established that Sweet-Breath kills. It is not the business of their firm to knock their product. Oh, come up with a fresh victim of Sweet-Breath and they will never contradict you head-on. If the widow cries political murder, they won't print her statement, though they'll allow a tacit silence, as long as she has her facts straight and doesn't get too morbid. But long range, their job is a quiet atmosphere and untrammeled power. They'll observe a silence about Sweet-Breath for a decade or two, clean up their product a bit, and then, what do you know, a fresh bust of Sweet-Breath with a kindly handlebar moustache is standing secure and fatherly by the Kremlin. A lot of people may have been eliminated; but Sweet-Breath kept the firm solvent.

This elimination of dialectic process from inside Russia lies behind the system of forced confession of treason engineered by the Soviets. To attribute the trials to Stalin's paranoia is historical self-indulgence. Certainly, he was paranoid; but whatever his paranoia, it was also a successful and lifelong strategy of power and survival. Those engineered confessions came like a monkey wrench in the tight dynamic of process of the Russian Revolution. They were undertaken, not to get rid of a few thousand fanatics, but to work dialectic confrontation out of the very nervous system of the Party, to eliminate basic social change by a conditioned reflex, in trial after trial, and thus change a dynamic confrontation to a vegetable process of growth. From now on, Russia was all establishment, opaque and uniform. The rulers pulled the rug out from under any antithesis as it found a head. The rebels cried confrontation; the rulers sent in their Pavlovian secret police. Thus, by execution, torture, slave labor camps and forced confessions, Russian society was conditioned like a salivating dog to go dead on "confrontation" in its system. Honest disagreements on policy can shake an entrenched establishment no matter who wins the debate. That isn't good enough in Russia. The debaters must be reconditioned by a fatherly mental hospital, totally ignored or sent to prison. A world that has arrived can tolerate no suspense.

Any aberrations of Stalin's temperament are thus inherent in his position. Quite simply, we regard Stalin as a Zeus who successfully replaced Saturn, who successfully replaced Uranus. If this Zeus is not himself to be replaced as king of the gods, castrated, imprisoned forever, he must maintain a constant alert, nail Prometheus to a rock, enslave the titans, maneuver for secret information, and kill all his male sons at birth. So Stalin becomes that strange figure, a Zeus who has kept himself the final synthesis and put a stop to essential time by freezing the state apparatus and meeting the public only with programmed patter. Mistrusting a continuing dialectic revolution, mistrusting, indeed, its very shadow, he first petrified the party bureaucracy, and then got rid of Trotsky and the rest in a conspiratorial process. This Zeus survived then by killing all his male infants in their cradles.

As society froze and process became bureaucratic, old Slavic instincts again absorbed the Russian soul. Conservative ideologies, brushed aside by the Revolution, began to appear again, in fiction, in cinema, in public positions on issues. Thus, land is again the mystical body of Holy Mother Russia, as in Dostoevsky and Tolstoy. Individual characters come flatter, less significant than the vegetable processes of a landed people. So Sholokhov rose to supreme legitimacy, writing epic chronicles of the Don and its spreading countryside where characters blur and melt into one another like thick vegetation.

With the change, Soviet Communism ceased to be a Revolutionary force in Soviet Russia and in every advanced non-Communist country in the world—in Europe, North America, large parts of Asia and South America. Communism is now a political party, with candidates, a program, pretensions and decent strength. Here and there, it may be the most decent thing around; you line up and decide, casting your vote. Its threat today is staying power, not revolution. Like a chain of J. C. Penney stores, with well-located units, stable management, central buying and a careful chain of bureaucratic controls, the Communist parties support their firm, and believe that sooner or later they will take over the market. After twenty years, members of the same family come to look and act alike. So a conservative, slow-moving, entrenched, landed empire like Soviet Russia would hardly relate to firebrands and revolutionaries. The last thing the Communist Parties of France and Italy will ever do is revolt, what with their entrenched bureaucracy, their hierarchy of officers, their careful system of thought control, their hold on organized labor.

This is a truth the revolutionaries have increasingly registered. Their growing revolutionary disillusionment with the Soviet Union is well known, their cry for a revolution within a revolution; but they have failed to read its implications. They read personal sluggishness into the Soviet bureaucracy, and have no sense of how implacable the historic forces involved are. There is no dialectic in the Soviet Union today, nor within the parties and nations dependent on her. Therefore all revolutionaries who work by an inner dialectic are barred from the workings of the party apparatus. Ignorant of the present historic reality, committed to an archaic metaphysics, to bookish memories of factories of a hundred years ago, they maneuver for fissures in the entrenched working class, to win the workers over to the mentality of Karl Marx. Feeling alienated from Soviet Communism, they blandly shift toward Chinese Communism—whatever disasters Mao's cultural revolution brought, he conditioned confrontation into the texture of Chinese society. Lacking capacity to examine or criticize their own mystique, lacking the most rudimentary knowledge of who they are, and what they are doing, they make romantic gestures with live dynamite, futile self-definitions in atonal music.

The style of talk among Orthodox Communists has no personal edge. Having programmed the ego out of the party, they never betray personal ambition or allow ego in anything they do. Even personal animus comes in small asides, never in direct rushes of emotion, always programmed, as when the entire Russian literary establishment rose in horror upon Boris Pasternak's winning the Nobel Prize. Once the conversion experience takes place, all personal matters enter the chew of process.

Stalin's rule thus closed the dynamic of history, and settled Russia like a rooted oak tree. At its best, this suggests an attractive stability. Russian culture comes through in the media with whole-some, four-square directness. On his American visit, Khrushchev stomped out of a Hollywood showing of the can-can—though he thoroughly enjoyed himself imitating the dancing. A riverful of happy Muscovites welcomed him back, swimming on their day off from work. The Russian prisons are not schools for hardened crime; home visits are occasionally allowed, and some form of family life. So too there is the system of infant massage and touch-care in the nurseries.

But this blunt wholesomeness has levels of darkness. At its core, it is, quite simply, a bald lie. There is no such thing as arrival at any final form of history. All societies are a tenacious churning of process, a chasing and climbing of establishment, a surge of prole-tarian withdrawal, and impulse to revolution. Marx's parochial be-stowal of the name *"proletariat"* on the workers of a hundred years ago was arbitrary; the name no longer fits the position of labor in society. To maintain that lie, however shipshape it keeps the present establishment, distinctions must be smashed and blurred, or cease to exist.

So Soviet achievement has an aggressive exhibitionism, with brutal consequences for the social misfit. Quite simply, to look dis-satisfied in a society in a beatitude is to be nuts; one who looks so is properly thrown into a mental hospital. You may be emotionally adrift—the Russian social machinery doesn't sift that closely; but if so, it must be underground and in quiet. Any confrontation of a restless artist, any meeting with radical discovery and growth on both parts, smacks of genuine dialectic. But what thesis and antith-esis is possible after the final synthesis has been hammered out? Dialectic in Russia today belongs with the dinosaur skeletons in the museum. The Russian dissidents are by this reasoning out of touch with reality. The synthesis must have its nature slammed down; so, their blurry minds can grasp it.

The edge of anguish in Soviet Russia is duller today than under

Stalin; but the essential process remains that of manipulating the public image so as not to allow any dynamic of change to break surface in Soviet Russia. So geniuses are coached into realizing their political stupidity, artists are locked up for having a sense of purpose, scholars are put to work in slave labor camps so they may learn where true happiness lies. Political comment in Moscow is exceedingly oblique. The ultimate taboo is confrontation. In Paradise, nobody ever confronts anybody.

Stalin's death left an ominous element alive after him. Quite simply, Stalin so put his stamp on the Russian establishment, he eliminated so many potential successors, and kept others so subservient, that no public testing of candidates for supreme office has ever taken place to establish a new Face, nor does one seem likely in the foreseeable future. On the contrary, the rung below Stalin's on the ladder of power was slippery with self-effacing assistants and ambitious underlings who were overthrown and have disappeared. Its present rulers are therefore a Shadow in power. Now Brezhnev, a mediocre and colorless slug, sits immobile on the seeds of change. He knows very well that imprisonment and legalized murder have eliminated his brighter competitors. His talent is his staying power, and he is using it.

This situation produces a self-righteous stuffiness about Soviet policy. The Russian mystique of labor and soil is not native to Czechoslovakia, Hungary or Poland. They are not "Holy Mother Russia," but permanently occupied countries, whose desire is to labor more effectively and not become parasites. Economic relations with Germany, France and England would simply make their labor a great deal more meaningful. But Russia holds them in a vise of stuffy holiness. The position of Russia resembles that of the Roman Catholic Church during the Reformation, when the Inquisition moved armies of the counter-Reformation into a country as it went Protestant to maintain a cast of mind. Czechoslovakia and Hungary thus resemble Belgium and Holland in the sixteenth cen-

tury. Confrontation? Dialectic? Competition for goods and services? What have they to do with countries in beatitude? So process
is waterlogged with bureaucracy; what cannot be killed outright is
dulled and manipulated into meaninglessness. The final curse of
life behind the Iron Curtain is not poverty, imprisonment, or economic control, all common enough in the West, but the curse of the
boring lie. Russia moves its armies by twitches of threat and withdrawal. The broader its explanation, the better—nobody can prove
wrong a formula that has no content.

Thus, the recent Czech occupation was depicted, not as a coup or
seizure of power, but as a brushing aside of a few misguided, irresponsible officials. As it happened, the "misguided" included the
entire Czech working class, all the students, the journalists, the
government, the army, the entire city of Prague—all of them
sullen, misguided children. It was all arranged fast, like a medical
invasion to heal some social influenza, a spontaneous reaction of
the international communist movement to an odd aberration—the
soldiers no doubt all put on sterilized surgical gloves on the plane.
The Czechs coöperated beautifully, taking the overthrow of their
government on cue like an unfair shuffle in a bridge tournament. So
adult control was reëstablished over a boyish irregularity, a whim-
sical wish for freedom, a self-indulgent attempt to improve the national economy with better markets, a perverse hunger to move and
talk where they wished, and to tell the truth for once in their lives.
Such self-indulgence!

The Russians vaguely hinted at an invasion of Hungary and Yugoslavia, proclaiming their right to invade dissidents at any time.
Rumania and Yugoslavia muffled their protests about Czechoslovakia, thus offering the twitchy dinosaur the blackmail-payment of
silence; they partially mobilized, threatened to fight back hard,
and laid out detailed contingency plans. Russia would win; but an
extended fight behind the Iron Curtain might suggest dynamic confrontation in a world frozen and beatified out of circulation. Their

patchwork justification of the invasion of Hungary—"just straightening out a few local Fascists, reactionaries and perverts"—stank over Europe. A longer fight might expose the truth about Russian controls. So Rumania and Yugoslavia were left alone.

Stalin's successors are a Shadow committee of politician-moralists, all cautious and slow-moving, ruling an enormous and complex empire. They have absorbed Stalin's vegetable dynamic, and made it theirs. Having time on their side, they never extend themselves unnecessarily. They like socialist environments—also oil, ships, engineers, top pianists, building cranes, harbors, and oriental religions. England means less than Yugoslavia, not because England is not socialistic—the difference is one of degree—but because the Iron Curtain does not border on the Atlantic. They detest Israel, whose Knesset has two communist parties represented in it, and extol Egypt, which has exterminated its Communist Party with Russian support.

Russia's international politics is slow-moving because Germany, not Russia, is the economic center of Europe. The best hope for fresh markets is for things like gas, oil and caviar. Their manufactures are poor, their designs archaic, their engineers heavily committed to the armaments industry. They turn to Fiat or Henry Ford for automobile factories, a gesture unthinkable in Western Germany with its Volkswagen and Mercedes-Benz. Open-market competition must therefore be kept out of eastern Europe at all costs. The Second World War gave the Russians a monopoly of more land than they had ever thought of controlling. They invaded Hungary as John D. Rockefeller might have invaded Massachusetts in the free-booting days of Standard Oil. A shaky franchise on a large underdeveloped territory does not allow an open market. Russia would not mind extending its controls by an ugly word or a squad of planes, but essentially its European politics are those of a mountain cat over the fresh body of a dead buffalo. Lethargic, it snarls occasionally, and does a lot of feeding.

Russia is thus more sluggish and conservative today than in Stalin's day. Its dinosaur-twitches toward areas of power, though appalling, remain slow, heavy, occasional and manipulative. Adventures bore it; genius scares it; social stirrings stir it not at all. It has outgrown any dialectic in history. Having inherited a power base, it wants to sit on it and watch it grow. It is building an empire more cautiously than Great Britain did and is a bit more doctrinaire—but politics today generally comes more doctrinaire. It is nervous as a starved bird in its competition with the United States. When the first Sputniks went up, Khrushchev snorted about American grapefruits in the air; then, mysteriously, Russia dropped the subject as it lost the race to the moon. Its public media have a complete apparatus worked out for the steady belittling and vilification of the United States, feeding items and photographs in controlled amounts as a matter of public relations. This is not a matter of economic warfare, but is intended to condition the people, who might otherwise note how regimented and dull are their own lives. The vilification is obnoxious, but given the increasing American air pollution, population growth, and assorted other problems, vilification may soon no longer be necessary to keep their meager country quiet. There is no present stir to war against the United States. The stir is at present against China—the Russians can beat China.

The Soviet collective mind works by an entrenched, self-righteous pragmatism; the USSR is one of the most solid, conservative countries on the face of the earth. Were Russia not so priggishly monopolistic, Coca-Cola and Chrysler would be welcomed with open arms; but Russia wants a monopoly like AT&T, and sells in eastern Europe by forced mail order catalogue, not on the open market. In the nineteenth century, England and the United States were far more revolutionary than Russia is today.

Stalin put his stamp on Russia by solidifying the dynamic of revolution to a steadily growing social vegetable. The crunch in his lifetime cost millions of lives to effect; but by now it is all over, and Stalin's formulation holds. The revolution that once inflamed Europe now sits like a marvelous mechanical egg on a shelf in the Kremlin. Outside its borders, Russia will support Egypt, its ticket in the Middle East, against Israel, as Richard Nixon might fish for a ticket in California. Stalin would not have undertaken such imperialist ventures; yet it is his Russia, not the Russia of Lenin or Marx. The land he gave his inheritors is ideologically solvent; they are now in business for themselves.

Our discussion of Stalin bears strongly on the role of a great man in history. It seems clear that the drama of a strong man's spirit must be responsive to deep elements in his nation's spirit. Thus, France, long engaged in a fairly pedestrian drama of rational conservatism, accepted elements from Charles de Gaulle agreeable to its temperament: de Gaulle's conservatism, his administrative solidity and his scorn for a shifting, all-powerful legislature. But when de Gaulle reached for a world drama of power equilibria, a drama suited to his temperament but not to France's, the French voted him out. His gifts to France were simplicity, conservatism, and entrenched self-respect. Similarly, Trotsky's drama, like Lenin's, was one of ideological revolution, a drama that proved ephemeral. Stalin's was a drama of manipulative bureaucratic controls, sanctified autocracy and entrenched administrative superstition, all Russian elements inherited from Czarist times. Stalinist paranoia has abated, with its elements of personal malaise; but his stamp is today the stamp of Russia.

The prospect of a fresh Face ruling Russia is not sanguine. In government offices, as in universities and corporations, Shadows reproduce Shadows. Hack administrators reproduce after their kind, as do all things in nature. The bigger the hierarchy, the more entrenched the Shadows, the deeper their controls against surprises. The complex bureaucracy of the Russian government is a series of fine sieves that catch and trap any fresh Face as it moves up. There is thus an aggressive self-righteousness of consensus in Russian literature as in Russian politics, a steady, collective reinforcement of collective attitudes. A society which requires of every novel a socially satisfactory ending has reduced its literature to the level of the *Ladies' Home Journal* and *Redbook*.

It is time to stop discussing socialist realism in the abstract. Today socialist realism in Russia is as helpful and inspiring in governing taste as the shape of a box of breakfast cereal. The only great literature produced in Russia is produced underground, if not illegally. Socialist realism today is a sentimental moralizing patina that spreads its dull monochrome like dirty glue in a varnish over the creative spirit.

Serge Eisenstein, Russia's greatest director, betrays in his career the freeze that gripped Russian creativity. His first movies essentially followed a Trotskyite dynamic; his revolution was a process in the dialectic of history. *Strike*, his first movie, depicts straight class warfare. Its opening shot is a long still of a fat rich employer; then comes a profile of a revolutionary intellectual—a synthesis and an antithesis, of which the following action is the synthesis. As the movie unfolds, the workers relate to their factory machinery, as to their own bones, twining around it and swarming in secret to plot their moves. Terrorist provocateurs swarm out of cisterns; a field produces workers' corpses at the end. Russian society was not yet ready for its moment of truth.

That moment of truth arrived in *Potemkin*, which amazingly parallels Trotsky's *The Russian Revolution* in its plot. Thus, the action begins, not with any intellectual leadership, but in a spontaneous gathering of sailors, the navy Proletariat, who like energetic atoms stir to political activity. The crisis comes as Russian battleships surround the harbor to pin down the mutinous boat. Then, like Trotsky's Cossacks, the sailors, when ordered to blow the mutineers out of the water, raise their guns and allow the rebellious boat to slip through. Communication has been established, and the will of the people is triumphant.

Eisenstein was severely restricted and controlled—indeed, his very life was saved by an old chance acquaintance with Stalin. The effect shows: In *Alexander Nevsky*, land has replaced social process as the decisive factor. Thesis and antithesis are no longer displayed within a society; the enemy is a foreign invader, the Teutonic Knights, an international religious cartel who, by military discipline and a fanatic ideology, attempt to control and enslave Russia. His land invaded, Alexander Nevsky retires to Nijni-Novgorod, the last unconquered Russian stronghold. Riding, lounging, feasting, jousting, close to the soil, he establishes a corps of comrades who breathe the free air of Russia. He then mobilizes his forces and returns to battle the enemy.

It is thus Mother Russia, not Alexander, who defeats the invading Teutonic Knights. Too heavily armed for her spongy soil, unable to maneuver, their troops sink in the marsh and are drowned, outfought, killed or dragged away for ransom. This is no synthesis of history, no dialectic of social process, but a tale of Mother Russia, swallowing up invaders like an aroused bear. If *Potemkin* follows a Trotskyite dynamic, exploring a new dialectic of history, *Alexander Nevsky* is thoroughly Stalinist, and follows exactly the dynamic of Tolstoy's *War and Peace*. The Czarist landed aristocracy had just that mystique of the land.

Eisenstein's last surviving picture, *Ivan the Terrible*, Part I, offers the full horror of a freeze in time, the dynamic reduced to a vegetable process, the vegetable then glazed and petrified. The land is not a setting for action, rather the bodies appear like grotesque Slavic battlements, with towers, bays, curtains, fortifications, and a stirring of foliage in their hair. The action stirs like an animated landscape, a choreography of stylized gestures, the elongated motions so in tableau that they lose the savor of action. The landscape is like Flemish egg tempera painting, with soil, trees, hills, people and gestures, all rendered equally real on the screen. The characters are not detached persons, making surprising choices and living their consequences, but stylized aspects of the movie's dominating spirit, Ivan the Terrible, who is depicted as degenerative, insane.

The analogy to Stalin is irresistible: he also, we note, was the presiding spirit of Russia who first forged a state, then froze and hardened all action out of it in caustic mistrust, reducing its inhabitants to bits of landscape. Indeed, rumor has it that *Ivan the Terrible,* Part II, had its prints destroyed, with only a few mutilated bits of action passed by the Soviet film boards, when the authorities grasped the entire epic as an allegory of the life of Stalin. For all their suspicions and controls, they had been had by a genius. *Ivan the Terrible* was the last film Eisenstein was allowed to make.

Russian culture has now relaxed from its Stalinist period of paranoid uniformity, and leans towards a sort of loose Victorian moral control, a sentimental self-righteousness about the drab pablum that is allowed in print, while more exciting underground material is not regimented too closely. Thus, the products of an official book industry, run off on official presses under government editors and supervisors, are available at book stores. Another library of surreptitious material often smuggled in from abroad, passes from hand to hand, copied by hand or on typewriters. The sheer labor of copying such bulky materials and the lack of publicity, keeps the work from circulating too widely; the broad masses thus get only the official pablum. In Russia, as elsewhere in the world, to him who hath shall be given. The government could quickly suppress the secret material, were it determined to, but it leaves well enough alone. So too certain painters who never exhibit in official galleries do sell by personal visit and word of mouth; only, they are scarcely ever discussed in articles or publicized. Indeed, public art in Russia is so poor that collectors of taste will only buy underground.

Russia today is thus quite Victorian, with one culture subject to a decaying censorship of dull, official taste, and another, a surreptitious culture, vaguely immoral and politically suspect, tolerated as long as it keeps itself in hand. The authorities control dissent with the pragmatic rule-of-thumb by which the police tolerate homosexual culture in New Orleans and Atlantic City. Like small-town cops in a resort area, they do not make a storm in the atmosphere of the best of all possible worlds, as long as the disturbances are tolerably quiet. So Solzhenitsyn is ostracized and his works repressed, yet he is left untouched; but Andrei Amalrik, the author of *Will the USSR Survive Until 1984*, is sentenced to three years in a forced labor camp. Intellectuals are controlled, not like people, but like microbes, in proportion to their power to infect and the expense of suppressing them. Meanwhile, a whole literature of the "Other Soviets" like the literature of the "Other Victorians" is gradually coming to light, with fresh material escaping each year. To the Victorians, sexual freedom was the hot underground commodity; in Russia, it is the seamy truth of Russian life.

Russia is piecing together an empire that is fairly sluggish and unwieldy. Its absorption of eastern Europe is not yet established as final; but what is ever final in this world? Marx conceived of society as a metaphysical process producing class conflict, the dialectic of history, a dictatorship of the proletariat, then a gradual withering away of government machinery to leave a loose association of free workers around the world. So far, the opposite of such a withering away has taken place. A dynamic intended to produce a socialist democracy has become a blueprint for monopolistic control of a vast empire. Quite simply, the Soviet Union is a company town constructed on strong Czarist foundations.

Russian officials are then cartel executives. They talk of a school system bending talents to their proper outlets, so that natural process may allow the coming rulers of Russia to manifest themselves; but General Motors explains its selection of executive vice-

presidents by the same rationale. Judging by reports from eastern
Europe, Communist officials tend to live exceedingly stuffy, puri-
tanical lives, with a moralizing self-importance that compensates
for endless drab reports, and with a steady, faceless caution. The
reports of Svetlana Alleluyeva about Kosygin and the Soviet executive are shocking in their humorless moralizing and tape-recorder
speech. So too the Communist officials in Hungary are described as
atheist puritans, who dress without color, travel without company,
dine without appetite, and govern without personality. Lately, they
have improved their public image by allowing themselves to be
ridiculed on television. Nor are these executives answerable to an
annual stockholders' meeting. That company is closed. Like mo-
nopolies everywhere, efficiency is not their bag.

None of this should surprise us. These are atheist priests who
administer a metaphysical process by administrative fiat. The latest production figures replace mystical truth. They are priests
with power but no grace. Their parades lack festivals; their celebrations lack mysteries. An atomic missile is the wafer displayed at
the Kremlin on May Day. The self-righteousness of this company
town is entrenched and aggressive. They know Alexander Solzhenitsyn is the most talented novelist alive in Russia, and treat him
gingerly as a piece of anti-matter among the half-finished Chevro-
lets along a Detroit assembly line. They give him no job and no
prison sentence, no publication of his work and no slave labor
camp. He simply hangs in the air and writes. If he keeps moderately quiet, he will be let alone. Then, if he wins a huge foreign
reputation, once he is safely dead, by the ineffable process of the
metaphysical absolute, he will be allowed to arrive. Meanwhile the
Russian literary establishment has reacted to his receiving the
Nobel Prize like an organization of village harlots when the town
virgin wins a beauty contest. Shocking! Simply shocking!

These words are written in discouraged befuddlement, but not in
downright pessimism. There is a strange tenacity in social groups

that continues once they have defined themselves, in spite of changes of fortune. So the Soviet executive, having begun as Shadow, will continue as Shadow; but they are only a few human beings doing their thing. They are not the Russian people. Russia is rising in power, for all its slow piecemeal development, its self-righteous ostentation, and blunders in policy, and seems likely to become the dominant power in the world. But as Stalin's Shadow thins with the passage of time, a younger generation may grow up whose close dedicated leadership was not exterminated by secret police and broken in slave labor camps, nor participated in the bureaucratic thralldom of eastern Europe. Such a youth can coalesce into a fresh Proletariat, indifferent to its Shadow rulers.

Yet my own sense of the situation, I must say, is not optimistic. The truth is not being told in Russia: The obedient Russian tankman who first landed in Prague, were screamed at, spat at, and cajoled by patriotic Czechs in their own Russian language—their first real confrontation. They were quickly replaced as unreliable by other, fresher units, having been contaminated by real talk. The future is a loose dark mystery; but beneath the immediate opacity of silence grows acquiescence, blandness and smaller, more Latinate ambitions. Such a consensus leans towards a sort of giant Portugal, self-righteous, blindly aggressive, and socially trivial.

Meanwhile, Solzhenitsyn works in silence, surviving as one survives under censorship and an Inquisition. He is a creature of intense reserve and a princely silence. He knows more than he says, and says nothing without integrity. His silence is pregnant with implications. We dare not stop listening to it.

PART III

THE WAYWARD AMERICAN DREAM

dies like Shakespeare's *As You Like It*, where the clearing is in the Forest of Arden, and, as a political blueprint, in More's *Utopia*, which is set in a secluded island off the seacoast. Even the medieval monasteries were clearings in a wilderness, not indeed of natural, but of secular, barbarism. All had in common a sense of barbarism around them, and the need to clear an area for a more human island of life in its midst. So the earliest cities, whether in the Near East or in Switzerland, were planned cells of human life in the wilderness. Indeed, Eden itself was seen as God's clearing in the primal wilderness, where the original Adam Smith crawled out of the mud.

Utopian plans have popped up throughout history as idyllic visions. What made for a uniquely American version of the Utopian myth was the changing of an idyllic project into a dynamic program for setting a continent. The more static European version of Utopia did occur, most notably at Brook Farm, with the transcendental presence of Emerson and the brief visit of Hawthorne, who contemplated its golden heap. Indeed, throughout the nineteenth century, such eccentric colonies sprinkled the nation, introducing polygamy, communal property, simplistic economic theories, and messages from heaven. New religious rituals were generated that added God and salvation to the goods to be shared communally.

These more static utopian colonies were a significant minor variation on the colonies more aggressively on the move. Even the Amish colonies in Pennsylvania though static, settled, and old-worldly, had colonies in Ohio, Indiana, Idaho. As for the Mormons, under persecution and attack, they kept vehemently mobile, aggressive in making conversions, with a program and territorial ambitions. These "clearings in the woods" were no poetic retreats, but the germ of a utopia put to technological purpose: to keep America on the move. Puritan New England had a different tradition from the colonies along the central seaboard and yet its method of expanding westward was the same: a series of carefully planted units, clearings in the woods—the Puritan villages; the covered-wagon trains across the Mississippi Valley; the square, new hard-edge western states; the towns sprinkled like Shasta daisies across the California mountains. Today, "utopias" still spring up everywhere in suburbs, one behind the other. The metropolis is corrupt, old, heavy, shot through with crime and dope; but there are still fresh suburbs spreading like yeast, each a clearing with a slide, a teeter-totter, and a row of swings, all little touches of utopia you can call your own.

Alongside the myth of the clearing in the woods came a very different myth—the myth of the frontiersman. This solitary wanderer, the civilized counterpart to the "noble savage," is not an eighteenth-century figure, but a Romantic Age figure who belongs to Rousseau, not to Voltaire. His purpose is not to reduce the frontier by a cell of fresh civilization, but to blend and mingle with it on his own. Exceedingly competent at his best, he has the smell of civilization about him—the abandoned pariah is another creature entirely; yet the frontiersman has shrugged off civilization as an effete or tawdry corruption. He chooses rather to roam the wilderness serenely and at will. Wordsworth, as a Romantic poet and a sort of village frontiersman, unlike Marvell a century earlier, visited no garden for fulfillment, but found his mystical fulfillment in the wilderness around Tintern Abbey.

Both myths have very old roots, and come with ambiguities; but the ambiguities of the frontiersman myth are greater than those of the "clearing" myth. Just how much civilization does the mythic frontiersman slough off in returning to the wilderness? Simply table manners and life in a civilized small town, as Huckleberry Finn renounces, or more basic moral traits also? There is a long tradition that depicts the frontiersman as exceedingly civil, innocent and human—Wordsworth's wandering mountaineer, Cooper's Deerslayer, or Tarzan, a modern frontiersman in darkest Africa. Even more committed is the medieval frontiersman moving through the wilderness of life on earth. So, Dürer's engraving of the wandering knight in armor, beset by demons, depicts a medieval frontiersman, bound on his pilgrimage through life. The heroism here is more savage than that in the romances—it has a Teutonic brutality—but the same mystique pervades books like Spenser's *The Faerie Queene*. Rendered somewhat more secular, it pervades Rembrandt's portrait of the Polish cavalryman, calm, self-reliant, wedded to his role in life. Even as a workman and outcast wanderer, a man may build romance into his profession, as in the Old English poem, "The Seafarer," with its muted harmony of openness and harassment, servitude and freedom.

But the knight with a mission is too armed and embattled to blend with the frontier; his victory lies in not succumbing to it. And Deerslayer is too pastoral, too static and idealized to hold up with finality. After a while, we begin to sully him: we ask carpingly why he never gets married—just as we follow a Superman with a Supermouse. So we grow aware of another order of frontiersman, the man who has not only left civilization, but also the role civilization brings with it. This figure flounders not only beyond the city limits but also beyond the pales of grace. So, in the wilderness of a modern city, Holden Caulfield, in *Catcher in the Rye*, is a sort of latter-day Caliban, floundering on the fringes of society, refusing to go home and refusing to go to school. So too Ralph Ellison's underground man is a sort of black Caliban on the move in a white wilderness, cut loose and berserk. But the ambiguous commitment to the wilderness can reverberate with guilt, and not just a loosening of constraints; it may even become a gesture of depravity. The mythic frontiersman is often a criminal in flight. Thus Stephen Rojack, the hero of Norman Mailer's *The American Dream*, at the end is on the move across America, having murdered his wife and escaped the criminal charge. His role is that of Cain, murderer of his brother Abel and an eternal wanderer. It is ominous that in the Bible the tools of civilization are invented by the sons of Cain. As today, the wilderness is inside man as well as beyond the frontiers. The damned belong in the wilderness, refusing to be their brother's keeper.

But even when legitimate, even attuned to the national temper, even if, as in America, its founding is a supreme expression of national destiny in the great trek westward, the clearing in the woods is exceedingly transitory; it has no secure continuity. All the clearing presumes is a radical innocence on arrival, in the first brush against the alien wilderness; the restless urge to movement and fresh arrival is there. So Hamlin Garland and others document the urge to continue westward. Furthermore, civilization does not leave its virginity long unsullied. On the contrary, Satan characteristically arrives by the second packtrain. Indeed, even its initial innocence is open to question. The American clearings, unlike their European counterparts, while expressing an impulse to live in Eden, were also the tool of an aggressively expansionist society. Who then, was using whom in sending out a new settlement? That question is echoed about the American constitution; that document was intended to make a clean slate for a new civilization in the American wilderness, yet Charles Beard and his followers have colored the charter of American freedom with economic motives.

When all is said and done, the clearing in the woods expresses, not a civilization, but its expansive force, the eternal innocence and strength by which it meets the wilderness at its borders. As such, the clearing in the woods has no staying power. Indeed, the myth of the frontier is a myth not of enduring civilization, but of romantic achievement. Inevitably, the second packtrain arrives with Satan on board to corrupt the now settled town; and a push to a new clearing is called for. Even if the moving is not a gesture of flight, the frontier itself is too much on the move. Pursued with single-minded dedication, the clearing in the woods suggests, not a magic ring protecting all civilization within it, but a magic ring of life, a thin circle, with primordial wilderness around it and civilized wilderness within. So the frontiersman of the second myth is an eternal romantic wanderer, who shrugs off the enormous waste as he leaves the settled towns behind. He looks only forward.

The wandering frontiersman, while courageous on his terrain, has exceedingly gingerly relationships with human beings. Alone, on the move, a solitary, experienced male, he is necessarily free of family ties. Even when strong in his sense of selfhood, he is to some extent a family outcast, the road male, a wanderer without roots. When he travels in gangs, his gangs are all family outcasts. Marlon Brando's *The Wild Ones,* like Hell's Angels, and all motorcycle gangs on the road, are road males, who move with the mark of Cain. But the bitter reality is that the wanderer is seldom that well-adjusted. Road gangs are also poor little sheep who have lost their way, emotionally amputated half-men, rejected sons, forever on the road, destined never to arrive at a secure home and surroundings. So Huckleberry Finn flees to the wilderness at the end of the book, at least in part a fixated boy. But rejection can produce darker emotions, impulses of savagery, jealousy, and revenge. Cain killed Abel because God had accepted only Abel's offering.

Flawed or not, both myths strongly work in America today, in the romantic slighting of established institutions, the hunger for the new and the unknown. Yet both myths grow increasingly sour and ironical as the truth registers that the geographical frontier is gone. Fewer and fewer clearings have the bloom of innocence; the wandering knight in armor steadily gives way to the road male. Thus a steady split, full of ambivalence, divides the brand of brothers who settle in established towns and cities from the anonymous wanderers of the modern city and highway, the town people from the street people. The band of brothers may settle in civilized protective neighborhoods, but they are conformist, hedgy, defensive. The wind is in the teeth of the male horde, family outcasts on the road, the tribe of Cain, multiplying and expanding, but condemned to eternal wandering. These are the depression hobos, the motorcycle riders in *Easy Rider*, Hell's Angels, the street people in Berkeley and Cambridge. The magic ring of the frontier has broken up and disappeared. Now, as time passes, Satan engulfs more and more clearings; more and more of the men of the road bear the mark of Cain, the eternal wanderer.

Indeed, behind the darkening of the frontier myth lies a deeper reversal. When America was first settled, the opposition was between the frontier and the outer wilderness. Civilization was shrugged off; the Apache and the mountain lion were confronted, gun in hand. But gradually, as the wilderness shrank and finally disappeared, and the settled areas grew in size, the opposition reversed itself, to turn against the settled areas. The impulse to confront and withstand as a free wanderer is now directed against the wilderness of settled America, against which a frontier impulse rages without a purpose or a place to go.

This reversal of opposition, from the settled city against the wilderness to the frontiersman against settled land, is characteristically American, and marks a full-scale arrival of the wilderness. In most ancient times, cities were slapped down by a plan, square and straight, inside a wall whose line violated the roll of hill and valley. The idea of a city was thus a *Ding an sich,* preceding the act of building it. So the original frontier was a means to an end, the ground cleared to allow a settlement. The ancient epic does not explore waste space for the adventure, but as a voyage of control and arrival, for the heady zest of handling dangerous seas and threatening spirits. Thus, the wilderness adventure serves to render the wilderness inconsequential, and to establish the empire of the human mind.

So, in the supreme grand voyage in Greek literature, Homer's *Odyssey*, Ulysses is driven off course by the gods, as he seeks his home after ten years besieging Troy. He repeatedly struggles to look homeward, but is trapped, imprisoned, driven astray by storms. Finally, in a huge vindication, he reaches his home and rejoins his wife, his sea adventures at an end. And yet his adventures, while they do not celebrate the frontier, are fixed on it in fascination, strongly establishing the supreme power of the man of experience, his empire, body and mind, over all obstacles. Yet he is a captive frontiersman, approaching his goal with resilience against monsters, whirlpools, and forbidding deserts. Once comfortably settled and arrived, he ignores the unknown that still stretches around Ithaca, enigmatic and threatening. For the present, his travels are over.

This same epic balance of city and frontier, of the goal of arrival and the frontier adventures on the way, controls the *Divine Comedy*. Driven back by three beasts as he moves towards his City of God, Dante undergoes a penitential journey through the afterlife, exorcising spiritual terrors as he explores all cosmic space and human types. Finally, a seasoned veteran, he enters the being of God as an infant returning to the womb, or Ulysses his wife's hearth and home. The poem finishes with the catharsis of arrival where he belongs.

Indeed, Ulysses, not Dante, is the dedicated frontiersman of the *Divine Comedy*, who sails off for sailing's sake, but is drowned below Mount Purgatory. This tale is closer to the American frontiersman myth, though the archetypic frontiersman, Cooper's Deerslayer, was profoundly at home in the wilderness, hunting and fishing, masterfully secure, with no driving ambitions, while Dante's Ulysses is an alien to the ocean he is exploring. The frontier is not his home; what he experiences is an urgency to seek fresh encounters, to explore unknown territory, to strike out for the far beyond, not live at peace with his familiar home. We suspect unuttered blasphemies. Cooper's Deerslayer would never have attempted Mount Purgatory.

The frontier, as at once a geographical reality and a fascinating value unto itself, came to the fore during the Renaissance, when territorial expansion made the unknown expanse of ocean porous and familiar. The parallel spread of Greek cities across the Mediterranean had not been an encounter with the wilderness, but a series of new cities, engulfing and digesting fresh bits of wilderness. But the Renaissance brought to the fore a restless urge to strike beyond the bounds of civilization in a baptism of ocean and wilderness, penetrate fresh land at land's end. The same Renaissance urgency came to a head in the realm of knowledge, the urge to occupy the frontiers of knowledge, steadily to amass fresh bits and pieces of knowledge, civilize the unknown, and reduce it to the domain of the mind. But this was still the urgency of a confident, expanding civilization, not the liberation of the frontier as an end in itself. The opposition was between the wilderness and the established city, only the city was now looser, more dynamic, expanding into the wilderness, creating landed solidity and the cultivated garden. Yet a growing library of voyage books described life on ocean and in wilderness, making familiar, even attractive, the strange new life of the outcast wanderer.

In Shakespeare, exile is a form of execution, and yet it also sometimes suggests the "clearing in the woods." The record is mixed. In *Richard II*, Bolingbroke manages to return from his exile and rise to the throne; his enemy, Mowbray, wanders Europe to his death. Yet exile and open country can also be a blessing. In *Midsummer Night's Dream*, the two adolescent couples leave the city and fall in with Oberon and Puck in a thin, stylized pastoral. In *As You Like It*, the outlaw band in the Forest of Arden builds a radically decent society, simplified and purged of corruption, finding "tongues in trees, books in the running brooks." These outlaws decently mark time until they can return home; meanwhile they occupy a clearing in the woods.

In the late Shakespeare, the city has lost much of its mythic force. The Rome of *Coriolanus* is not the flexible, resilient metropolis of *Julius Caesar*, but an adjustment of political cliques, stupidly complacent as they organize political claques. *Antony and*

Cleopatra hangs in a strange ambivalence. Self-exiled, Antony escaping the constrictions of Rome sighs over the abundance of the East; yet he is powerless, lacking any steady purpose. Octavius will obviously win against him, having his native city behind him. But not until the last comedies does nature become wondrous, healing, laden with power, and the city corrupt, weak and sterile. In *The Tempest* the hierarchy of state is manipulated like puppets, the lords put to sleep, awakened, teased, fed and denied food. Prospero finally leaves his magic isle in weary obligation and self-sacrifice to return to his dukedom.

This gradual shift toward a "clearing in the woods" moves several notches forward in *Robinson Crusoe*. Crusoe, supremely bourgeois, carves out a republic on a desert isle with a single man in it, himself. This is appropriate. The open market needs citizens only for what they can contribute; so Crusoe founds a new state holding a single self-sufficient citizen. He is not a true frontiersman, a Deerslayer of the ocean; nor does he seek out his desert—his ship is wrecked there. He is merely exceedingly practical, settling down for survival and comfort as close as possible to his comfort at home. His clearing in the woods is no innocent spore of civilization in the wilderness, but a make-do arrangement. When the opportunity arises, he handily returns home.

In the modern world, only America made the clearing in the woods a supreme myth. The frontiersman, the solitary wanderer who can confront the unknown, a myth of exceeding tenacity, even with its ugly modern overtones, came slightly later than the "clearing" myth. Small Puritan townships built New England, steadily pushing westward. So while solitary fur-trappers skimmed the western plains, long wagon trains effectively penetrated them. Daniel Boone, perhaps the noblest actual frontiersman, cleared forest trails and founded his own city at Boonsboro; other clearings in the woods spread at a churning pace.

And yet the classics of American literature never trusted the clearing in the woods as a secure ideal. The frontiersman comes to a noble flowering in Cooper's Deerslayer, a solitary woodsman dressed in furs, peerless on the hunt, peaceful, yet a crack shot, the friend of Indian and white man. This idealized version of a tenacious, yet exceedingly problematical mythic figure has nothing wrenched or crippled about him, though he lacks a wife, children or a steady home. Whatever elements are missing in his life are the imposition of the reader. Yet Cooper is a romantic, celebrating the frontiersman as an ideal; the clearing in the woods as a seed of civilization does not win comparable adulation from him.

The Adventures of Huckleberry Finn more closely approaches the reality of the frontiersman's problematical life. Indeed, the entire novel is a gamy adolescent story, telling of how a frontiersman is born. Thus Huck's opening choices are limited to the settled town (the area behind the frontier, with Satan pushing hard to be the next mayor) and the river as the unknown wilderness. Impossibly pressured at home, Huck strikes out blindly and stumbles on Jim. They flee together along the frontier of the river. Briefly, in the most rudimentary way, their raft becomes a clearing in the woods, the locale of a new society, where generous human beings sift language and history, attuned to each other; but even this idyllic period is scarcely taken seriously. They explore the story of Monte Cristo as they would have explored Monte Cristo itself, had they ever gotten there.

But the raft as a clearing in the woods moves with a savage gentleness, against the grain, southward, not westward, ever deeper into slave territory. Buffeted by storm, in hiding, threatened by every passing boat, every town, it can go only toward destruction. Finally two fourflushers (the Satans of the second packtrain) calmly take over, transform the raft into a shelter for boondoggling thieves, and sell Jim back into slavery. Twain had too sober a sense of the Gilded Age to feel secure in the clearing in the woods. As the book ends, Huck's adolescent Garden of Eden is gone forever. His final choice falls between city and frontier. Unlike Jim, who finds the city tolerable, Huck heads off for the wilderness, stubbornly committed to play the frontier boy forever. His choice was apparent from the start. He was like a baby in the womb on the river; on land, he disguised himself, assumed false names, made up stories and played roles in them. From the beginning, his true self belonged on the frontier.

Melville's *Moby Dick* is a more savage attack on the myth of a clearing in the woods. Ahab sails his whaling ship, the *Pequod*, back and forth, seeking the being of God in the body of a whale; he moves, not as a frontiersman, but as leader of a sailing covered wagon, its society a little city full of civilized crafts, its crew a survey of all the races of men. But the trip is laden with irony. The *Pequod* gives itself to the pursuit of Moby Dick by a mock social contract, creating an illusory clearing in the woods by a ritual with overtones of magic, that commits everyone against his self-interest. The broad wastes of ocean are a good emblem for the American plains; yet they can never be settled, never incorporated. The sea's savage power, far from succumbing to anchor and plow, rages at its pleasure and eventually swallows up the ship. With imbecile dedication, the crew work like factory hands to catch and store the whales, doing the job of the commercial establishment that hired them.

Furthermore, their entire commitment to the hunt of Moby Dick is a ghastly illusion. This is already the second *Pequod* run. On its first, the ship may indeed have been an innocent clearing in the woods, with Ahab as a straight frontiersman—Whaleslayer, cousin to Deerslayer—but during that voyage, Captain Ahab had lost one leg. Now, he is on his second voyage; Satan is on board, and hunts whales as a mask for hunting God. Like the Mississippi townsmen Huck Finn brushes against, the ship's crew are a grab bag of jaded human experience, all road males, committed to spiritual slavery on the broad expanse of the ocean. Powerless and corrupt within, the *Pequod* finally sinks before the supreme force of the oceanic wilderness, Moby Dick. Only Ishmael, the solitary who sifts whale blubber through his fingers, pops out of the last smashed whaleboat to bob directly into the water, saved.

But Melville and Mark Twain no more trusted the frontiersman than they trusted the clearing in the woods. So Ishmael, the solitary surviving witness on the *Pequod*, is a shadowy individual, easily swayed, but gradually slipping away from the essential drama of the boat. His endurance is a gesture of survival, not a ringing salvation. So too Huck Finn, our frontiersman in the making, remains an adolescent boy, pliable, mistrustful, somewhat passive, morally open, ready with the easy lie, innocent, suggestible, yet wary. To him, women are odd creatures who write grotesque poetry and draw pictures with too many sets of hands, or bewildering housewives, who read his mind with riddles and abruptly send him packing. He finally sees them as overbearing mommas and runs away, a frontiersman.

Since the closing of the frontier around the close of the century, both frontier myths have been treated with even darker mistrust by our great writers. Thus, Eugene O'Neill has a strong sense of the bitter paradox of the compulsive wanderer with nowhere to arrive. In an early play, *Beyond the Horizon*, a pallid frontiersman in the making, gentler than Huck, has his trip aborted, and lives out his life on the edge of wilderness, without the tough fiber to settle his affairs at home. As an added irony, his brother, Andy, who has no deep-seated wanderlust, is pitched into the wilderness at losing the girl he loves, and finally returns home rich, a speculator in wheat futures. In *Desire under the Elms*, two brothers take off for California; callous, self-indulgent animals—frontiersmen—they grab cheap satisfactions chasing after gold; while the brother with soul, who has the family birthright, is jammed at home and finally goes out, to his execution. In *Mourning Becomes Electra*, Lavinia and Orin, the Electra and Orestes of this play, return to the homestead from an abortive trip to the Pacific, still with their guilts upon them, for suicide and permanent seclusion. So, in play after play, O'Neill denies that there is any true frontiersman, or any clearing in the woods. The wanderer cannot go home again, nor the home-body escape the house. The Oedipal bond flagellates life into the very grave, with worn illusions to distract sentiment and precipitate folly.

Steinbeck's *The Grapes of Wrath,* an epic tale of the American depression, recounts the tragedy of a community jarred loose by the universal poverty, and gradually sinking out of sight. In the great migration, an Okie family crosses the western desert to the promised land of California, a truck their covered wagon, made into a clearing in the woods by their tenacious loyalty and simplified existence. And yet the book is finally a tragic chronicle of the loss of the American frontier. There is no primeval wilderness. The Okies cross endless deserts only to arrive at more wandering. Any good land they cross is legally closed off. The geographical frontier has dissolved away, the economic frontier, the hope of new money in a new life. The Joads flounder from desert to abandonment to deeper chaos, and gradually sink out of sight.

The novel ends with a dubious catharsis. The truck gradually sinks under the flood water; a crowd of Okies are all washed together. In a sheltering barn, Rose of Sharon, her still-born baby blue and mummified, nurses at her breast an aging and starved stranger with grown children. Her crazy fulfillment is no overflow of charity—her breasts have milk to get rid of. The irony is savage. The girl's Biblical name, Rose of Sharon, her taking refuge in a barn, her giving a stranger life, all make a Christ story, but without focus, hope, or direction. These woods are impenetrable. Steinbeck, then, sees the great American voyage gone senile and accomplishing nothing. The truck will emerge from the flood, the trek continue, but all its clearings are ephemeral; the American wilderness grows steadily more sullen, experienced, and savage.

This literary skepticism and ironic withdrawal in Melville, Twain, O'Neill and Steinbeck, in the teeth of the great American adventure, have formidable implications. The myth of the clearing in the woods is deeply hallowed in our country. The Declaration of Independence cleared the ground of old forms of government, gone wild, clumsy, and uncivilized with abuse:

> . . . when a long Train of Abuses and Usurpations, pursuing invariably the same Object evinces a Design to reduce them under absolute Despotism, it is their Right, it is their Duty, to throw off such Government, and to provide new Guards for their future Security. Such has been the patient Sufferance of these Colonies; and such is now the Necessity which constrains them to alter their former Systems of Government.

Our revolution sought to clear away earldoms, dukedoms, baronetcies, coats of arms and coats of armor, stained glass windows, entailed estates, inherited seats, all vested loyalties and all oaths of allegiance, to allow a new relationship among men. Economically, its open market was a clearing in the woods, its emblem the town square, where surrounding farmers might push their wagons on market day. Indeed, its social contract carried fresh winds of a social openness where free individuals could meet as equals and bind themselves to one another. That is how our government came into existence. This myth of the clearing in the woods may slide over bad education, political deceit, economic manipulations, enslavements of body and mind; but it remains the American myth, the myth of clear, open areas that allow free movement and uninhibited choice.

Bordering a vast frontier which it soon penetrated, settled and absorbed, white America began overhung with the myth of the great unknown. All the colonies were a string of fresh-cleared townships on the edge of a wilderness. As such, for all its classic simplicity, its measured enlightenment, the American dream was expansive and romantic, on the move all along the borders, but subject to rapid waste, crowding, and disillusionment in the hinterlands. The urge of American colonial society was more to establish its civilization than guard its careful continuity. Either it was expansionistic or one of its basic impulses tended to go to sleep. So, as the frontier drew away, old disillusionments hung in a pall over the heads of the more expansionist idealists; this temper is caught at its height in the record of Hamlin Garland. The weight of age sat too soon upon the country. As economic and social difficulties set in, the urge came again for a fresh clearing in those now cluttered woods.

This Janus face of the frontier impulse, at once to chafe and fret at the tawdry settled areas, and to hunger with a transcendental urgency for the new, the open, the virginal, could not die with the disappearance of the geographical frontier. The implications of the break-off line of the Pacific Ocean, of the Rocky Mountains, Oklahoma, and the last reservation, have worked slowly and mysteriously to reverse the direction of the frontier spirit. Instead of dying, it now bore upon the settled land behind it, and grasped it as a civilized wilderness, more virulent and hostile than the old one had been to newly arrived pioneers. Civilized corruptions, like educated germs, having survived two or three inoculations, shrug off the next shot. The primordial wilderness could be cleared for a fresh seeding of human order; but the metropolis is paved in asphalt. The jungle of reinforced concrete refuses to be cleared, and exacts casual vengeance from its would-be pioneers. Geronimo has faded into the National Guard. The clearing in the woods has turned into a sour dream.

But the urge to shoot out a pioneer expedition and penetrate the wilderness is too programmed into our society to lie quiet. With increased congestion, our present clearings in the woods grow emblematic and unreal, to be faced on television, not experienced directly. So celestial covered wagons leave Cape Kennedy for the moon just as the old covered wagons left St. Louis and Kansas City. So we propose a fleet of ships of white hope to sail around the world, fleets of helicopters to bring aid to the hungry and the diseased. So Timothy Leary, the hallucinogen prophet, founds a commune of believers to eliminate private property, meditate and feast together, free from all evil. These are covered wagons all—the covered wagons of an expansionist America. But the quieter, more static clearings-in-the-woods have their latter-day resurgence, too, in the hippie communes, now increasingly spreading as the hippies withdraw from a hostile society, sharing homes, farms and stores. Theirs now become clearings in the woods; yet they themselves become "noble savages" within them, producing an improvident confusion of communes that have nowhere to go and no way to stay put.

Steadily, in contemporary America, the myth of the frontiersman becomes dominant over the myth of the clearing in the woods. The clearing of course is there—the commune. So the double bents of the hippie—the bent toward the frontiersman's life, and the bent toward the clearing in the woods, street people and hill people— cross and tangle. But the power-driven wanderer—the motorcycle nomad, Hell's Angels, the greaseball and hophead—grows increasingly anarchic, more and more on the run, often criminal, cutting through the indifferent jungle of cities that never turns him on. So the jalopy Ford, carrying a colony of hippies, crosses the Georgia hills at exactly fifty-four miles an hour, trailed mile after mile by a highway patrol car with an arrest warrant ready, should the hippies once, accidentally scratch fifty-six miles an hour. The jalopy moves the way its ancestor, the covered wagon, rolled through hostile Injun territory; but its dream frontier is now blurred. It is stalked by jail and legal guns, not by bows and arrows. Its riders may see themselves as noble savages, wild as the woods they can never find; but that is mere sentimentality. They are just another collection of road males, rejected and on the run.

In the same way the frontier of science, once a vast wilderness of frightening ignorance, has been stripped of its frontier texture, as it has been cluttered with technical libraries, specialized laboratories, atomic accelerators, power commissions and measuring apparatus, thickening like suburbs overloaded with township laws, municipal commissions and land controls. The scientific establishment hedges in our imaginations, so that we no longer grasp the great bordering spiritual wilderness, the unknowns of mind and body, broad ocean and virgin wilderness, that once hemmed us in.

Arrowsmith, perhaps Sinclair Lewis' finest novel, depicts the situation of scientific discovery early in our century. The ideal laboratory then was still obviously a clearing in the woods, related to other free laboratories elsewhere in the wilderness, its discoveries public knowledge, shared by all, its participants a community responsive to one another and dedicated to a clean solving of problems. But Lewis saw such a community as corrupted by the large incursion of administration and of laboratory equipment, an investment and pressure that chose the problems to be attacked by considering their public relations value. So *Arrowsmith* records the strange path in life of a practicing physician who eventually becomes a scientist; in a rearguard action to clear a fresh area in the woods where clean research can be carried on, as his present institution is taken over. Yet no new clearing will be any more permanent than the last; in each case, the usurping administrators will arrive on the second packtrain, and he push off again to start yet another laboratory in the distant woods, a solitary frontiersman of science.

The myth of the scientist as frontiersman is a haunting one, with his air, the cool menace hanging in the ignorance around him, the diseases he works on, his eerie powers, the uncoded messages rising to his hand, messages that constantly elude his grasp and trained eye, as he keeps his test tube and his muted torch always ready, shifting from problem to problem. But now, along the frontier of knowledge, areas of the unknown that crawled with scientists twenty years ago are being abandoned as soon as they are settled, for they are no longer interesting to the scientific frontiersman, and new areas of ignorance open to the oncoming swarm. As a frontiersman, the scientist is part Deerslayer, part Huck Finn. He may be on the run from personal problems, from the need to mature in a mature society; but he pursues the unknown in the laboratory, the raw, the exciting domain of ignorance, not his adolescent urges, his hunches of malice.

He makes a pretty hero, the frontiersman of science; but he is as old-fashioned as the frontiersman of the wilderness. The scientific community has changed from a domain of free frontiersmen to one of fixed company towns, towns worth, potentially, a great deal of money, when producing, say, a new contraception pill, a blended tranquilizer, or synthetic chlorophyll. This is less true of the scientific establishment at the universities than of that in private industry, but only slightly so. The university laboratory is still organized with its team, its equipment, its prestige to maintain, its system of government grants, its graduate students to launch into careers. Indeed, its leading figures are not Daniel Boones, solitaries of the wilderness, but Napoleons of scientific organization, who marshal their companies in urgent competition to crack the secret of power by fusion for industrial purposes. As for industrial laboratories, there corporate controls, patent claims, industrial spying and directed investigation soon usurp the initial dream of a dedicated band of brothers, settling together on the frontiers of truth.

So the traditional fear of the scientist as heretic, atheist and armed psychopath—an abandoned son of Cain, the sinister figure of Dr. Faustus, the scientist beyond the law—now has a narrower source in the settled man's fear of the jungle of ignorance and pollution around his habitation, of the uncontrollable, the sudden upset of the nature of things that the scientist may trigger off. This is not fear of the frontiersman, but fear of the frontier itself. But there is also a fear of the scientist not as Faustus, but as would-be Napoleon. This fear has an element of the psychopathic: it is a fear displaced onto an ambitious Napoleon, when it should be fear of a moronic *golem*, the bland administrator and moral imbecile. The scientist as a scientist is an adventurer and a solitary, a frontiersman in the regions of truth; the man we should fear is the engineeradministrator who commands an area of research as his empire, using his scientific unit as his team to move as he directs them, meshing laboratory, scientist, engineer, factory, and billions of dollars, to build the atom bomb, to land a man on the surface of the moon, to fuse the atom and produce limitless energy. So the clumsy dance continues, enlarges, and goes berserk, the square dance of pioneer ignorance, of the frontiersman and the clearing in the woods; in both, the landscape grows cluttered with communities, and the frontier grows choked and elusive.

Thus, in its popular culture, America has steadily woven a balance between the frontiersman and the clearing in the woods, the call of the prairie and the call of the homestead. Old-time cowboy music is essentially frontiersman music—songs like "Home on the Range," that celebrate solitude, restless meandering, and an eternity of homelessness. Such songs steadily come in an even flow out of Tin Pan Alley. How recently did we cry for "Land, lots of land, under starry skies above—don't fence me in?" That song quickly blended into a cry for "Spurs that jingle, jangle, jingle." On the other hand, the square dance essentially celebrates the clearing in the woods; its programmed spins, kicks, and turns, its exchanging of partners by a prearranged plan, but returning each to his own, are a dancing pantomime of making a homestead and having good neighbors. So its grand march of two by two, as described by T. S. Eliot, "denotes harmony":

In that open field
If you do not come too close, if you do not come too close,
On a Summer midnight, you can hear the music
Of the weak pipe and the little drum
And see them dancing around the bonfire
The association of man and woman
In daunsinge, signifying matrimonie—
A dignified and commodious sacrament.
Two and two, necessary coniunction,
Holding eche other by the hand or the arm
Which betokeneth concorde.

The younger the viewer for whom movies, comic strips and television are geared, the more likely the hero is to be a legal champion, a policeman or his equivalent; but even then he tends to be
detached from any natural community. Old faithful Dick Tracy, a
veteran comic-strip hero, is still a regular plainclothesman with
close family connections; but the Lone Ranger, also a deputized
Texas Ranger, wanders in solitude, with only an Indian, Tonto, for
a companion. His mask contradicts his badge; he is a government
official, sprung loose to be a solitary frontiersman, roving at his
discretion. Superman, too, is a sort of self-appointed cosmic policeman, though he comes from another planet without badge or
legal authority; his ordinary appearance as Clark Kent, a private
citizen and reporter, is a disguise. And as the audience moves
through adolescence, we have a flock of private eyes and solitary
"guns for hire," who make pedestrian the talents of regular policemen and government officials. The hero of *The Maltese Falcon*, for
example, is a solitary frontiersman in the jungle of modern life,
quite outside the apparatus of the law.

This concept of the hero controls a steady, though very slow,
bent in cowboy movies. Once the typical hero of these films was the
local sheriff, who maintained a clean community, single-handedly
holding his town against invading thieves and rustlers. Indians, in

the early cowboy pictures, were invariably barbaric nomads, to be subdued so a town could be established and civil life advanced. The settled community held itself like a fort against oncoming villainy; but it often had insufficient staying power; its citizens were lazy, greedy, imperceptive. It was the sheriff who righted the balance by his heroism, and kept the town alive and free, preserving the original town innocence left behind as the frontier pulled away and oncoming evil swept up to take the town over.

High Noon was a dramatic break with this old order of cowboy pictures. There, the local sheriff remained the hero, but hero of a community so apathetic to the oncoming danger that they left the sheriff alone. Like a wagon train attacked by a war party who indifferently continue on their way, they let their leader meet the enemy single-handed, instead swinging around in a circle for the common defense. The sheriff finally met the gang at high noon, killed them one by one, and cast his badge in the dust before the townsmen. The town was too brutalized to be worth preserving. All innocence was gone. There was no clearing in the woods, only a human wilderness. The hero gave up his badge and became a frontiersman.

Cowboy pictures have increasingly narrowed to the wandering frontiersman, the solitary rider without family, home or community, who drifts across the wilderness, free, mythic, fearless of death. Even when he wears a badge, as in *True Grit*, he remains a free-floating frontiersman, there for hire. Now Indians become nature's innocents, in danger from white man's ways. The clearing in the woods is suspect, or altogether corrupt. Typically in these films, an indifferent amoral hero, a man who can keep riding and not be pinned down, enters a town controlled by established criminals. At first he doesn't mix in; but then some helpless victim, perhaps the local schoolmarm, intrigues him to champion her. He then frees the town and wanders off, still the solitary frontiersman. As a solitary wanderer, he is an undefined enigma, not one of the band of brothers. The heroine, at least temporarily, joins him to society by his bond to her; but he may simply ride off at the end, as in *True Grit*. Similarly, in the wilderness of cities, movies like *On the Waterfront* present an ambiguous hero, joined to society by the bond of love.

In more recent pictures, the wanderer is altogether corrupt, a social outcast, too far gone even for his sweetheart to draw him back. Slick and pleasant as it finally is, this is the mood of *Butch Cassidy and the Sundance Kid*. Indeed, in the recent cowboy pictures made in Italy and Spain, movies like *A Fistful of Dollars* or *For a Few Dollars More*, the town he fights over may be utterly destroyed. The cemetery he leaves behind testifies that the land is only a wilderness to wander over.

This wandering westerner who wants his fistful of dollars and a clean getaway has an edge of sour finality. A true bourgeois dollar is an investment, a down-payment on a house, a coming career, power, security; but his dollar is a figleaf of bourgeois respectability. The wanderer after money is a false bourgeois, with the moral blob of the brutalized horde. Any pleasure available to him is ephemeral, sudden, expensive; it ends abruptly in more wandering and hardship. He recalls the medieval knight-errant and chevalier. When he plays the guitar, we hear echoes of the medieval jongleur. Yet his identity suffers a strange impoverishment. The jongleur had a specific social role in medieval society: he performed entertainments on festive occasions. The knight-errant had a similar role, keeping his lance unattached and available for any moral cause, the more morally alert for being free to wander. But the cowboy wanderer after money is a floater who gets more morally blurred, picture by picture.

Indeed, modern America has had several generations of cultural frontiersmen, classes on the move, fringe Proletariat, bordering the established culture. So the current hippie, a complex beast already on the wane, at once increasingly established and increasingly under attack, sharply differs from the Bohemian of the Twenties, the hobo of the Thirties, or the Beat generation of the Fifties. The styles become so rapidly generalized that the reality underneath is already difficult to piece out. We know them already as a way, an ethos, that periodically disappears in a patronizing, ignorant blur.

The Bohemian of the Twenties was the most cosmopolitan of the lot in taste and life style. He dislodged himself from the established society and gravitated towards the metropolis and on the seaboard, here and abroad, to follow after culture and give it shape, settling in New York, Chicago and San Francisco, in London, Rome and Paris. To him, the seaboard metropolis was the crossroads of the worldly man, the place with the broadest cultural horizons. He sought cosmopolitan associations, a steady fingering out for connections with novelists, poets and painters. His fiction writers sought a European ambiance—Ernest Hemingway, F. Scott Fitzgerald, Gertrude Stein and Anais Nin. His leading poets, men like Eliot, Pound and Wallace Stevens, had Olympian vision, and straddled centuries of cultural history. He loved chamber music and the classics, and would have found rock music and folk-singing shallow and trivial. He produced cultural catalysts. In Paris, Gertrude Stein became the center of a Bohemian cell, welcoming Hemingway, seeking out Picasso. So in London, Ezra Pound gave substance to the imagist movement, editing T. S. Eliot, meeting William Butler Yeats, working to launch fresh publications. In New York, Edna St. Vincent Millay shaped herself a Bohemian life. Wallace Stevens briefly mingled with them before settling down to insurance work in Hartford.

The Bohemian shrugged off the patriotic harness that typified the American heartland, the Puritan code with its emotional dynamic of sin and depravity. This was an age of emancipation and self-fulfillment, of art for art's sake. The Bohemian chose good music, good cooking, pleasant work, and sexual fulfillment, over

Nietzschean self-affirmation or a technique for moral instruction. Indeed, his experiments in imagism, in symbolism, in natural speech, vigorously expanded the horizons of expression, giving style a fresh dynamic. So too Dada and Surrealism widened the frontiers of art. The music of the Bohemian was essential, cultivated, elegant, not folksy or turgid with emotion in a group hypnosis. He worked to "turn on" to culture and history, escaping the cutting strands of the surrounding culture. To sit in groups and folk-sing was too provincial and adolescent. In personal style, the male added style and color to the figure of the male as the well-engineered social tool. He dressed for comfort, but kept his masculinity intact. This style was no gesture of Unisex; but sexual walls were softened. Men could be expressive, creative, emotionally open; women could carry jobs and circulate more freely. A woman now could wear sleeveless dresses, loosely draped, a bra and panties instead of corsets and petticoats. The flapper generation often dispensed with bras too. She wore bathing suits she could swim in; she could smoke in public and admit she enjoyed sex.

Socially, the Bohemian ethos curiously combined Face and Proletariat. The Bohemian was Face because American culture officially supported art, with its established museums, trained orchestras, and literary classics. Indeed, he was the new Face of the American hunger for culture. Yet he remained part of the Proletarian avant-garde. The salons of Paris denied his best painters admission. His writers first broke into print in esoteric little magazines. He formed long friendships after exciting personal discoveries among people of good will who shared his taste. In a wilderness of Puritan utilitarianism, he struggled to stay on the frontier of the arts. A refugee from small town and established university, all he had to offer the world was his wit, his originality, and his ability to reverberate to the cultural experience of man. Yet as a Proletarian, he touched off large chords in the human spirit and crossed international borders. Here and there, he achieved international recognition; yet having no official channels to power, his Proletariat status stayed intact.

And then mysteriously, the Bohemian artist advanced from enigmatic ambivalence to simple Face. He became official, editing magazines, sitting on the editorial boards of major publishing houses, directing new museums, publishing and performing in every country. As his work became the text in university courses, the Proletarian romance disappeared, leaving a few individuals working to advance their careers and keep their country's culture intact.

Obviously, I am, to some extent, jealous of that rarest of breeds, a Proletarian Face that has authentic talent. This is the sweetest Proletariat in history, restless, mobile, a coming aristocracy, with a sense of sweep in a brave new world of art. They touch to life an old, romantic hunger, a yearning for a group who need never pay a tragic price for the romantic life in their frontier clearing. I am too enamored of their ethos. The human tangle sits waiting in truculent isolation. I read closer, down notations of alcoholism, estrangement, jealousy, and suicide. Fitzgerald's wife went mad; Hemingway's Robert Cohen won no boxing championship. And what of Fitzgerald? Of Hemingway himself? There is no security in a "moveable feast."

The hobo of the Thirties was a tougher breed; yet elements of his ethos rose to a strange dignity above the bitter grind of his existence. He came from the working, not the middle, class, and was flung into his role by the depression, untrained or semi-trained, permanently without a job, a worker who kept moving or starved to death. To stay alive, he shifted across state borders, jumped freight trains, took any job, or visited a soup kitchen and slept in the fields. The migrant farm worker might travel in a family or he might travel in a gang. And yet his poverty cloaked a deep dignity. He wore gray, durable clothes, made to last. Skinny and undersized, he paid a heavy price for being long out of work. That price rocked family life; but his woman had her faded durability, and a peasant survival instinct.

Inevitably, he too gathered a Proletarian ethos. Starved worker that he was, as he grew elemental, he disproved the American prejudice that finds the ideal man sterile and solid. He grew intuitively creative with no adolescent posturing. He knew the score. So his experience on the frontiers of hunger welled up in deep songs of homelessness and starvation, of labor and wandering. He produced perhaps our greatest folk singer, Woody Guthrie, and a folklore of campfire and the hobo jungle, of riding the rails and cooking weeds for food. He wrote with homespun realism, painted the realistic social comment of the Thirties. The WPA produced a people's theater. For all the bitter starvation of his life, the photographs of the depression hobo breathe a quiet, austere dignity. He belonged to the American heartland, to Arkansas and Wyoming, to the Sierra Nevada and the continental divide, his spirit strictly American, his starvation and hunger, and also his free life.

In a bar, an old Arkansas painter once lighted up a pipe as he told me how he first got started. He ground his jaws, lips closed; then one gnarled hand nervously tapped the bar. "I was plowin' the back tater patch, hot as crea-tion, when I saw maw comin' across the field at me. I waited, lookin' at her, leanin' on my plow. It had to be serious, her stumblin' so fast and hard in the sun, skinny, her face worked up, not skeered, her bony fist flyin' up, talkin' though I couldn't hear a word. Finally, I heard her yell, 'it's on the radio! The WPA is payin' peeople to paint! You git down to Little Rock!' I left those two mules and the plow in the furrow, cut for home, packed a kerchief, and got on the Little Rock road, hitchin'. I been paintin' ever since."

And yet the call of the New Deal packed the wanderers home in the tens of thousands. The hobo got government support in relief and job training. The CCC offered work on the land for youth. A battery of alphabet agencies produced public work projects, price control, wage boosts. His channels to government power tamed the Proletarian hobo to a Shadow. His folk songs faded, his poignance, his universal vision, leaving a herd of poor workers, struggling for a job.

The Beats of the Fifties were not Proletariat nor Face nor Shadow. Radical social dropouts from Joe McCarthy, the Cold War, and the Eisenhower administration, they simply did nothing. The concrete mix of American productivity had hardened into something fundamentally artificial, destructive. The Beats wanted out, they wanted just to be fulfilled in a steady, quiet truthfulness. They dressed quietly, in dark blues and browns, in denims, shabby tweeds, dungarees, clothes of the patchy woods. In a way total conformists, they violated nothing, confronted nothing, undertook nothing; but their tolerance hid the deepest seeds of rebellion. They were the break-off point, no longer open to social return, as the Bohemians and the hoboes had been. Their clothes were respectable, but they were neutral, durable clothes, without style or individual taste. They began the Unisex phenomenon. Men and women dressed and lived pretty much the same; either was open to a letch, a mad, or a hunger for faraway places. More fundamentally, they rejected all games and all role-playing. As such, they sometimes slipped out of western achievement culture, and groped for some Buddhist orientation.

Socially, they lived low-key and private. I've met some sluggish, inarticulate depressives among them, others with a deep simplicity of movement. Drugs weren't that common, but they drank a good deal. Overtures were meaningless; you either tuned in or didn't bother. They lacked the sweep of a Proletariat, though a touch of elemental truth carried the Proletarian aura. They didn't talk much, just wanted to be a watershed of non-participation in an America locked in Cold War politics and national success. Their violent break made going beat a sort of low-key suicide, choking themselves in. Their names reduced to a laconic Biff, Jero, Priss. They weren't particularly creative. Some advanced jazz came along, some cryptic free verse; but that was it. The emerging civil rights movement suggested meaningful social change, and the beats melted into more active groups.

The hippie is a more complicated critter than his daddy, the beat. He plays the frontiersman, and acts out a lot, with his shaggy clothes, his openness to the outdoors. He has made permanent the break from social return first begun by the Beats. A creature in rebellion, he is in part defined by his opposition to the established society: The bourgeois reverence for property as secure continuity he transforms into a feeling that property is material to be enjoyed; the bourgeois sense of living to secure a future he transforms into a Bohemian sense of living to celebrate the uninhibited Now. The bourgeois anchoring of goods in their ownership he dislodges into the view that goods are to be shared by whoever needs them. The bourgeois organization by nuclear families he dissolves into his loose groups of drifters and hippie frontiersmen. So his communes, families, and digger stores, and his group farms, are all fresh clearings in the woods, a new society of clean relations and decent people in the wilderness of bourgeois America. These are gathering in force, as the more innocent frontiersmen are mugged and driven out by established society, as happened in the first Puritan townships that appeared around Massachusetts Bay.

The temperament of the hippie is a strange mixture of established culture gone berserk and the heady excitement of the social frontier. His hair is ego gone mad, physical, productive, finger-painting all over his head, the negation of the bourgeois haircut. So too his robes are the negation of the bourgeois suit and creased pants. But this frontier escape, this Huck Finn adolescence, carries a vehement assertion of the broad wilderness. The hippie wants his poetry now, out loud, from the man's lips, not on paper from a printing press. His is an art of communion, not of isolated genius.

So he sniffs around the social frontier. His commune women often insist on group marriage. Once private ownership is surrendered, they want to share love like food, clothing, tools or shelter. So again, the commune walls out the wilderness to allow a new, more elemental community; but again restlessness, crowding and the spreading Satanic weeds gradually choke out the clearing. Publicity bleaches his culture to death, and a new breed of street people stirs under his feet.

Why is America so loose and berserk as to chase a nonexistent frontier rather than build with dignity a tough nation that can shape its fate? Every Alice has her Wonderland, every Isaiah his vision of paradise, every Plato his never-never Republic. Why does America act it out again and again, propelled by an expansionist economy, in a spendthrift wooze? The English transcendentalists drew up utopian plans: we pushed across to the Pacific. The English Puritans organized tight churches; we draped Mother Hubbards on all the Indians. The English bought and fought and robbed and gutted strange continents; we gut our own continent in a pioneer spirit. We're the country that tramps from pioneer project to pioneer project. Europe boggled the Suez Canal from country to country; we organized an engineering job and dug the Panama Canal. Germany diddled with an atom bomb; we slammed the pieces together and set it off. Russia loped a Sputnik around the earth; we organized a team and landed a man on the moon. When we undertake a job, we line up our team and do it. Our team wins —that's how we beat Hitler; and then the crowd gets bored and sleepy. We've won our ballgame; now we trail back home, watch TV, and wait for the next game.

Neither of the two myths we live by is entirely to be respected. Nothing is as ephemeral, in a country on the move, as a clearing in the woods, a Brook Farm financed by real estate operators, nothing as pointless, wasteful and evasive as a souped-up frontiersman riding his white Mustang into the Twenty-First Century, his tank full of gas, his brain full of ass, riding the spaghetti frontier and dreaming he's Mick Jagger. Each wayward dream represses a darker reality. The clearing in the woods initiates the waste of the American city. We may organize fresh projects, suburban communities, industrial task forces; but we end up living in a municipal sprawl; our easy rider is a soured, twitchy escape dream, gone hippie because it has nothing to do with its time. Thus, the restlessness of the latter-day frontiersman engulfs and reduces to itself the older clearings in the woods. In a dramatic encounter still coming to a head, the street people are engulfing and chewing up sections of Harvard Square, to produce the Haight-Ashbury of the East Coast.

Our dreams grow rancid; they do not keep. The sprawl of our cities is again wilderness, but too dense and cranky now for an easy clearing. Surrounded by suburbs and bedroom villages, our dream-city gradually becomes megalopolis. The energies that once built cities are now diverted into random greed that engulfs the asphalt jungle. We have no social father; and our band of brothers —suburban youth, students, the boys at the Y—turns into a street horde, into city frontiersmen, loners inside and outside the law. We inhale the chaos and glamorize the outsider who lives as he is. Our cities end up as a sluggish congestion.

The hippies want out with their own communes; but inevitably, Satan comes jogging with the second packtrain. So the tourist agencies first killed Haight-Ashbury by bringing busloads of sightseers. Reporters clutter the city communes—business promoters, sick dogs turned on to revolution, freak-outs, dealers in hard drugs, yes, and stray runaways, wobbly, with milk behind their ears, acidheads, hardhats, political eyes that eat up the commune walls like acid. Surrounding ranchers and freeloading frontier visitors harass the farming communes in Arizona. In California, some Hell's Angels policed a Rolling Stones concert with beatings and a murder. The busted festival at Powder Ridge stranded thousands of loose campers like pilgrims who had their mass forbidden at their shrine. The crowd slipped into hard drugs, and had a thousand bad trips. So the mammoth rock festival sinks six feet under.

With the quick sour and choke of the inevitable second hushed arrival, second-string Satans take over the clearing. Charlie Manson, the pint-sized thief with the wicked-baby grin, built his own commune on flicks of feeling, twitchy controlling tantrums, and threats of physical violence, stealing cars, taking over ranches, his soul sisters on call in the commune family in a system of free lays. But as the months passed by, Charlie got sour-mad and bossy, and organized some random killings, with Walt Disney terror-words scrawled in blood on the walls and scratched on the dead bellies. His bald commune women sing his songs in the courtroom corridor; and he sits in the dock and grins. But his crew are copouts from broken and distracted homes, determined to go down with their ship. His commune family should call itself the Pequod, on its second journey through whale country. Linda Kasabian, the female Ishmael, flounders in the water as she tells her story; and the Mother Goose ship sinks, its sails still flapping in court.

Hippie festivals come and go. Rock festivals like Woodstock are an old American ritual, with roots in various types of revivals going back to Colonial times. They call for their own *Woodstock Tales*, after Chaucer's *Canterbury Tales*. Tens of thousands of participants gather from around the country like holy-rollers, camping in tents in the woods, under tarpaulins, in the backs of trucks, sleeping on the ground in sleeping bags, cooking on an open fire. At the shows, rock group after rock group makes the festival a revival, one dedicated to music, not to God. The crowd takes off its clothes; groups of them snake dance down to the platform. The dry sweet smell of grass-smoke thickens like the heady wash of incense. Squatted on their hams, the crowd feels the music percolate along its bone marrow and stab along its blood canals.

At Delphos, the oracles sniffed steam the rock emitted, turned on, and prophesied; but in these festivals, entire crowds turn on to the steam of grass, the chip of acid, and cry messages to the rock groups and the slam of music. No more the hacky city world, full of pigs and private property, no more draggy subways, PhD degrees, carbon monoxide and parking regulations. This new society comes inside a mountainside of music, an atonal earthquake under the stars. All the young are spaced out, turned off on mind, time, money; turned off on hooks, glue, zippers and long, invisible ropes; turned off on connections, and turned on to love, love, love. Nude bathing is a fun baptism for this clearing in the woods. Clothes are like property and marriage, obligations that hold you down. Old John the Baptist is on the tenor sax. After eleven months of chlorinated water, you're washed in the snows of soul.

Summer brings in a daisy chain of festivals, all clearings in the woods. The pilgrim packs his knapsack, hitches or rides his motorcycle from shrine to shrine. Some festivals happen and some get busted; some have good toilets and plenty of hash, and some farmers who charge five dollars for a cup of water; some pigs bust your head and some take a neighborly drag on your joint. As the summer lengthens, the easy riders engulf the festivals, motorcycle solitaries, latter-day frontiersmen, hippie believers, who can pack a joint and can travel. Families drift apart; parties get lost. A spell of rain piles bodies under any loose tent like lumber jammed along a river bank. Sister hunts sister, but all are sisters, turned on to the beat, the hills, a thousand campfires, a hundred joints. Who is that girl, grinning at the monkey in my head?

The festival is the Disneyland of the modern frontier, a bag bought for what's in it. And yet, when the sheriff says yes, and the cops keep the traffic moving, when the portable toilets stand in rows and helicopters fly in food ahead of the mob, when rain don't bust your head, the loudspeaker delivers and the lake doesn't ask questions, when worried nurses work overtime as the smoky sets pile on top of one another to sizzle the stars and crackle the moon to a sliver of sky-skin, then Joe Cocker takes the front of the stage in a fieldhand shirt, all runny-colors, his sideburns like a North Atlantic frigate shaggy with seaweed, his hair parted in the middle and swept back like cold Atlantic breakers, his spastic hands twitching up in strobe, and he delivers dry restless kick talk—the talk of a mad train, getting started with too little grease but plenty of coal, and a long way from home, and gradually picking up steam charging across the prairie; or Joan Baez, in a white peasant outfit, draws up tall on the big stage at Woodstock, a baby in her belly, a dry shine suspended inside her face, and belts out "Swing Low, Sweet Chariot," slow and easy, wood ripples in her voice, our peaceful pup-critter, riding her sweet chariot till the grass-covered earth stirs in its sleep; and while she sings, the hills feel like home.

But the festival can turn sour, like the rock festival in Downing Stadium, eight-fifty a ticket, with an arm-long list of rock groups, and Ravi Shankar, too. I went early, to catch the opening numbers and the smell of Klieg lights coming on, to see the first speed-freak throw off her clothes and make like music. Downing Stadium is closed in and four stories high, with no mesh fences to climb over and get in free. The fees paid should have bought a lot of action.

The long, oval stadium had the feel of an eerie, panoramic 3-D nightmare, a dream sequence of a Roman vista in Fellini's *Satyricon*, a slum-city Colosseum, with a mammoth stage at one end and concrete bleachers all around a football field in the middle. New York was in a brown-out; the smog arched over the Stadium in a gassy shimmer that darkened and glazed in the sun, as though a hundred thousand subdued incinerators had pulverized their garbage and whipped it up shimmying. Big jets kept heaving over the stadium from La Guardia, each trailing its long tobacco-shit exhaust. They rose so easy, the dense stadium air seemed to be lifting them like heavy pool water lifting an unconscious body. A New York traffic helicopter angled about, drowning out the stadium noises. And gradually, rising into the cape of smog, the hot, eerie lights, the exhaust gases that spread over the football field, there rose the dry, crisp, insidious smell of burning joints of hash and grass. That stadium was turned on.

Forward, under the stage, the crowd sprawled; it filled the first third of the bleachers, with stray parties in the back bleachers, and solitaries lined along the section partitions like subway riders taking the wall seats. Several thousand were already there, and more steadily trickled in, not slum kids, not at eighty-fifty a head, but college students at loose ends between semesters, high school grown-ups, dropouts with parents who don't ask questions as long as they keep out of jail.

In the stadium, I took a seat low in the bleachers. The MC made a long boring procedural announcement, the kind obviously dragged out to kill time before the entertainment. The stadium loud-speaker had a booming reflector that jammed his charged, nasal voice so I could hardly catch the words. I wished he would sit down —the noise of the traffic helicopter overhead was more entertaining. Finally, he lifted his fist and shouted, "Power to the people!" and sat down to a sluggish silence. I thought to myself, the program is half an hour late getting started. At eight-fifty a seat, I didn't need his adolescent nasalities.

And then, deep in the back of that mammoth stage, a solitary boy sat on a low piece of lumber, plunked his guitar, and occasionally sang a few lines about his mood. Were we marking time until the programmed entertainers got started? I looked around at a crowd like nothing I had ever seen. More than half were turned on; the others blended with their mood. This was hot-rock, power-to-the-people, youth-defining-itself. The crowd squatted in thousands under the stadium loudspeakers, smoking, marking time. Hardly anyone listened or noticed what was going on. They slowly wove across the football field and milled listlessly, while that solitary guitarist communed with his mood. It was summer; and they didn't have air-conditioning at home. The stage was a giant 3-D screen that offered only one channel; so they sat patiently, waiting for the next program. The stuff was dull; but they didn't come to listen anyway, just to sit in each other's company and not have to talk.

I looked at my watch. Half an hour had gone by. Bored and restless, I got off the bleachers and joined the strollers weaving around the field. Thousands of people were scattered about, but totally fragmented, sitting or moving about alone. No one connected with anyone. A willowy fourteen-year-old passed in an Elizabethan costume, then a paunchy black, bare-chested, with sideburns and a sombrero. I passed the booth for an underground university—no curriculum, no program, no statement of purpose, not even the address of a campus, just a table with leaflets.

And then I saw, between the underground university booth and the mammoth stage, an eight-foot, soft, green, beautifully shimmering marijuana tree, growing out of a green wooden barrel, the thing itself, alive, fresh and beautiful. People twitched around it in awe, smiling at some secret joke—it looked so uncanny. And then I started—the plant was made of rubber. I looked up; the North Vietnam flag was flapping in the smog, probably also made of rubber. The stage was bare, and a record started to play. Nothing moved, only the traffic helicopter, growling its figure 8 over the Triborough Bridge. Everyone sat, quietly waiting for the program to change.

I started to leave as a murky dark mingled with the brown-out glow over the city. Far off, the Empire State Building glittered. Queens spread in a flow to the east. New York, the most awesome city on earth, was stewing in imbecile power. I looked around at the young throng, patiently squatting, zonked out, dumbly waiting to be booted into adult living, a herd of frontiersmen on the latest American frontier, out of it, out of sight, in the wilderness of psychedelic living. They wanted to space out in a wild new world, leave the wilderness of the city they knew. Too intestinal for any ideology, they just huddled in Downing Stadium. The old dreams had gone sour. The youth was out of it, waiting for a world they could call their own.

TOWN AND CITY

WHEN WE examine how nations came into existence, with their great capitals—London, Paris, Madrid, Rome, Berlin and Moscow —the nations seem clearly outgrowths of their original capital city, rather than the reverse, the capital the outgrowth of the nation. Here, the United States is the solitary exception. Only here did a nation newly-formed touch its capital into existence on the shores of the Potomac. Indeed, across America, there is a weakness in sheer native vitality in the cities, as megalopolis spreads everywhere in patches. New York spills its millions out in every direction; Boston, Los Angeles, Chicago—all are clusters of cities, municipal stews that overflow one another for hundreds of miles. Yet the cities themselves are strangely listless, engulfed by suburban growth, the posh service villages that feed on and ignore their central city.

The politicians keep cities listless, for cities can cause trouble. The French and the Russian Revolutions, the Long Parliament, war and national policy, all came to a head in cities. America, which has only sprawls of population, keeps the cities suspect and marginal. The foreign immigrant is kept alive and working there until he is socially sanitized; and so are the various ethnic minorities, the Blacks and the Chinese. Minority disturbances, Black Panthers, Fem Lib, the pacifist movement, all these are essentially metropolitan activities. The city is the warehouse for the dole. The suburbs, much more docile, bargain for utilities, but don't go crazy. Cops aren't shot at from suburban windows. No, the American city, an overgrown, unwanted municipal baby, is kept a political golem without a soul. Indeed, in the future, it will be increasingly ignored. Essentially, America has no cities. Ignorance of the ways of the city is so great in this country, that one must step back and look at our municipalities to see what impoverished paralytics they are.

Historically, the first nations were not countries, but city-states. A nation took hold when the tribal élite threw up a protective wall to contain a palace, a temple and a core army. Family life, crafts and local marketing centered around the countryside villages. Villages and city interacted, but had a clear division of function: the city collected taxes, guarded the borders, stayed in contact with the gods, and arranged war and peace; in the villages, people worked and lived. Indeed, the modern suburb is a good equivalent of the ancient surrounding village, except that it is cut loose, without a city to relate to.

The ancient Hebrews remained a collection of tribes, with sporadic national activities, until David forged a nation, not by defeating the Philistines—national enemies had been defeated before—but by giving conquered Jerusalem a royal palace, a national temple and a standing army. When census, taxation and national administrators were instituted, that went so against the national grain that a revolution split the country. And yet, in the process of history, the ten northern tribes slipped away, successive wars coalesced the national élite, pilgrim festivals softened tribal divisions—until the Hebrew nation became Jerusalem, a city-state, and its hinterland.

Ancient Greece began as an association of city-states, Athens, Sparta, Thebes and the others. Having a walled town as their prime political unit, the ancient Greeks were civilized; the barbarians had no cities. So the bordering regions were an amoral jungle, where a random wanderer like young Oedipus might murder his father for the right of way. The city was man's pillar and protection with the gods. Jason was a wanderer, a moral barbarian. Theseus, a supremely civilized man, settled down as king of his city. This myth is the polar opposite of the myth of the American frontiersman, whom the Greeks would have thought a perverse outcast and wanderer, not being settled in his own city.

The Hebrews became a nation in a slow and painful growth from tribal villages into a city-state. The Greeks never achieved nationhood; the original city-states absorbed their loyalties, organized their lives, administered their holidays, and under attack, sent them swarming to protect their municipal mother. The idea of a league of cities forming a nation was first realized only centuries later, in Switzerland and Holland.

Rome began as such another tough city-state as Athens or Sparta. There is a stubborn sense of biological continuity here. Indeed, the entire *Aeneid* tells of a municipal succession in which Aeneas, the last survivor of the royal family of Troy, sails westward under divine appointment to keep the family seed alive in a new Troy, greater and nobler than before, in the city-state of Rome.

This sense of an apostolic succession pervades European cities, and controls much of their folklore. By Roman Catholic tradition, Peter, first bishop of Rome, got two keys from Jesus, and so made Rome the supreme bishopric. But each early church father also claimed his bishopric as supremely important; each medieval city became a little treasure chest, holding its stains and relics, its cathedral, its apostolic succession, its claims to political authority.

But if apostolic succession gave a city holiness, power, validity, sovereignty of empire, the succession most maneuvered for was the mantle of Rome. The Holy Roman Empire slid Rome north of the Alps: and glory be! Vienna was Rome. The King of Prussia was called Kaiser, or Caesar: and Berlin was Rome. Constantinople became Byzantium, or eastern Rome; then, when the Turks captured

Byzantium, Imperial Russia assumed its mantle of holy authority, making the Czar the eastern Caesar, and Moscow Rome. The name Britain has been traced to the legendary Brut, a descendant of Aeneas; he made Britain successor to Troy: and London was Rome.

Myth aside, Rome, a municipal city-state like Athens, Thebes or Sparta, established an enduring political empire, whereas Greece and Macedonia had been unable to do so. Perhaps the key administrative action here was the extension of Roman citizenship to all free-born Italians (after the military unification of the peninsula) and to select citizens in the outlying provinces. This action created a tenacious double focus. The Roman élite were citizens of greater Rome; and that gave the Empire a geographical spread of top administrators. At the same time, a Greek municipal tightness intimately controlled every province. Citizens, they ran Roman affairs, their tough training and municipal loyalties reinforced by huge financial and legal benefits. The Roman Empire was thus not a nation, but a city-state thinned, honed, and sitting on an empire.

But strong as was its social texture, its established élite was hammered dangerously thin. Underneath the tough bond of the Roman citizenship, there were millions of ordinary people, the free provincials inhabiting the empire, who were not members of the body politic, but only had their affairs administered by the law. And underneath these, there were an enormous number of slaves, whose affairs were not even administered by the law, but by their masters. This situation created a strange new creature, the underground, or invisible man, legally part of the nation, and yet, by law and emotional orientation, neither citizen nor slave. Such a man can move about, own property, make a living, respect village tradition, and yet, in the political system that covers his world, he has slipped underground. As with one born colorblind, it may seem to him that nothing is missing in his life; and yet he finds the activities of government alien. Patriotism is not a factor in his emotions. Underground, no flags wave to be saluted.

The Roman Empire was slowly sapped by the pallid loyalties of its people. Emotionally castrated, the slaves remained herded solitaries, animal property, replenished by military capture, kidnapping, legal enslavement for debt, penury, or crime, amortized like cars. Moreover, the vast bulk of provincial inhabitants without Roman citizenship moved in symbiotic relationship with their Roman rulers, not fighting, not ruling, piling up bureaucratic machinery between themselves and authority, machinery behind which they worked, robbed, bought and sold, traded and produced. Helpless to change anything, they were the disenfranchised half of the Roman Empire, living a flaccid, provincial existence. When the Goths invaded, they shrugged their shoulders, and labored to provide what was demanded. The Goths were more barbaric, but not as practiced in rapacity as the Roman masters.

The Roman government, whose rule was absolute, stood over and apart. Its governors stole, extorted, taxed and held for ransom, until entire provinces groaned under the load. Mountains of gold were amassed, entire provinces shoveled under with debt; Rome was not concerned—these were provincials to be administered, not citizens to be protected. And through the centuries, the city-state of Imperial Rome ineluctably changed into a giant cartel, a cartel with a shifting, sliding balance of power, a flexible technique to run its armies, and a tenacious continuity of management. Company loyalty replaced municipal patriotism; but tenacious cartel ways offered thin emotional support, and fostered instead private philosophies—of Stoicism, materialism, Epicureanism—and also the substantial rewards of organized thievery.

One might call this the wisest and most balanced of all possible governments, as Gibbon certainly did; but to us, the springs and equilibria of domain of spirit gradually shrivel among slaves, provincials, a career army, and a cartel of administrators. The slaves would not reproduce. Family bonds were everywhere violated. Loyalty to the cult replaced loyalty to the state; and an underground hunger for a fresh bond of spirit spread Judaism, Manicheism, Zoroastrianism, Gnosticism, astrology, fertility cults and cults of magic. Following his own genteel eighteenth century hedonism, Gibbon read politics as a marketplace of vital consumer goods, where Christianity peddles grace and the afterlife. Following Toynbee, we read the rise of Christianity as a blistering up of Proletarian religion, once the national Face has settled into a sterile, rigid mask over a vacuum of spirit.

The modern nation, a balance of citizens and social classes working to maintain a society, was born in the waning of the Middle Ages, first in England, France and Spain, then in Holland and Switzerland, then in Germany and Italy, in the United States and Russia, until the idea of nationhood had spread around the world. While religious, military, and economic factors were all involved, as well as the ineluctable glue of language, the European nation grew either as an expansion of a core city, as in England, France, Germany or Russia, or as a league of cities, as in Switzerland and Holland. Spain and Portugal were born as alliances that shifted with the sheer movement of armies throwing the Moors out of Spain. This expansive camaraderie that widened and consolidated the peninsula, crossed the Straits, circled the coast of Africa to India, then crossed the Atlantic to shape a vast new empire in South and Central America, was an association of the city-states of the southern Pyrenees, writ large and fused into a nation. So France was the kingdom of Paris writ large to become first a unified people, then an overseas empire; England was the expansion of London, Germany of Berlin, Russia of Moscow under the Muscovite Czar.

Indeed, the national will is still forged around London, Paris, Berlin, Moscow—the tougher the capital, the tougher the nation. In Europe, every country was subject to sudden onslaught from a hostile neighbor or an alien horde from Africa or Asia. The capital city was their fortress; when all else failed, they fell back on their capital. So Vienna finally held against the Turks, Paris against the Germans in the First World War, Moscow in the Second. The capital is, as it were, an armed homunculus, that will spring up, reborn, when the invader is beaten back. So provincial seats hoary with age and martial experience come to be assimilated as provinces: York and Lancaster are cities, and not simply distribution centers for the London wholesalers.

When this instinct for protecting a fortress-capital and mother-city is missing in a country, the nation suffers a loss of nerve. That is why the Weimar Republic was a makeshift democracy. Bonn is somehow an ersatz capital; its national policies read as administrative adjustments, rather than as the will of a nation shaping its political being. The mildest European nation, Italy, had its capital forced on it by a provincial conquest from the north—Italy was completed, not begun, with the acquisition of Rome. Today Italy seems crumbling back to the provinces it grew from.

But the European capital is central not only in national origin and as a military bastion. In all other ways, it leads its country. That nation has a head whose leading city conducts its commerce, regulates its bankers, expands knowledge in its university, makes political decisions in its parliament, and shapes its plans for war and peace in its military headquarters. Without its capital, it would indeed stand decapitated. So Shakespeare wrote for the King's Company, the one that performed on state occasions; Milton was born in the shadow of Parliament; Donne was private secretary to the Keeper of the Seal. Their pages breathe personal acquaintance with national affairs. The London fog, the sun of Paris, the Berlin winds, stir with a bite of national effectiveness, a quiver of decision.

American power is vastly greater; but its nodes of power are scattered. Wall Street is in Wall Street, the President in Camp

David, war plans are on file in a Pentagon basement, electronic computers hidden under some cornfields, atomic rockets in the next county; goods are bought and sold in Chicago; rockets nose toward the moon out of Cape Kennedy; *Better Homes and Gardens* grows homy as tassel corn in some midwestern town; Coca-Cola belongs in Georgia; and in New York, Jewish and Negro playwrights compete for the dwindling Broadway market. Could the city of Washington rise against the Pentagon in indignation, as the city of Paris attacked the Bastille two hundred years ago, or in 1968, sent de Gaulle flying in secret to Germany? Washington is not a city to begin with, but a national road junction with slums. Indeed, no American city has registered as a bastion of strength in wartime. What American city has ever come under such attack as Paris? Only some southern cities during the Civil War; and they all fell.

The theatrical floodgates of ostentatious national contempt—spite to the flag, spite to the army, spite to Washington—theaters of realistic toilets and stylized mental hospitals—intercourse on stage, nudity, perversions—you don't know from which elbow the beards will be growing next season—the entire barrelful of vomit that opens each year with more desperate urgency—all that is not simply social protest, but also animal outrage at the absolute pointlessness of the artist in America today. The welcome given the work of the outraged artist by New York audiences is a cry of recognition and camaraderie—they have both been had. New York City today, the metropolis of the nation, has unbreathable air, disintegrating subways, avenues bulky with wealth behind concrete walls, and miles of slums where families are discriminated against by Welfare. New York has lost its nerve. It is a pauper and politically without power. Its courts, its schools, and its jails suffer from arteriosclerosis. Furthermore, it is gradually getting worse, and it knows it.

In economic history, as in politics, the European city played a key role. The western European state is typically an aristocratic area, bourgeoisified as the city shed its older aristocracy and acquired provinces piecemeal. In Switzerland and Holland, perhaps the most tenaciously enduring governments in Europe, a league of Protestant, bourgeois cities, fighting for survival against a Catholic empire, put the stamp of their collective religion, their morals and their resilient way of life on a tough, independent state. During the sixteenth century, the Tudors used bourgeois London to thin out and bring to heel the old aristocracy of the North and West. A new aristocracy was appointed; and a close bourgeois squirearchy held unified national power in England. In France, bourgeois Paris sent the aristocracy to the guillotine to establish the French Republic. So, in more or less clumsy fashion, bourgeois cities expanded into economically viable nations.

This confrontation of bourgeoisie and aristocracy, city and province is irrelevant to the American experience. For all its rambling regionalism, the loose squirearchy of the South and of Dutch New York, America was thoroughly bourgeois, at its core and from its inception. Land in America is not an aristocratic heritage, but a chartered wilderness, acquired by perseverance, consignment and hard work, uninteresting and begging for development. Blending with the wilderness carried no romantic mystique. The first Pilgrim was not here to build bridges to Indian culture or to give himself to the soil. To him, trees cluttered up good land; cleared, trimmed, and nailed in logs, they provided him with a house and left land ready for a farm.

We see then that the myth of national expansion in America was a bourgeois myth; in Europe, the myth was one of conquest of land from lesser people. The Germanic wanderings, the Slavic expansions, were heroic activities of pitched attack and vindication through victory in battle. Each culture knew where the present battleline was, and by folk-legend how far it had once extended—in the Mongol invasions, in the wars between the Moors and Catholic

Spain, in the Crusades, in the Turkish invasion to the very gates of Vienna, and then their slow withdrawal—the *Drang nach Osten*, the *Drang nach Westen*, the wars between neighboring kings and nations. Shakespeare's *Henry V* dramatized no opening of any French wilderness to settlement, but the vindication of the divine legitimacy of the British as a more tenacious soldierly and princely race than the French.

In America, land was acquired by bourgeois expansion, not by heroic victory in battle. The Revolutionary War and the War of 1812 were waged to throw off British rule, not to seize British land. The Ohio Valley was open from the first; the settlers simply pressed deeper into the wilderness to establish civilized farming. So in the Louisiana Purchase, some administrative debris was cleared away from another stretch of wilderness. Manhattan was never acquired in battle, but bought from the Indians for twenty-four dollars.

Indeed, the relative slighting of the Indians in our history was not intended to whitewash the record. Had the victorious whites thought more of the Indians, they would have dwelt more on their victories—equally brutal wars of conquest in Europe produced a spate of chronicle and legend. More basically, land was acquired in America in a bourgeois dynamic of which the Indian wars were no integral part. The Indians were rather cleared away with the raccoons and the wild grass, and Puritan farms spread through New England by sober application of the religious elect. The gun simply made the acquisition tidier.

Even the Mexican War, which resulted in an enormous land acquisition, was not, like the wars in which Spain defeated the Moors or Vienna rolled back the Turks, a manifest destiny triumphing over barbarians. We had no ambition to take over Mexico itself; we only wanted a clear strike at the wilderness. The Pacific was our manifest destiny, not Mexico City or Ottawa.

This bourgeois land acquisition cut the city out from any major role in the growth of America. On military grounds, the city was not a bastion; economically, the city did not serve as economic pathfinder or vanguard, but only as a rearguard consolidation; it did not put its stamp on the American character. Indeed, Colonial America had no cities, only villages and provincial capitals. Thus New York was a reshipment center on the line between London and the wilderness; Plymouth was its eastern terminus. The frontier laid down our broad bourgeois base; its myths parallel those of the European city. The American city had power, money, industry; but it was also suspect, parasitic, full of unstable foreign elements. New York rolled the railroads across the country; but agrarian liberalism grew in the Middle West. In New York or Los Angeles, you lived in a seat of power and a backwash of the American temperament.

Thus, the American Revolution, an internal bourgeois revolution against a slightly less bourgeois master, was not a revolution at all, not a revolution, that is, like the French or the Russian Revolutions, where one class threw another out, but rather a local consolidation, where the provincial bourgeois, and landed squirearchy, dominant already, declared its independence of the mother state. A shift of bourgeois power that had already taken place was finally legalized. Issues like local taxation are matters of bourgeois rule. In the original Declaration of Independence, Jefferson had proclaimed the inalienable rights of "life, liberty, and property"— "the pursuit of happiness" was a later Quixotic substitution. The first American political parties aped the very names of the English divisions of Whigs and Tories.

Just as the colonial cities failed to shape a nation, so they lost out in the American Revolution, which was won by the New England villages and the middle-state and southern squirearchy. The cities were riddled with Tories and vulnerable to an organized British assault. True, Washington fought skirmishes on the outskirts of New York City on Morningside Heights and built a fort on Washington Heights; but New York itself did not rebel as Paris had done in guillotining its king, and the St. Petersburg workmen touching off the Russian Revolution. Only Boston among American cities fought in the American Revolution; and it could not put its stamp on the broad American character. The Washingtons and the Jeffersons overshadowed the Lowells and the Adamses. Flank attacks won the Revolution, skirmishes, and cross-country marches, not battles in the streets of Manhattan or on the Brooklyn docks.

Later it was the states, not the cities, that consolidated a confederation after the villages had won in the Revolution. The American élite looked westward, not to the seaboard. As a result, even today —this is our most amazing eighteenth century anachronism—the United States is still an agrarian bourgeois democracy of villages. We are a thoroughly bourgeois country, with no tradition of blood ties, people's marches, mythic kings, and knightly supremacy in battle. On the contrary, the face of George Washington moves every quarter and dollar bill. We bang the dust out of Congress almost as often as a successful businessman changes his new Buick. And we slight and mistrust our cities. They didn't fight our wars; they didn't stamp our character; they didn't shape our truth.

In New England, which was closer to the European city tradition, the largest city can still be the state capital, Boston in Massachusetts, Providence in Rhode Island, and Hartford in Connecticut; but New York legislates its schools, arranges its taxes, and programs its poor relief in the upstate village of Albany. If ever there was a move designed by a team of political hacks to make sure no talented man ever ran for the New York legislature, it was to condemn him, if he won, to spend his winter in Albany. So Pennsylvania has its capital in Harrisburg, not Philadelphia; Illinois in Springfield, not Chicago; California in Sacramento, not Los Angeles or the Golden Gate. Our national village, Washington, got its first mayor a few years ago. As a senator, Jack Kennedy had to keep flying to New York to see a decent play.

The rationalizations are endless and wearisome: cities are subject to mobs, overrun by immigrants, poverty-stricken, politically corrupt, subject to newspaper whim and fancy—all the self-righteous excuses of the small-town bankers who run America from its towns and villages. In actual fact, a mob can be met by troops. The only time Paris ever beat France (it tried more than once) was in 1779, when the bourgeois of the nation stood behind it; otherwise it lost every time. France runs Paris, not the reverse. So England runs London, and Italy runs Rome. But a European capital wants the charge of a metropolis beating around its debates on national affairs. So, when all is said and done, none of the considerations we have listed has swayed a single European country. However conservative, European nations grew out of their principal cities; they are not national associations of villages which through the years have castrated and impoverished their largest cities to keep them docile and well-behaved.

The American city is not a cultural or political center, but a metropolitan service station. Indeed, American cities tend to come in two kinds: manufacturing cities and distribution cities. The manufacturing city is raw, ethnically more emphatic, more vulnerable to depression, with a population fresh off the land or out of the mine to work in its factories. It will often have a curfew to control its youth, suddenly flush with money. Its police are a bit more violent than elsewhere. Its money comes hot and cold, as in Birmingham, Alabama; Gary, Indiana; Seattle, Washington; or Akron, Ohio. The distribution city spends its money more coolly, handles its minorities more suavely, with more native city people, more concern for its image, as in Atlanta, Georgia; Portland, Oregon; St. Louis, Missouri; Nashville, Tennessee. In both cases, the city is a service city, not a cultivated garden, or a crown of the countryside.

So, when American poets celebrate the city, it is seen as teeming with power, abundance, fertility, a sort of urban wilderness, a metropolitan frontier. Whitman strikes this note in his "Mannahatta":

I was asking for something specific and perfect for my city,
Whereupon, lo! upsprang the aboriginal name!
Now I see what there is in a name, a word, liquid, sane, unruly,
        musical, self-sufficient,
I see that the word of my city is that word from of old,
Because I see that word nested in nests of water-bays, superb,
Rich, hemm'd thick all around with sailships and steamships, an
        island sixteen miles long, solid-founded,
Numberless crowded streets, high growths of iron, slender
        strong, light, splendidly uprising toward clear skies,
Tides swift and ample, well-loved by me, toward sundown,
The flowing sea-currents, the little islands, larger adjoining
        islands, the heights, the villas,
The countless masts, the white shore-steamers, the lighters, the
        ferry-boats, the black sea-steamers well model'd,
The down-town streets, the jobbers' houses of business, the
        houses of business of the ship-merchants and money-
        brokers, the river-streets,
Immigrants arriving, fifteen thousand in a week,
The carts hauling goods, the manly race of drivers of horses, the
        brown-faced sailors,
The summer air, the bright sun shining, and the sailing clouds
        aloft,
The winter snows, the sleigh-bells, the broken ice in the river,
        passing along up or down with the flood-tide or ebb-tide,
The mechanics of the city, the masters, well-form'd, beautiful-
        faced, looking you straight in the eyes,
Trottoirs throng'd, vehicles, Broadway, the women, the shops
        and shows,
A million people—manners free and superb—open voices—hos-
        pitality—the most courageous and friendly young men,
City of hurried and sparkling waters! city of spires and masts!
City nested in bays! my city!

Celebrated here is not the city as civilized, but as "aboriginal," "that word from of old," a wilderness or an ocean, masts rising like trees over water flowing everywhere, combining both wildernesses of America, ocean and forest. Its inhabitants move like innocent animals, radically at home on native ground. This is a clearing in the woods for the newly arrived immigrant, and Whitman is a frontiersman of the poetic spirit, celebrating his abundance.

This same American sense of the city as a metropolitan, primitive wilderness, though more violent, more brutalized with the advent of power, not the suggestion of a virginal first wilderness, yet mysteriously riding its Satan, rather than being ridden by him, is present in Sandburg's "Chicago":

> Bareheaded,
> Shoveling,
> Wrecking,
> Planning,
> Building, breaking, rebuilding.
> Under the smoke, dust all over his mouth, laughing with white teeth,
> Under the terrible burden of destiny laughing as a young man laughs,
> Laughing even as an ignorant fighter laughs who has never lost a battle,
> Bragging and laughing that under his wrist is the pulse, and under his ribs is the heart of the people,
> Laughing!
> Laughing the stormy, husky, brawling laughter of Youth, half-naked, sweating, proud to be Hog Butcher, Tool Maker, Stacker of Wheat, Player with Railroads and Freight Handler to the Nation.

Sandburg gives us a service city, but primitive, a city seen as a dog, a savage, half-naked—not an aristocratic garden. His treatment echoes Whitman's celebration of the urban wilderness; but "Chicago" was published in 1914, after the geographical frontier had disappeared, and has a more congested violence. As in *The Grapes of Wrath*, here is a frontier gone berserk, a Huck Finn grown up, powerful, contemptuous of niceties. Satan has arrived; but the frontiersman rides him.

For a picture of the city as a majestic garden, we must turn back to Wordsworth, and his "Composed upon Westminster Bridge, Sept. 3, 1802":

Earth hath not anything to show more fair;
Dull would he be of soul who could pass by
A sight so touching in its majesty:
This city now doth like a garment wear
The beauty of the morning; silent, bare,
Ships, towers, domes, theaters, and temples lie
All bright and glittering in the smokeless air.
Never did sun more beautifully steep
In his first splendor, valley, rock, or hill;
Ne'er saw I, never felt, a calm so deep!
The river glideth at his own sweet will.
Dear God! the very houses seem asleep;
And all that mighty heart is lying still!

This city—London—is not half-naked, but wears "a garment" of extraordinary beauty. The word "majesty" echoes later in "all bright and glittering" to suggest a crown, halo, or nimbus. "Towers, domes, theaters, and temples" encompass the civilization of a city, its culture, its faith, its halls of justice. The attribution of radical innocence to it makes the city momentarily a Garden of Eden, thus adding the garden image of a civilized city, such as Europe aspired to, and America scarcely acknowledges.

Ignoring the lyric celebrations, one of the sad truths of American political history is that small towns have always run American states. States convene; cities never convene. As a result, throughout

American history, virtually every constitutional convention has rigged its charter against its cities by establishing a two-chamber legislature and giving the state Senate, a chamber based on areas, veto power over legislation. So the very incorporation of a city is according to state rules; the state determines what is a city, and once it is incorporated, what moneys it can spend and how. The state is sovereign; the city stands hat in hand before a grudging legislature rigged against it to ask what it can and cannot do.

In a major decision, the Supreme Court finally established the "one man-one vote" rule, forcing a voting redistribution in every state in the Union, to prevent the rigging of their legislatures against their cities. This sounds like a major power shift, giving the American city a voice at last in its own destiny. In fact, however, that national champion of village power, Everett Dirksen, introduced an amendment through the state legislatures—thus bypassing national attention in Congress—to abrogate the one man-one vote rule as a threat to the American small town. He quietly got it within two or three votes of passing, and then it died. It sounds then, as though the cities had won; but they didn't. The most recent census indicates the suburbs are sharply increasing in population vis-à-vis the inner city. Dirksen's amendment failed because the politicians knew there was nothing to fear. The Supreme Court decision shifted legislative power from country village to suburban village; our cities remain helpless paupers.

The effect of living in a nation of villages must be spelled out. There is much revolutionary talk, for example, about the establishment, its insidious thought control, regulating every detail of a man's behavior, etc., etc., etc. My principal objection to Roszak's *The Making of a Counter Culture*, and a host of other studies, novels, plays and journals, some by the most subtle minds at work today, is their presumption that there is some new, insidious malevolence, an electronic Madison-Avenue-cum-Wall-Street-cum-General-Motors conspiracy, to shape the collective mind. For example (this is from the horse's mouth) the establishment lets me write this book because its electronic apparatus knows I serve its dark purposes. I'm the green chlorophyll bottle on the smoking-room shelf that freshens the social air. My words harmlessly disperse aggravations (I'm the freak with a tie on) and help prevent a revolution. So the establishment leads me on with contracts, with air-line tickets at State Department expense—to Copenhagen, say, for lecture engagements—my fee is substantially lower than Kenneth Galbraith's—with literary prizes—are you listening, Stockholm?—with movie-scripts—my number is in the phone book—to keep well-oiled this safety valve of controlled independence for the electronically enslaved.

I must say, despite the extraordinary unanimity of men I deeply respect, their sense of discrimination, their detailed exposés of that super-cartel of the GNP, the establishment, I am deeply skeptical about its very existence. Oh, there is an establishment—and a substantial one. America more or less controls its rebels; but what is new or unique about this? How on earth do our underground innocents who stand aghast before the "establishment" read human history? The constant of human life is the way a society makes minds subservient and mauls and seduces its rebels. What made Japanese warriors from Samurai days to the present commit harakiri, if not the Japanese establishment, shaping their minds? What shifted thousands of English churchgoers back and forth between priest and Protestant ministers, but the shifting Tudor establishment? What is *Huckleberry Finn* about but the Mississippi establishment? Or Zola? Or Voltaire? What was Milton fighting for in his *Areopagitica* but freedom from censorship by the English establishment? What does the American establishment have that is unique—television? I can subscribe to the *New Republic*, while your television can go on playing "Jingle Bells."

Calling such an insidious brain-control system the "establishment" even has unpleasant echoes of the condition called paranoia in which the patient thinks some power is generating electric waves, or manipulating the environment to control his thought and behavior. The truth is uglier: that virtually all independent human thought since the beginning of time has struggled against some established system. Leo Strauss has a dumbfounding thesis that many western intellectual rebels—Maimonides, Descartes and so on—wrote in code in order to slip their books past the censors and avoid being burned at the stake. That's what all the threatening fires of history have been about—the lynchings in the south, mental hospitals in Soviet Russia, autos-da-fé in fifteenth century Spain, children attacked by unidentified gangs, smirking laughter on the village green. All this huddling, this whispering "The Establishment," as though some electronic King Kong jiggled the words of every *New York Times* editorial, is too easy an escape from spiritual loneliness and the benign indifference of the modern age.

Even the core establishment that runs the American economy—Wall Street and the banks—is not a tight, controlled operation. Wall Street (if we may mix our metaphors) is a jungle with traffic cops, not a civilized city. Furthermore, Wall Street and the banks do not get along that well: in an inflation, Wall Street expands, with more speculative money available, but banks lose money, when the inflation makes worthless the fixed interest on loans. The evidence is strong against the Marxist theory that there is some core of power that makes the real decisions for our country. For example, the American establishment no longer supports the war in South Vietnam; it has lost too many billions of investment dollars in the current long decline of stocks. Every peace rumor sends Wall Street prices soaring; yet politics keeps peace from arriving there. The core establishment is a jungle, not a brain; and that jungle is open to any key of finance or special talent. Indeed, a jungle-on-top is an expensive luxury for a civilized country, even if the jungle has policemen.

In relationship to the ordinary citizen, the establishment is generally loose, overweight, punchy, bored, warmhearted, and utterly indifferent. It is moderately cranky, not out of kindliness, but because it is secure, testy, mentally self-indulgent, and socially wasteful. Fundamentally villagey in all its twitches, the American establishment has no concern in anything I do. I can say anything, read anything, move to Honolulu and back: no one gives a damn, as long as I don't try to blow up the George Washington Bridge. The image of an establishment trigger-happy to attack its thinkers is hardened into a ubiquitous reality by speakers who cannot bear their cultural loneliness and political impotence. The Roman Stoics had a more philosophical vocabulary to discuss oppression.

What is limited about the establishment are its nervous twitches and tics; it works like a village, not like a city. Much of the confrontation between freaks and squares is not simple persecution, but a subtle invitation to live through the *Easy Rider* experience, to amble down Main Street at the stroke of noon packing a six-gun for the coming showdown. Any man who knows he'll get shot at, busting through Louisiana with shaggy hair and an American flag painted on his helmet, can change his helmet and head for Maine. This is not to wash one's hands of a killing, only to understand exactly what is being said.

So the romantic talk about the "underground man" is wishful thinking. The Weathermen are underground, because the FBI is after them for planting bombs. In our slippery society, the decor of Face and Shadow easily reverses itself in particular situations, though the strain of the reversal can be severe. I know a heterosexual composer who became the invisible man when he brought his wife to a musical gathering where she was the only woman present. You choose your neighbors by the shape of your beard as much as by the morals in your head. Decor aside, America has no true underground because it has no true overground, just a lot of conformist conventions, cheatings on the law, cultural jangles, social impotence, and also a lot of good living—these in no way contradict one another.

Indeed, our village structure invites social unrest by a vacuum on top; it has village elders, but no national figures. Town engineers shape our style, but they create no myth either of national leadership or of national direction on which the young can climb. Roosevelt, with traditions of Dutch New York, created such a myth; so too did Kennedy, whose Boston had city traditions rare in this country. But these are both cases of fortunate Old World touches. Nixon's campaigning is deft, his political moves experienced; his social engineering would perfectly manage Wilmington, Delaware. So we grumble at the vacuum on top; and after a while, we begin to yawn. The Proletariat of England was kept relatively quiet through the nineteenth century by the Methodist revival as they were gradually given the vote; the Proletariat in America is stultified by our vast clutter, and finally rendered comatose by television conditioning. The Republican Party rules by the controlled yawn.

We cry enough. Our chafing is not at the lack of perceptivity of the establishment, but at the insulting indifference of its village methods. In Soviet Russia Stalin destroyed the kulaks, the village property-owners, to consolidate a docile nation. In America, the kulaks won the revolution and are still in control. As a result, we are a nation of villages with a world responsibility beyond the kulak's grasp, with whatever resulting dulling of our national awareness vis-à-vis the consciousness of other nations.

Municipal loyalties, population figures and all else to the contrary notwithstanding, New York is *the* city of the United States. This is not a metaphysical absolute, but only our national reality. As a writer, you break surface in New York; in theater, you arrive on the New York stage. In opera and ballet, other audiences are regional—the New York audience is national. Wall Street is in

New York, so is Madison Avenue, so is Park Avenue, so is Tin Pan Alley. I myself grew up in a scuffed corner of Akron, Ohio, and now have a flat on upper Broadway, on the fringes of Harlem. To say in Europe that I live on Broadway raises the temperature in the room. New York City has a status like no city in the world; yet it is a stepchild in Albany because, as in every other state, New York City is run by distant village politicians.

Indeed, beyond the village level, this country has scarcely any community spirit. We have discussed the establishment as a jungle-on-top. Were any village remiss in a simple matter like sewage disposal, town meeting after town meeting would explode until the problem of sewage disposal was settled. Never mind socialism, free enterprise, the collective mind; that village wants clean streets. If the waste escaped the sewers and poured down the Main Street gutters, and the mayor appealed for patience and did nothing, he would be impeached. Our villages are organized to meet communal needs. Our trouble is that patches of megalopolis spread like a skin disease across areas of organized villages. So poison pours by the boiling bucketful out of factories, car exhausts, power plants, exterminating our lakes and rivers, poisoning our beaches, polluting our soil, contaminating our atmosphere—and an uneasiness is felt by all. We know very well what is producing smog and poisoning our air—essentially car exhaust is doing it, that is, General Motors and Shell Oil, Ford and Esso, Chrysler and Texaco. It distresses us, the way nothing seems to straighten out. We swallow hard, exercise patience, and appoint a commission. The problems in the area of megalopolis are communal; but we have no tradition of regional communities, nor political bodies to foster them. Holland does; but then Holland has self-respecting cities.

I am quite pessimistic on the subject. To be perfectly blunt about it, this country will very likely do nothing basic about pollution, as our waters are poisoned to extermination of sea life, our ears are deafened beyond repair, and our children grow into a warped existence, not because we are greedy monsters, but because our nation is a collection of organized villages. Any problem beyond that level is met by a commercial twitch reaction called "free enterprise." "Free enterprise" is the slogan that enables Main Street sheriffs like Barry Goldwater to sit in cheery catatonic indifference, presiding over the poisons spreading under their good-looking boots. Were his village pond getting poisoned like Lake Erie, today the Dead Sea of North America, Goldwater would soon put a stop to it; but when a national waterway is steadily pumped full of poison, we appeal to the industries to find other outlets for their poisons. We are told regulation would raise the price of their product. We sigh in distress and resign ourselves to patience.

Beyond the village level, government works in an aggressively hedgy fashion. To apply our earlier terminology, our villages are Face, our cities Shadow with all Shadow's special traits of inferiority complex, clique mentality, compensations, blocks against creative thinking on problems. Our village leaders weigh the village; our city politicians weigh minority group demands. So, in Congress, committee chairmen scratching eighty tune in to the village mind back home. Even the Pope has decreed that Cardinals cannot participate in a papal election when they are past the age of seventy-five. Surely our Congress need not be more conservative than the Vatican in Rome. On the state level, our legislatures are entrenched holding companies for village interests. As a result, our large cities are paupered beggars with no community sense whatever. The paralysis of the American legislative function is well-known; but the paralysis of the executive function is equally gross. There is no serious metropolitan planning, as everywhere in Europe. In communal decencies, our nation is not a mind-controlling establishment; quite the contrary, it is an equilibrium of special-interest commissions and villages that maintain a bored vacuum.

I do not exaggerate. Our ugliest single social horror is the handling of the problems of Welfare. Speaking quite simply, a man out of a job is socially sick; an unemployable is a social cripple. By paying Welfare allowances without a straightforward program of job referral and job training, we multiply a race of unemployable parasites. The ready answer, that job orientation costs money, does not work, since its absence costs more. New York City recently passed an awesome divide when it paid out more money for Welfare than for the school system. This means that the New York school system is essentially bankrupt, since it doesn't train the young for jobs when they grow up. The city has now cut its Police and Fire Department rolls because Welfare is such a growing drain. Moreover, once Welfare becomes socially acceptable, marginal students become like school girls who stop trying because they will settle down soon; then why bother? Welfare spreads like a gray shadow, softening effort, encouraging drug abuse, fattening and dulling any sense of the dynamic of a job to be done. We sicken our poor, and pay them to multiply. But our Welfare budget, vast and growing as it is, is an excuse not to have to think. It is our hush money, paid to save ourselves from having to become communities.

It is bad enough to strip a man of self-respect by giving him a dole and no way to a job. But we do worse when we dole out money to mothers without a man around which is denied if a man is around. We thus force divorce and abandonment on Welfare families, and systematically destroy family life among the poor. The poor are not only rewarded for being unemployed—their family structure is engineered into wreckage. Such procedure results in a weird city of floating male studs and multi-mothers on relief. Nixon's recent proposal of a guaranteed annual wage in place of Welfare might have preserved family life among the poor, and given them some hope of crawling out of Welfare; but Nixon wobbled in its initial presentation and the plan faces a Congress with no planning on its mind.

Indeed, our system of Welfare is a contributing cause of our present drug epidemic, which is spreading as the bubonic plague spread through medieval Europe. Legalistic as we are about such drugs as heroin, opium, and cocaine, we are so ignorant and complacent about drugs themselves, that we do not think constructively about their social roots. In America drugs are tenaciously native. To vary Rap Brown's celebrated quip about violence, drugs are as American as Coca-Cola. It is a well-known fact that Coca-Cola contains caffein, a mild but habit-forming drug.

Cigarettes, that trigger lung cancer, are also habit-forming, containing nicotine. For a twenty-year chain-smoker to quit is like a heroin-break, especially for a chain-smoking woman. A boiling, craving hunger chews up the bone marrow, and produces twitches, nightmares, crazy talk. The most charming minuet of the century is the dance of respect between Congress and the tobacco companies about cigarette advertisement. We can't forbid cigarettes, can't even label the package like rat-poison; but at least we can block all ads! Did cigarettes cause cancer in a single village, the matter would be settled very quickly; but an entire nation goes paralytic before the Face of free enterprise.

Even with more suspect drugs, the paralysis occurs. Perhaps the worst drug is speed. A man off heroin can hope to build himself a new life; but speed degenerates the nervous system. Speed kills. A speed-freak is a wrecked and gutted car. A heroin addict may turn criminal; a speed-freak is an incurable maniac. Yet heroin is forbidden in this country, while speed—I mean the amphetamines—is openly manufactured by legitimate drug houses in vast amounts, almost all of which, unless it is secretly plowed back into the soil as fertilizer, ends up on the drug market, and the manufacturers know it. A small amount is needed in special cases of weight reduction, though I dare say other diet-techniques are available. All the rest pours by the truckload into the drug market. Knowing all this, with real courage, the government asked the drug companies voluntarily to manufacture only the amount legitimately needed. The request was shrugged off—business is carried on in normal fashion to make money. The government sighed, and hoped things would improve. Thus our community abets the flood manufacture of the worst known drug. Every manufacturer who blindly produces by the barrelful drugs needed only by the bottleful should be tried as an accessory before the fact. In a village, this would be settled overnight; but in national affairs, we mumble "free enterprise" and smile for the camera.

All the gingerly legal niceties about drugs must be kept in mind in considering the relationship of the heroin epidemic to the present Welfare system. The heroin addict is the slave of his habit. Clinical investigation shows a wrench in his basic psychic equilibrium, with no father figure in his unconscious. Heroin-addiction is thus pre-Oedipal. Taking a shot blanks out consciousness, satisfying a starved craving to slide back to the tissue level, with the illusion of the womb. There is a relief, a sense of arrival, of sliding back, of murkily curling up in momma's belly. But with it comes a sense of being cheated, robbed forever of will power, of freedom, of one's adult destiny, a sense of being perversely reduced to tissue slavery, one's life castrated and destroyed. All these elements, the false security, the hunger for the womb, the sense of being cheated, trapped, in chains, a yearning for death, the muffled, wistful desire for revenge, combined with the sheer expense involved, give the addict a blank check for compulsive, brainlessly mechanical thievery.

Our system of Welfare creates the predisposition for heroin-addiction by forcing the father out of the home at pregnancy causing detached mothers to raise large families—each child is worth bounty money on Welfare. The poor thus live in a cloud of non-family, with no father around to work for the family living—only a series of male studs, and a momma who sits at home on Welfare. This is a hothouse to produce drug addicts and permanent parasites. In blunt language, our Welfare system is designed to make permanent freaks, perverts, and emotional cripples of municipal youth and to thrust the city poor into the raging inferno of the drug epidemic. By denying the poor the possibility of a supportive father figure, we create habits only steady thievery will maintain. In a word, we engineer Welfare to maximize perversion, thievery, and crime. Mr. Nixon, Mr. Rockefeller, and Mr. Lindsay, would you cut down the heroin traffic in New York City? Find a way to stop pushing fathers out of the homes of the poor.

The problem is serious. Civil rights leaders are concerned—and rightly—about computers tracing all our citizens, a sort of computer-on-top. They are distracting themselves from a more essential problem. As we know from physics, nature abhors a vacuum. What the United States suffers from most basically is a vacuum-on-top, a vacuum of community that is being filled by computers. What is more, almost nothing is going on to solve the problem. The national politicians were perturbed at the last election by the Princeton proposal to allow a two-week vacation just prior to the national election to allow college students to participate in the election campaign. Their disquiet was soon allayed. Political awareness on a national level is so lacking in this country, only the most intermittent gestures took place outside the machinery of the political parties.

What is needed is to penetrate the blank wall of the village mentality in this country. First, in the most fundamental way, we have to change our attitude to village and city. I once hitch-hiked a bit in the Ohio Valley, where I grew up. I crossed peaceful small towns, with deep lawns, wrap-around porches, and the quiet decency of settled folk. Once, hungry, sleepy and broke, I stumbled onto Bowling Green, Ohio. The serenity of that town, its handsome, spreading campus, the sheer size of its elm trees, left me feeling it unbelievable. I suddenly stopped hitching and started walking, my eyes drinking in the town. Here Shakespeare could retire after a twenty-year storm of creativity.

But let's face it: we need the contagion of contact with alert metropolitan minds, not just the serene greenhouse of a university village. I sometimes drive north for miles up the sweep of Michigan Boulevard and the Chicago Lakeside Drive, past the broad beaches and spreading vistas of park, overhung by luxurious skyscrapers parading like dogs in a show in ostentatious competition to be designated the sleekest sky-burdening monster. Compared to this wealth and explosive building, these rows of reinforced-concrete thoroughbreds, most of New York seems like drab middle age. So too the ripple of steady money runs through the ocean harbors of San Francisco and New Orleans, with their open-air sculpture houses, the trees smelling of ocean, the streets a mingling of Main Street, a Latin regatta and the distant Orient.

But finally, my city is that malevolent, brutalized beggar, the city of New York, with its enormous loneliness, its waste, its empty power of brute anonymity. Here is no stagnant reservoir, but a stark human ocean—millions of people choking the Broadway gutters between dead concrete monstrosities, and the smack of talent on my talent, smashing its way to the surface along these canyons. Here I confront in a moment maturities I never knew existed. After my two weeks of expense-account living in Las Vegas, that glittering village, with the high-toned, sentimental show biz of yesteryear, I found more original talent in one Manhattan block than in all Nevada. Like, some of my best friends live in small towns.

The recent Supreme Court decision of "one man—one vote" has made the suburb the coming political hub, but the suburb is just the bedroom of the city. We have graduated then from a nation of villages to a nation of bedrooms; but our cities are still not political centers. One proposal of Norman Mailer in the recent New York mayoralty campaign blazed in the face of every candidate running: that metropolitan New York become a separate state. The world's biggest power center should not stand like a petitioner in Albany, waiting for the word of Ithaca and Syracuse on its schools. And a New York City-State would mean Metropolitan New York, its natural enclave, and not a few boroughs which cannot breathe for the choke of bedroom cities surrounding them. And so too, a greater Chicago, a greater Philadelphia, a greater San Francisco. Recently, Bella Abzug has kept the idea from dying.

The step is necessary, not only to allow the city to plan its own destiny, but also to advance the general good. As things stand, our largest cities are doped into such inertia that a political opportunist and hack like Mario Proccacino can bark, "Law and order!" to a few relatives, and capture a primary. As a collection of villages, we're so sluggish, our national power is gradually fading. Our youth moves with indolence; our best talent holds back from the public treadmill. We articulate no collective purpose, but only muddle and wait, supporting the status quo. Essentially, we do nothing, lacking a metropolitan grasp of our problems.

An occasional charismatic president can bring a surge of national energy by suggesting a metropolitan approach to national problems. So Franklin D. Roosevelt gathered fresh talent in Washington to plan an end to the Depression; his administration finally became just more governmental machinery. So Jack Kennedy attracted fresh talent to Washington, suggesting a metropolitan community like a fresh breeze through the country. Even Eugene McCarthy made angry campus youth look respectable and spread a sense of civil life through a sluggish country, just by talking like a metropolitan citizen and not like an aging village undertaker. But these precedents are ephemeral and spotty. The truth remains: a nation of self-righteous villages moves its congressional leaders like village folk to hobble the most charismatic leader. What we need is not charismatic good luck, but metropolitan centers to attack the problems that undermine our self-respect and threaten our survival.

Our cities should take sober stock of what they are, how it happened, and where they go from here. The truth is, New York City has been hobbled, hamstrung and gerrymandered into triviality. Furthermore, the future looks bleak. The middle class slips into the suburbs, and so may Wall Street and investment companies. There is no oil under Manhattan. Yet with its great harbor, its people, its equipment and historic tradition, New York could evolve a program for its own affairs, grapple with its Welfare problems, its schools, its transportation—Shadow the program into being, or know what blocks it. It should support candidates pledged to its emancipation from political peonage, to achieving for it self-respect through self-government. They would be hard to beat.

The core question is, how do we establish national communities? About our only effective community outside the village is the corporation, a closely organized group of men who think, plan, and work together; but that is a community honed to make money as an army is honed to win a war. When an industry settles in a town (except a company town), it steadily spars and negotiates for zoning, cleanliness, access to highways, etc. Those two communities have to get along. Free enterprise will not first paralyze a village, and knock the hinges off all its doors to allow entry to promoters. Should an industry pour buckets of poison where the town swims, fishes, and draws its drinking water, the mayor will not simply appeal to the industry to be concerned about its poison, any more than one appeals to an army not to hurt anyone. The army is organized to win a war; the industry to make money. The question is how to make an industry behave that is polluting an entire nation.

Here stands the brilliant and elemental proposal of Ralph Nader to impose representatives of the community at large on the board of directors of every great corporation. A trained professional with a serious job gears his attitude to the morality of his job. Quite simply, a large corporation is a company town with a flat, one-dimensional purpose: to make money; however, it functions as a wholesome community, promoting good work relations, a reliable product, etc. Our nation is locked in with numbers of such company towns whose final purpose is to produce a flat product, money. But such company towns, unless they mesh with the larger nation they feed on, become parasitic growths, clinging to and weighing down a half-dead tree.

Let's not stand too primly outside the company town of General Motors and hope like rejected stepchildren that something will be done about the pollution of our air by car exhaust. No revolutionary gesture is needed. Corporations are fictitious beings who exist at the pleasure of the public. For the law to put a public representative on the board of a corporation requires no further step. Furthermore, the action can be taken even without a law, by a vote of the stockholders. Universities and churches are themselves entrenched communities; let them share in the communal concerns of corporations they substantially own. I tell you for a church dedicated to human uplift to consign its investment capital to the flat pursuit of the dollar is downright unChristian.

Now that political power is being shifted from the country village, the community that seems most worth developing is the Shadow metropolitan community. Farm villages are isolative and entrenched; suburban villages come in shifting clusters that share communal problems. So the cluster of suburbs around New York should go metropolitan on metropolitan problems. The Long Island Railroad is near bankruptcy; Penn Central is already in receivership. With their massive resources, their political leverage, and their stake in safe, speedy transportation to the city, the collective suburbs of New York should move first for a metropolitan problem-busting authority to attack the transportation problem. Their rising political weight could bring in their own specialized TVA. So too with power, and with water and area pollution—problems for which a metropolitan address seems so eminently constructive that only an entrenched village politician hiding behind the banner of "free enterprise" could move to block it.

Such a metropolitan community could not only attack the problems in the areas concerned, but also tap the energy, vision and talent asleep in this country. The United States is suffering more from a galloping case of premature hardening of the arteries, than from any excess of revolutionary energy. Village hacks who sound like James Stewart on television get elected governor; and fresh blood hardens behind village valves. The widespread sense that our country lacks a head is an unfair exaggeration. We have a head: a head the right size for Wilmington, Delaware.

The revolutionaries who act out their complaints about the establishment are tediously adolescent. There is no establishment. America is a jungle-on-top, an arena of random enterprise whose sclerotic passageways village policemen keep somehow open. Politically, we are jammed in; but the roadblocks are stupid enough to let themselves be hammered open. The hammering has to come from that strangest of all Proletariats, that enigmatic willful child, American youth, when it begins to take itself seriously.

9

THE TRIVIALITY GAME

A SENSE of the trivial comes in occasional, sudden starts, when I least expect it. I loop around a turnpike feeder, then bear hard to the right in a quick figure-eight under a feeder onto my parkway. It's a gas, maneuvering in a dull haze. All around me, major arteries course into the main drag, eight lanes. They open neat as a pod around a gas station, then fold around it, seamless. The gas station belongs to the parkway, and the parkway to the cars; the system straddles a land it never touches. We're all machinery in the American space ship, meshed, engineered and in operation. It's under control; no danger is possible. We're coursing over Key West, or some outlandish Bermuda.

Suddenly, it's all a triviality game. Like, two minutes ago, somebody put a dime in a pinball machine and I popped up, a marker in a highway game, zagging along my slot. I speed up, pass, cut lane; I want a full play for my dime in the slot, before I pop down again, dead until another dime pops me up again. A rusty old Dodge hurtles close by me in the next lane, too close, too fast, and a little wobbly. It needs a wash badly.

Suddenly I check my speed. Have I reserve gas? Is my direction under control? How solid are my tires? A road marker flies by me. I breathe easier—I'm in the right direction. The black asphalt supports my tires with a rolling pressure. The trip is under control; I relax for the driving.

A row of black silhouettes pulses by to my right against the distant, dusky city glow. Are they stage cardboard? Live wood? Nothing matters in the flow of driving, the wind, the passing cars, the highway unrolling. Turned on again, I pass another filling station, folded in, neat as a bean in a pod. It's a gas, maneuvering in a dull haze. The station belongs to the highway, and the highway to the cars; the system straddles a land it never touches. We're a system—the American space ship, meshed, engineered and in operation; but what of that rusty, wobbling Dodge? Cars like that should be ordered off the highway—they don't belong! But how are my old tires? Is that a slick on the highway? If I skid into a crash, my head will get crunched in like a raw egg. It's risky, driving. I have to buck the triviality game.

A department store with too many piled stalls sometimes sets me wandering, a slot in the triviality game, or rows of chuck steak in the supermarket by rows of shoulder steak, rows of T-bone, rows of sirloin. Did a well-trained cow in back tear itself apart that neatly? Or magazines in an over-stocked stationery depot. I mean, how much *Life* can a man take?

I once passed several acres of shiny used cars, red, white and blue banners flapping all over, a white sales office on the corner, its windows framed in red, white and blue neon, the salesmen all in white uniform. The cars looked funny; as though a row of long asphalt rugs had been rolled open from the curb, side by side, with fenders glued on top, blue, pale green, gold and mustard color, and shiny car-tops plunked down the middle, to produce this spread. The cars couldn't be real, not that many! And that spanky shiny? Those cars couldn't have real heft! No, this was Sleepy Lagoon Cruise Ship, sailing up the Caribbean, its deck done up for the evening show, "One Summer of Happiness in Detroit."

But then a truck trailer rolled out the back lane, lugging eight more used cars, one with a dented fender. It slowed, lurched on the bump—the cars bounced inside the trailer; and then it carefully worked its load back to the garage for cosmetic treatment. The cars were real; so what was I playing, the Triviality Game?

Partly it's the size; connections are so vast in this country, administrative details spring loose. When a hot air machine gets too complicated, it springs a leak somewhere; all the gas runs out, and it goes flop.

I had the feeling our campus strike wasn't for real, not like at General Motors, where cars stop getting produced, wages are interrupted, we know what we're bargaining for, and we do the bargaining. This was a demonstration-of-anger strike, a let's-get-the-bad-air-out-of-our-system exercise; as a progressive summer camp might have a let's-have-a-strike activity, then shift to a session-at-the-United-Nations. Only who was I kidding? That strike was a partial social breakdown, with threats of a drug bust, a fight over the grading system. The school was closed. A storage building was burned down. Meetings cooked all over the dormitories. I negotiated marks and term-paper assignments with individual students. I had to stop playing the Triviality Game.

Little by little, I began to sense it was happening too neatly to be just an occasional game. Something inside me was sporadically taking over and getting it started—nothing as dramatic as Dr. Jekyll and Mr. Hyde; and yet, before I knew it, I was on my guard. Who was he, this shadowy figure, playing the game? What was he like? It was a fine state of affairs, like suddenly casting a shadow, and no light behind you to cast it. I kept watching for a clue. It certainly reassured me, that nothing he did was scary. He never talked or pushed. In fact, he was boringly predictable, a cheerful, reassuring chap you could instinctively trust and automatically ignore.

Without thinking, I gave him a name, Mr. Triviality. A moment later, I was sorry. Dr. Stampfer and Mr. Triviality hadn't the ring of Jekyll and Hyde. It was comic silly—like, what was he, Mr.

Triviality, Snow White's eighth dwarf. It even gave Dr. Jekyll a simplified cast, a variation of Dr. Soul and Mr. Hyde. Most souls I know have twitchy hides. Except my Hyde was puffed up to agreeable, Latinate Triviality.

A moment later, the name felt right.

Names are deucedly sticky. Now I'd named him, I started to dig him. He certainly had his habits. I never worry what I wear; any old shirt will do; but Old Triviality wore only a suit with a tie, shipshape inexpensive stuff, all from a discount store. You don't play games with Triviality.

Old Triviality is squarer than I am, waspish, but low-key. He's too mousy to join the John Birch Society, at most a sort of reliable canned pig, bland and experienced. You'd never put him in charge of anything; and yet he had a hard, quiet, level edge that didn't attract trouble. His life had a bright shine, rather attractive in a cheap, steady way, like I tangle and mesh with people, but Old Triviality floated on puffballs and neon tangles. And he dragged me with him. After a while, I could smell him on my face, my hands, in the subway, behind the wheel of a car, at first only occasionally, but he soon dogged me close. Old Triviality—he carried it off, trivial, normal, safe, a bit slippery, but thoroughly dependable. You could never pin him down.

For a while, it made me giddy, he violated so much I believed in. I even sort of got high on him. Imagine, a serious, dedicated Joe like me! It makes you wonder, the things I worry about, while all the time there's that cool, shiny brass, steady and reliable as silverfoil. I started thinking in a flipflop. Like the real me was funky old-fashioned, low-down, difficult, private, out of it, while Triviality kept linking up with Shiny Flakes, Dairy Delicious, Cayute Cars, TV spectaculars, Miss America, and the Four Leaf Clover smell. Why, triviality was important! It was all over America; and it always worked, like a computer. It always had the right time, and season tickets to a dozen movie houses. Old Triviality could rattle off the capital of every state in the Union, and what river it was on, and the president three presidents before Lincoln. Everything trivial was new and shiny—when it stopped shining, it turned to junk. It took over as during a stint of driving. When I drive, I'm steering a secondhand sedan with worn tires; but when Old Triviality took the wheel, like in all the TV ads, my car is a gun that will travel.

But after a while, I began to feel how thin triviality was. Maybe I was allowing too much, presuming a personality not really there —I'm always doing that for strangers. This wasn't Old Triviality —that's a joke, just a shiny chrome surface, like a cheap smile you sometimes put on to solve all problems, or at most a Walt Disney thing, Mickey Mouse, cheery-happy and trivial, a cartoon success, a shiny attitude that takes over and becomes a person. How did I even know it was a he—there's that male chauvinism again. Maybe Triviality was a woman, the ninety-second TV ad, to show you Pontiac is the car for men getting ahead. Worse and worse—that would make it Dr. Stampfer and Mrs. Triviality! But was she my wife or my mother?

Besides, it wasn't really there. It never listened. I could tell it anything. It wasn't even as deep as the nausea Sartre felt in France, or the perverse sadism of Hitler's Germany, where everything turned vomit-color. It just spread everywhere, pale, shiny, good-natured, meeting the eye, but shedding responsibilities; the way breakfast-food companies pour corn in the hopper, add granulated sugar and an artificial preservative, and out comes Shiny Flakes. Recently, most American cereals were attacked as empty calories—sugar-coated sawdust, almost worthless as food. After a while, the mills admitted they had once packaged healthier cereals advertised as foods; but they turned people off. Food made people uncomfortable. They liked the grab of Triviality, Shiny Flakes for breakfast, not food. Shiny Flakes never made them feel inferior or uncomfortable.

So that should have settled it: Old Triviality is the idea of cellophane, not a person—the shine of chrome, the feel of mass production, the smell of success. Something in me fought the rhythms of mass production; something else bought it. Why not? It made sense. A lot of people are divided like that. But Triviality reached farther than just cellophane and cheap watches. The war news I watched, a shot of a pile of corpses, student riots, letters from friends in trouble, all had that shipshape, shiny triviality. I saw a wrecked airliner as shiny-trivial, then a religious revival. That bothered me, Triviality over-reaching himself like that—let him keep his place. But there I was, giving Triviality a personality again! That finally did it. Triviality and I occupied the same body, where Triviality did his hard-edge thing, and I worried about the human soul. And then came the break.

One day, Triviality kept snagging and tearing on a series of nit-picky troubles, repeating old phrases like, "That's too bad," or "Oh, my!" or "Isn't that interesting!" But for the moment, it had a dull, sullen, hard-pressed edge, for all its bright surface, somehow rubbery, like an elusive Hallowe'en mask. For the first time, I felt something working underneath it, a more energetic twitch, responsibilities it couldn't really shrug off. No wonder Triviality had come through as laughably thin—something else was wearing it as a mask! I gave a nervous laugh—I mean, my personality was starting to get a little crowded. But insights, once they start, come in a rush; every time I felt trivial, underneath it all I felt bored. Then Boredom and Triviality came together; or rather, Triviality is the mousy face of Boredom.

Boredom had its own unpredictable personality, twitchy with impatience and not to be trusted. It sat so quiet you forgot it was there, then suddenly exploded. It was a drag to have around—you couldn't relax it, or get rid of it. It didn't sit comfortably, or listen to anything that went on. It was like an annoyed stranger sitting too close by your table for you to talk freely. No, I was relieved when Triviality took over. Boredom made me feel threatened. Triviality I was used to; it never really upset anybody. It was safer all around with Triviality. No more of the old existential proverb, life is lived in the face of death; after a tranquilizer and a proper embalming, life and death aren't that opposite. The current proverb should be, Triviality is lived in the face of boredom.

The two actually go together, Triviality and Boredom, like a married couple. I started to get giddy again. Triviality was the wife—I was sure of it, smoothing over difficulties and keeping her house in good taste. I fretted that that made Boredom my father, the dull master who just flopped around—the pig. Seeing what Triviality had to put up with in Boredom, I grew a bit more tolerant with her, even sentimental. Let's face it, an important thing can happen to me maybe once in a blue moon; but Triviality is around all the time. I mean, we get along. It made me feel good to vote for Nixon, that safe, shiny, trivial man. I'm like that myself, a neat package, small, bright, clean-cut and well-meaning. Being trivial, I am the common man. Let's admit it, most life is trivial. I identify with chrome, cellophane, breakfast cereals, carbon monoxide, a flag, a library catalogue. The blacks aren't trivial—that's why they keep getting shafted. They're too important to let alone, too difficult to spend time on. I get no attention; but I'm secure. Nobody shafts me.

So I adjusted to Triviality and Boredom together. Why not? They're a package deal; and Triviality can make Boredom disappear. But sometimes the package made me a bit wary. Boredom wasn't really involved; it was only biding its time. When I bothered to pay sudden attention, it seemed involved elsewhere. And then occasional explosions of violence gave a suggestion of still a deeper figure I could never face—Rage. It was like hauling an old chain out of the ocean—you never knew whose teeth were sunk in the other end. I mean, enough is enough. I fell back on Old Triviality.

I squirmed a little at all the loose responsibility around, but then shook it off. I wasn't responsible—Triviality had taken over, and Triviality couldn't be guilty of anything. Oh sure, there were crimes all around, wars, civil rights violations, babies maimed and murdered by their parents. The underground politicos wanted to label these super-crimes, put the screws on, then whammo, they'd slip a revolutionary pill into my open mouth. Who needed it? The whole production had a phoney ring. They were all in the Triviality bag.

So Triviality was in—I even began to talk her language; and yet she wasn't in, not really. She bored me. I mean, how much of that stuff can I take? She gets me mad, forever puffing up shiny, doing small neat things, and never really thinking. Everything ended in a pratfall so trivial you couldn't be bothered. Like Triviality had no guts. Whatever it hid was too inert to bother doing anything, so why worry? Its shine had stopped intimidating me. It had a more familiar look.

There she was, my gal Triviality—and to think I had taken her for a man! It was actually funny, all that shiny triviality, male. And then I went and took her for my mother! That just shows how she indulges herself. She really has to take off a little weight—she's new and brassy, yet somehow timid, like something real would put her in a sweat. The more modern woman can't stand her. And yet nothing fazes her. She tunes in on everything; but when there's pressure, she just disappears. She's everybody's housewife and the small-town slut; and yet she keeps getting pathetically lonely.

I mean, she's very sexy! She really turns me on. Like she's very cool, very tony; and yet she has an overtone of the cheap make behind the Woolworth counter. She often looks like a boy as much as a girl—a short, brassy stud with a soft downy upper lip and a lisp, and curly hair, just because he won't visit a barber, undefined not because he's so subtle, but because he's too lazy to bother. I can't figure out for the life of me how smart she is. She never says anything bright or original. She's slick, cheap, seductive—lives easy, and yet she has an edge of truth. She never makes a mistake. I swear after a while, her lisp has its own style, and begins to sound in, homy, and with it. Maybe that's her strategy for staying-power. I keep hearing her say with a cute whimper and a girlish chuckle—what can I do about cancer of the lung? Ditto pollution, ditto race, ditto population explosion, ditto sex, ditto hang-ups, ditty everything. It's refreshing, to have no hang-ups and be too mousy for trouble. In fact, it may be a bit perverse of me to admit it, but I enjoy sitting in her company and watching TV. Like Triviality could really turn me on.

But nothing ever really happened. She kept talking; but I didn't listen like I used to. Her face was too brassy for me, too shiny-boyish, too sly, the face of a compulsive prick-tease, who had been around too long, comfortably bossy and possessive, with no surprises left for her. You couldn't shake her; she was universal. In the Middle Ages, the body was trivial, but the soul was important. At the turn of the century, waste was trivial, but progress was important. Now everything was trivial! She shone with a steady light! Like Shiny Flakes was a real cereal—it was just my speed!

Triviality had an answer for everything. Nothing threw her off stride. And complacent? She was a neon quicksand, a Muzak swamp, an ad limerick I couldn't get out of my head; and yet it didn't mean a thing. Nothing meant anything any more. I figured, enough! Let me confront her, and see what happens. Why not? We've always been together; let's have a conversation, not Dr. Jekyll and Mr. Hyde, but Dr. Stampfer and Mrs. Triviality.

I glanced at the Triviality inside me, feeling rather timid and demure after all the preparation. It embarrassed me to have worked that hard to get started. She waited patiently. I finally opened our first conversation: What's boring you?

Triviality sighed—she was spoken to at last. As she moved, I was puzzled I had been so mistaken—what I had thought were her eyes and lips were the light shining on some cheap metal discs. She hung still a moment, then tangled up, all big and shiny, and gave me a breezy, cheerful smile: Nothing bores me; I'm very fulfilled.

I snorted: You fulfilled? You've been bored so long, you don't know how to keep awake any more. You're sleazy decent. You're such a bore, you're a waste of time. You're too tinny to register. It's impossible to pay you any attention without starting to yawn.

Triviality sighed peacefully—nothing had registered. I fretted a little. She gave a jiggle. In spite of myself, I started to grin. She sighed: Judah, what's bothering you? You don't mind my calling you Judah? I mean, Dr. Stampfer is just too much! We're actually much closer than you think. It's been going on since you were born. But what's bothering you? Why are you so worked up? You just make trouble for yourself with people.

I glared: Don't change the subject! You're so damned evasive. It's you I want a good look at for a change! You say you're fulfilled. I doubt that; but some experiences must fulfill you more than others. You must have taste in pleasures, even if you have no standards. What gives you real pleasure?

At this, Triviality swelled up confidently. The light glowed all over her face: Youth gives me pleasure. I fooled you there, didn't I? You expected another evasive answer. I belong to youth. Why not? I look good; I turn on fast, and change with every change in style. I've got experience, money, and the educated knowhow, especially in what's happening in this country. Like if you want to make it, get me under your skin, baby.

She turned my stomach, but my back prickled: Balls! You're so old, you could be my grandmother. You young? You've got so much junk on, I can hardly see you. What do you know about youth?

Here Triviality swelled like the center ring of the circus at the grand parade, as the light danced all around her: Youth is what is. I mean, youth is a celebration. This country has made it, because it's tuned in on youth.

My gorge rose: What mountain did you ever climb? What babies did you ever really care for? What passion ever stayed clean under your hands?

Triviality ignored me with a quiet patience: You want to know what youth is? Youth is triviality that has finally made it. I'm the way. Like the media finally get the message. I'm better than the passion; I'm the song their passion is singing. I'm what they're really after, because I'm really free.

I snorted again: What message are you? Nobody tunes in on you because there's nothing to tune in on. You don't mean a thing. You're worth nothing. You do nothing. You're a waste of time.

Triviality sighed with mellow, patient warmth, and started to turn all harvest greens and browns: Oh, the opposite, I do more and more all the time, but so agreeably nobody notices. I'm the shy type; but I'm what makes the cars go round, and politics spin. The money I control would astound you. That's because youth is my current kick. Classical records don't sell—the big orchestras are all in trouble, carrying grown-up music like that. Like what can you do to Beethoven except play him? In politics, I've got staying power. In government, you're a dead duck with a real issue around your neck. What you have to give is leadership; and that's where I come in! Like the rock discs are blasting wide open, to millions of dollars.

I scuffed my nose: Don't you talk about yourself and blasting. Don't you know about the coming revolution? What about the Weathermen? The bombs that get thrown? What about the crazies? The freaks? The four-letter-word men? What about the Black Panthers? What about social unrest?

Triviality brushed my hand with a hundred bells and gave a

syncopated kick. I jerked my hand back. She tinkled all over with shiny bells: Who, the revolutionaries? They're all my boys; they're my agents provocateurs. They're all show-biz men in action theater. Think they're for real? Haven't you talked to any of them? Those groovy cats run a country? Those spaced-out freaks build a dam or a big bridge, or plan a city? They've got their little thing to do and they're doing it. It keeps things lively. Oh, Judah, it saddens me to see you wasting your life thinking big. It makes you an egomaniac. You're my boy, too; and there's nowhere you tune in.

I chuckled good-naturedly: That's sweet noise you produce; but you're not my mother. Besides, I outgrew her a long time ago. Baby, it's not the egomaniacs who want a transportation system that really works. We need fast trains, and in a hurry, to take the glut off the highway. But what do you know about real needs?

Triviality licked her lips and smiled at me earnestly, with the kick of a dare in her lips: Why not? Sure, jet trains—absolutely. We'll slap them down. And we'll have them, and with real style —there's nothing wrong with style. Oh, stop hiding from life—to be young, and have a beautiful soul, zip along the shore in a snappy convertible with a cool sweet doll tuned in to you, or camp out at a rock fest, everybody tuning in on—it doesn't matter on what, tuning in on anything! And you need never ever . . .

I swung up a dirty finger in disgust: What do you know about youth? Youth is dull soap or it's nothing. In youth, you learn to carry a job, manage a tight budget, carry a loan, run a business, fight when you have to, find out what the truth is, what risks are, and how to take risks because important things are involved. In youth, you learn the price of love and its feel. Youth is when nothing is trivial. Tuning youth in on you is like asking an athlete to pose in a shop window and have Goldfinger touch him. Your talk is obscene! You look obscene, all done up like that! Besides, you're overweight!

Triviality giggled all over, and murmured agreeably: I'm light as a feather—I hardly weigh at all. I just look big because I impress you. Don't you like me?

I frowned, befuddled: You're much too big; you should trim down a bit. You're everything that's cheap in politics and mechanical in show biz. You look—promiscuous, that's how you look, available.

Triviality gave a little kick: Don't you like me?

I scuffed the ground: That's beside the point.

Triviality shrugged, then smiled enigmatically. Lights pulsed all over her with mysterious harmonies: All the other boys like me. I'm what helps you get ahead.

I scuffed the ground again: Into what, an air-conditioned Impala?

Triviality sighed: You think you know what youth is, but you don't. All you know are clumsy kids.

My eyes popped: That's what youth is, a bunch of clumsy kids.

Triviality lifted one glass eyebrow, and breezily shifted her position: You mean youth is what groovy kids tune in on. Youth is a Greek statue; youth is Viennese music. Kids are shnooks, most of them. When they shut up and look happy, they can be tolerated. Otherwise, they're a bunch of drags. Youth is Elvis Presley and Frank Sinatra, not a remedial reading class in a South Bronx high school.

I horselaughed: Elvis Presley and Frank Sinatra have been around. Like Sinatra is over fifty. He's retired already.

Triviality smiled agreeably: What's the difference how old they are? They cracked the formula for staying young. Sinatra is an inspiration. He'll be young forever.

I began to stammer: Look, never mind all that bullshit. You know what your reality is. Your followers are all middle-aged has-beens, with not one kid among them, except in a silly joke. You're a menace to anything decent. The politicians will throw you in the clink for leading minors astray.

Triviality swelled up even more, relaxed, pink with satisfaction: Who will throw me in the clink? The politicians? I'm what keeps politics rolling in this country. I'm their sweetheart, and they're all my heroes. Like we get along. I'm what turns youth on to Youth, all undulating and shimmering. When I finish, they have nothing to worry about. It's just beautiful, what I can do. I'm their best speech-writer.

I shrank a little—the way Triviality was sending neon runners out of itself, getting bigger all the time we were talking! Finally, I exploded: That's bullshit! Youth is frustrated because this country is middle-aged, small-minded; its arteries are calcified till it does nothing. It's you that turns them off the system and drives them underground. They want decent things to live for, and you're just a draggy bore! They're not interested in undulating in rhythm like a school of jellyfish, crossing the Caribbean. They want homes that make sense, bridges that lead somewhere, neighborhoods with steady jobs in them, anything that has some meaning.

Triviality shone with every color in the rainbow. She tinkled all over like a Radio City marquee, shaking with applause: Yes, meaning. That's the word for today. Judah, you've hit onto something; you really have. Oh, I love the way you put things! And you're so right! That's what youth is, a bunch of idealists, romantics, wanting homes that make sense and bridges—how did you put it?—yes, yes, that lead somewhere.

I spat: We've got nothing in common but a lot of gas. You're disgusting to talk to. You even make me disgusting.

Triviality applauded louder: Oh, you stick to that line; and you'll strike it rich! It's so manly! And youth is so manly. They march and sing songs. The quieter ones turn off and meditate; the angry ones go revolutionary and throw bombs. That's because they've got soul. Youth has soul. I love soul more than anything in the world!

I shook my head, grinning: You still riding soul, you devil, you?

Triviality turned dark rose and royal blue. Oh, of course, it's bridges they want, and youth will build them. It absolutely will! That's youth, eternal youth!

I stopped dead, and fought the cuddle of excitement out of my voice. Finally, I said flat: Look, to build a bridge, you go to a school for technology, plunge into politics, and then kick the ass off the human roadblocks. Like it's possible to handle the man with the permits.

Triviality shook all over in good-natured demurral, but also got very casual: You're such a romantic—but you're back with the kids again. Youth can't be bothered with kids. They aren't worth it. They're an embarrassment.

It bothered me, the way Triviality was getting shaggier as she talked, dropping down twiney vines like the vines in a Tahitian restaurant. I started to stammer, getting angry: What are you talking about? That's what this country needs, kids growing up and getting jobs. What does all this have to do with Youth? What are we tuned in on, Tahiti or some never-never land? This is a tough, productive country, the most productive country on earth, choked with engineering, technology, computers. It hasn't the time for Youth.

Triviality began to sigh like a Neapolitan wedding song: But that's just it! What does all that technology do? All that engineering? All those computers? They set people free at last, and give them something to live for—Youth! Beautiful Youth! And we can finally sit and enjoy it, now production has made work trivial.

Triviality began to hum softly, her hands shaking loose and easy. She distracted me; but I wrenched myself away: That's a loser's ploy, the consumer approach! You know what consumers are? Fat boys, supported by their mommas. Yeah, sure, we consume all we want, and turn into well-adjusted tapeworms.

Triviality hummed in a musical wheeze as I talked, then laughed good-naturedly, her whole body shaking with pleasure. I stopped short, disconcerted. Triviality sang out: Don't stop! I hear every word! I love to hear you talk! It's so silly and beautiful, and with it, I'm giving it a musical accompaniment. I could listen to you forever!

I shrank back. Triviality was blushing all over her glass body; the tangle of neon was getting larger. Silver threads were spreading all over, running along the neon tubes and weaving with the vines and over the leaves. I cried: Never mind the musical accompaniment! I want straight talk between us!

Triviality sighed softly, and subdued her lights and colors: You're so Victorian. Communication is a gas—don't you know that? Like we communicate with you talking and me singing. Better, we harmonize. Get with it, boy. Machines are like horses. They work and we ride them. For us to work also would be too much. We have to keep busy enjoying ourselves, change styles, find new wrinkles to relax with; or we'll produce our way to the moon.

I cracked my knuckles and snorted: Yeah, you've got the picture, a club of parasite fat boys, stranded on a pile of chromium junk.

Triviality clucked all over in a soft, minor key: Really, you moralize too much. It's out of step to moralize. Fat boys! Youth is beautiful! Youth has soul! Like what's wrong with enjoying life?

I kicked the ground in exasperation: This is the consumer answer to all our problems.

Triviality warbled in gentle annoyance: I'll tell you one thing—it's the only thing that works.

I ducked my head, chafing: You know the drug epidemic still gathering steam? It's the reaction of youth to being castrated. You've gutted everything they work for. They've got no will power left, because everything's computerized and overproduced in closed corporations. All they see are finished packages; so there's nothing left for them to do. You gave them a Jag, put the key in their hand, and then locked the garage door. Now all they can do is die of mono. You know what a drug addict is? He's a man whose mind commits suicide because his will has been castrated. He's like the fat girl who overeats because she thinks she's lost out on the main chance. She's a suicide in reverse: she gets rid of herself by bloating, simultaneously indulges herself and punishes herself, enjoys herself and makes sure she'll never enjoy anything. And it's because she's lost the main chance. That's the hard-drug addict; he commits suicide by bloating, drowning his will in consuming. And you did it. You chopped his will into packages of spaghetti.

Triviality warbled: What's his main chance?

I plunged right on: The will of kids—that's the main chance. To start something worth doing, and get it done. It's holding down a decent job, doing work that makes sense to your two hands while you're doing it. Take away their main chance, and you'll turn them into consumers—vegetables!

Triviality swelled steadily as I talked, until she hung over my head: Who worries about poor sick kids who fall into drugs? Get it into your head, I'm talking about youth that makes it. Who bothers with the garbage? Youth doesn't take hard drugs. Drugs aren't beautiful.

I leaned back with a tight grin: You're bluffing. Your youth comes out of some Hollywood movie. They don't make the Fred Astaire type any more.

Triviality tinkled bells all over my head: Oh, are you wrong! Haven't you read the papers lately? I'm the latest! Youth and the National Guard! Youth meets the FBI! I'm at the heart of all that's happening. Don't you know youth is finally a celebration?

I broke in: Youth, a celebration? You know what youth is in this country? Year after year of chickenshit—chickenshit courses, chickenshit classmates, chickenshit assignments to live in chicken-shit neighborhoods. That's what it means to be young in this coun-try, to hang around year after year eating chickenshit seven days a week. It always has been; and it always will be.

Triviality kept pounding its lights on and off as I talked. I heard a faint wheeze of "The Stars and Stripes," even a word or two of the Gettysburg Address. White banners began flapping in the breeze over its belly: Life has changed, boy. Parents don't teach children how to grow up any more; children teach their parents how to turn on. In a cool world, nobody tells anybody anything. The parents are with me now, like the politicians. Don't you know the score? Or don't you keep score any more? Parents and kids wear the same clothes; they borrow each others' cars. That's why a kid can rebel for ten years in school. His momma stands behind him no matter what. He can't lose!

I fought a panic, as Triviality slid all around me in an echo chamber, a Tin Pan Alley, arching all around. I fought an impulse to back out, while there still was time—but that would be chicken. I frowned in the technicolor flashes: Look, you're not total. Isn't power important? AT&T? US Steel? There's a lot of power in this country that's level and straight.

Underground winds blew all around me out of Triviality's sides, tearing up the dust: Yeah, power has taken over. But power isn't human. It's way out there, just a sweet dream, like youth.

I ground my teeth: Who needs all this? I'm a teacher. It's my job to tell the truth.

Triviality grew berries over the ground, towards, around, and over my feet: You know what your job is? You know what your school is? It's a four-year baby-sitting agency for young adults.

That blew my mind. Triviality was all around me now, like some leafy womb I couldn't back out of. I kept seeing a vague suggestion of a face; but it was like my own in a mirror. I blew my stack: That's why the colleges keep boiling over with trouble! It's not

Vietnam, nor the draft, nor the blacks, nor the pollution, nor the cranky world and smooth political patter. The kids want a handle it makes sense to move. They come to school to learn how to do something; and after four years, they're well-adjusted patsies. They want a man around who does things, to imitate him and be something real; but there are no men around. Nobody does anything; so they organize and do the rebellion song-and-dance; or they conform, and do the adjustment song-and-dance.

All around me, Triviality tinkled musically. I thrashed forward as best I could: What are you good for? You won't give me good food, or let me love you up, not really. You're not what I'm after.

All around me, voices sighed together: Teacher, teacher, what can I learn to do that's real?

I drew myself up: Cool it on the movements. Do things that are private and real. Take care of a barn, tutor poor high school students, read a fun book, buy your own slide rule, smell out local issues that have handles. Get the habit of doing things that work, because then anything can work. This country has no establishment. It's just a tough, crowded jungle, full of noises and guns. Nobody runs this country, just a lot of messy, draggy habits.

The lights started to go out. All around me, voices warbled: Yes, you are a teacher, aren't you? That's your role.

I looked around and started to shiver: It's dark in here. I can hardly see you. You've stopped talking—why have you stopped talking? And my voice don't sound the same any more. I mean, this whole conversation is a bore. You're not worth spending time on.

Triviality gave a sudden sigh: What can you do that's really worth while?

I frowned. Then I shrugged: I can look you in the eye, and piss.